WORK IS LOVE MADE VISIBLE

WORK IS LOVE MADE VISIBLE

Translating an enlightened vision into action

OSHO

PAN

Reprinted 2023

This edition published 2023 by Pan
an imprint of Pan Macmillan Publishing India Private Limited,
707 Kailash Building
26 K. G. Marg New Delhi 110001
www.panmacmillan.co.in

Pan Macmillan, The Smithson, 6 Briset St., Farringdon, London EC1M 5NR
Associated companies throughout the world
www.panmacmillan.com

ISBN 978-93-95624-41-1

Originally compiled and published in Hindi as Anant Ki Pukar. This selection of related talks by Osho were given to live audiences in 1967-1971. The first 12 chapters were first compiled in 2000, with 2 previously unpublished talks now included – Chapter 13 (translated from Hindi) and Chapter 14, an English language talk. Selected talks have been previously published as pamphlets, and in newsletters and magazines, both in Hindi and English languages. Audio recordings and the complete text archive can be found at www.osho.com

1 3 5 7 9 8 6 4 2

Contents

Preface vii
A Note about Language ix

1. A Gathering of Friends 1
2. A New Vision of Sannyas 22
3. Work Will Bring Its Own Wealth 42
4. Collecting Friends, Not Funds 53
5. Four Things to Remember 75
6. An Organism Built on Foundations of Love 97
7. A World Center 128
8. The Art of Living in a Juicy and Blissful Way 138
9. A Collective Vision of Religion 166
10. The Art of Work as Meditation 182
11. Making Meditation Centers 205
12. Facing the Ego 222
13. Beyond Office Politics 256
14. Liquid Organization 274

About Osho 291
Osho International Meditation Resort 294
Books by Osho in English 297
For More Information 301

Preface

All religions are against life. They say, "Renounce life," and life includes work, life includes love, life includes everything. "Renounce life, because your renunciation of life is going to be an entry into paradise after your death." But it is always *after* death.

All the religious people and the politicians are angry with me for the simple reason that I am telling people that life is *herenow* – not after death; don't wait. And life is in love, life is in being creative, life is in understanding your innermost being. Because only then can you become a constantly overflowing source of beauty, love, and joy.

Who cares about life after death? Life is *before* death, and if you can live totally there is no death for you. This is the experience of all those who have entered into silence. They have witnessed the greatest miracle: that their innermost core, their consciousness, is eternal. Life can take away the clothes, the bodies, but life cannot destroy *you*. But only the creator – and a creator out of love – transcends death.

As Kahlil Gibran says:

Work is love made visible.
And if you cannot work with love but only with distaste, it is better that you should leave your work and sit at the gate of the temple and take alms of those who work with joy.

If you cannot be a creator, if you cannot love work, if you cannot love life, then the only possibility for you is just to be a beggar. The lover is an emperor, the creator is an emperor – without invading the whole world. He has invaded the whole universe out of sheer, loving creativity.

Osho,
Reflections on Kahlil Gibran's The Prophet

A Note about Language

Spoken Words: Osho's books are not "written" but rather are transcribed from recordings of his talks. These talks are extemporaneous, without reference to notes other than copies of questions, stories or scriptures he has been asked to comment upon, or jokes he might use to drive home a particular point. He has asked his editors to preserve that quality of the spoken word in his printed books.

Pronouns: When hearing him speak, it is quite clear to the listener that generally when Osho talks about "man" he is referring to "human beings." His use of "he" as a default pronoun simply serves an ease and flow of speaking – in no way does it imply that "she" (or "they") is being dismissed or disregarded.

Osho's unique vantage point is good to keep in mind:

A meditator is neither a man nor a woman,
because meditation has nothing to do with your body;
neither does it have anything to do with your mind.
In meditation you are simply and purely consciousness.
And consciousness is neither male nor female.

~Osho

1
A Gathering of Friends

We have gathered here to consider a few very significant matters.

I had no idea that what I am saying to individual people would need to be made public one day. I had never thought about it. I talk to people according to my capacity and capability, about whatsoever feels blissful to me and whatever may be of help to them.

But slowly, as I have the opportunity to come into contact with hundreds of people, I have come to realize and begun to see that there is a limit to what I alone can do. No matter how much I may want to, I cannot bring my words to all the people who are in need of them. And many people have a tremendous need of them. This whole country, this whole earth is extremely thirsty and in distress.

Not counting the rest of this planet, this country is in a spiritual crisis. All the old values have been shattered. Respect, regard for all the old values has disappeared, and no new values have come in their place. People are just standing there with no idea where to go or what to do. In such a situation it is natural that man's mind should become very restless, very distressed and very unhappy. Every individual is carrying so much misery within him that if we were able to open his heart and look inside it, we would be at a loss.

The more I come into contact with people, the more puzzled I become as I see that what they are carrying within them is exactly the opposite of how they appear to be from the outside. Their smiles are false, their happiness is false and all their so-called rejoicing is false. An enormous hell, a deep darkness, and much unhappiness and misery have accumulated in them.

But there are ways to destroy this anguish, this pain. It *is* possible to be free of them. Man's life can become one of heavenly peace and harmony. And since I have begun to see this, I have also felt that if we don't share what it is that can take mankind toward peace, with those who are in need of it, we are, in a way, committing a crime. Knowingly or unknowingly we are committing sins of omission.

So I have started feeling that it is necessary to take anything that can transform people's lives to the greatest number of people. But there is a limit to what I can do. What I alone can do is limited. Alone, no matter how fast I run, no matter how many people I may reach, no matter how extensive this reaching out may be, when I see the vastness of life all around and this society with its deep anguish, there is no way I can deal with it all.

If we drop some dye into the sea, a small wave may be colored, but it will not make any difference to the vast ocean. And the interesting thing is that this small wave that may become colored will, in no time at all, be lost in the vast ocean, and with it the color will also disappear.

So we have gathered here to discuss how the color of peace can be spread far and wide in this vast ocean of life.

But along with this, I am also aware that a person who becomes only interested in his own peace can never become peaceful in the truest sense – because to be only interested in oneself is one of the causes of uneasiness; to be self-centered is one of the fundamental reasons for dis-ease. A person who becomes self-centered and who is only interested in himself, who wants to become oblivious to everything else around him, is like someone who builds a beautiful house and does not want to concern himself with the piles of garbage surrounding it. He will create a beautiful garden on his property without bothering at all about the stink surrounding his house. If the whole surrounding area is dirty, his garden, his flowers and their fragrance will not mean much. The stink will enter his house and drown the fragrance of his flowers.

People should not only be interested in themselves, but also in their environment. A religious person is not only interested in himself; he also takes an interest in everything around him. I feel that it is not enough to be just concerned with one's own peace. We have to make sure that the gentle winds of peace reach all the sentient beings with whom we are interrelated, with whom we are connected. This should also concern us. And a person who becomes eager and thirsty to bring peace to everything that surrounds him in life will discover that even though he may or may not succeed in making others peaceful, through his very efforts he will certainly become peaceful himself.

There is an anecdote in the life story of Buddha, perhaps it is a fictitious story but it is very beautiful…

When Buddha attained to nirvana, ultimate liberation, he reached the door of moksha, salvation, and the gatekeeper opened the gate. But Buddha was standing with his back toward it, so the gatekeeper asked, "Why are you standing with your back toward moksha?"

Buddha said, "There are many people behind me, and until they all attain to moksha, I will stop here and wait. I am not so hard, so cruel and so violent that I can enter salvation alone. All the peace I have attained is simply saying to me that I should be the last person to enter moksha. First everyone else should enter."

It is a very beautiful story. And the story goes that Buddha is still waiting at the gate of moksha so that everyone else may enter first. He wants to enter last of all.

The heart of someone in whom such a feeling has arisen has already attained to heaven. He need not enter any heavenly gate. For him, all notions of ultimate liberation become irrelevant. One in whom such feelings of compassion have arisen has already attained to ultimate liberation. Only people who are strongly inspired to spread peace all around become peaceful.

I feel that those friends who have become interested in this direction should not just remain interested in themselves, but become interested in other people and in their environment too – because whether this interest benefits others or not, it will still be very meaningful for the friends themselves. It will help them to enter deeply into a great silence, a great blissfulness – because one of the reasons for their uneasiness is their self-centeredness. One who radiates from his center to all those around him moves toward becoming peaceful.

So we have gathered here so that I can discuss with you in what ways the message of love, peace and compassion can be spread to as many people as possible. What methods can we find to make sure that this message reaches them? Is it possible? It is not propaganda, it is not to create a cult, it is not to create an organization or a group. We are not going to create a center which becomes powerful for its own sake. We are going to spread this message as widely as possible – without becoming a group, without becoming a cult, without becoming an organization, without creating any centralized power. And this needs a great deal of reflection.

If you want to create a cult then you don't need to think much about it; if you want to create an organization then you don't need to think much about it. Everyone in the world knows how to create groups and organizations. Thousands of cults have already been created. We are not going to create another cult in among all those cults. That is why it has to be thought through thoroughly so that we do not create a cult or an organization. And yet we still want to be able to share what we love and what feels blissful with everybody. We don't want to become propagandists, yet at the same time it may be possible to share it, to make it known.

Hence it is a very delicate issue, and it needs to be thought through very carefully and with great sensitivity. It is like walking on a tightrope. One option is not to share it at all because there is the danger of becoming a cult. This means we simply do not spread the message at all – to anyone. And the second alternative is that we spread the message, but end up creating a cult. That danger also exists. We have to spread the message, but it is absolutely necessary to take care that a cult is not created.

So it is a question of making this possible without propagandizing, without becoming a cult or an organization – so that the necessary transmission, the vital message, reaches to the maximum number of people. This is what you have been invited here to discuss. In the coming sessions, I will gradually tell you about the things that I can see. And I will also expect you to think about them. I will say a few basic things to you so that you can think them over.

The first thing is that our gathering of friends here today is not as big as the message is. An organization is not needed, only a gathering is needed. And the difference between an organization and a gathering must be clearly understood. A gathering means that everybody is free, has come out of his own freedom, and can leave out of his own freedom. The meaning of a gathering is that everybody is equal: nobody is higher or lower, nobody is in any hierarchy, nobody is a follower, nobody is a leader. This is the meaning of a gathering.

We are going to create a gathering of friends, not an organization in which there are authorities, hierarchies – higher and lower people.

An organization has its own infrastructure. There is a hierarchy from the bottom to the top, there are rungs and positions, and along with all of these comes politics – because politics is bound to enter wherever there is status and position. Those who hold a position become scared that somebody may replace them. Those who do not hold a position become eager to reach a position. So an organization has its own hazards.

We have to create a gathering of friends, not an organization. In the gathering everybody is equal and has equal value. Nobody is an authority, nobody is given more respect than anyone else, nobody is higher and nobody is lower. Each person is only to come to it out of his love. Except for love, there will be no other commandments to follow: no oaths and pledges which one has to fulfill, no vows and precepts to commit oneself to. A person will join in only out of his love and individual freedom, and can leave the moment he wants to. And even when he is part of the gathering, he is not bound by any dogma or ideology; even then he is free to have different opinions, to have his own thoughts, to follow his own ideas, to follow his own wisdom. He is not there to be somebody's follower.

So a gathering of friends called *Jeevan Jagruti Kendra*, the Life Awakening Center, will be created. We have to think along these lines.

Certainly, the rules around which a gathering of friends is formed are different from the rules of an organization. A gathering of friends is what we may call a totally anarchic institution. An organization is a well-planned system bound by rules, principles and laws. I do not intend to bind people by laws, rules or principles, because I am fighting against these very things. Such organizations already exist all over the world. What is the point in creating one more of them? Certainly there is more efficiency in an organization; there cannot be that much efficiency in a gathering. But to have efficiency at the cost of freedom is a very costly deal. Democracy is not as efficient as a dictatorship, but even though efficiency can be sacrificed, freedom cannot.

A gathering of friends means that it is a voluntary get-together of free individuals. If there are to be some minor regulations and systems within it they will be less important than the individuals, not more important. They will be functional, they cannot be the goal. We will be free to discontinue them at any moment. They should never have the power to hinder us. The regulations will be for us, not the other way around. It is important to keep this in mind.

Now, some friends think that there should be a charter, a constitution. Certainly there should be a charter, but not in the same way there would be for an organization. It should be created always remembering that it is for a gathering of friends. It will be a very functional charter; it will be utilitarian. It will be outlined with all this in mind, but there will be no insistence on clinging to it. It can be thrown out and burned at any moment.

And it is important to bear in mind that howsoever valuable the charter may be, our individual friends are more valuable than it is – because this charter has been formed for the sake of these friends, they have not gathered here for the sake of the charter. So we have to create a gathering of friends where the value and dignity of each and every individual is preserved. Obviously, the greater the number of individuals, the more varied their ways of thinking and understanding will be. The bigger the gathering of friends, the more differences there will be among them – naturally.

So, we should not attempt to create uniformity, otherwise an organization will start coming into existence. And the more we try to create uniformity, the more the individuality of a person, his dignity and freedom, will begin to be destroyed. The concern is not for uniformity but for the respect of all friends, even for their differing opinions – because the direction of my whole vision is toward the birth of freethinking throughout this entire country. If the very people who want to give birth to freethinking get themselves entangled in dependent thinking, that will be dangerous. Even toward me, this gathering of friends should not show any special reverence. Toward me too, there should not be any feeling of reverence. Toward me too, there should be a rational and an intelligent approach. If what I am saying seems right to you, if it is to your liking, if it appears useful, only then should you communicate it to people. Do not commit the mistake of communicating to people what I am saying just because I have said it.

This gathering of friends is not to be centered around an individual either, because that person, myself or anyone else, may become the center of worship. We will not have any worship, we will not be anybody's followers, we will not have any leader. Collectively, we are in love with a vision, a message, and feel that if it reaches more people, they will benefit. That is why we friends have gathered: because we wish to bring this vision to people.

So, first of all we will talk a little about organizations. We don't want to create an organization, only a gathering of friends. And we will try to understand the subtle difference between the two. It will be the responsibility of every individual to try to save this gathering of friends from becoming an organization. It is not in my hands alone. I can only say this, but it is not only in my hands – and if we are not very alert then there is a danger that it may become an organization. So it is necessary to be very alert. It has to be a very conscious experiment, so that it does not become an organization.

There are certain unknown ways in which a cult is formed. Before we have even become aware of it, a cult has started forming. So we have to be careful about this. And if we are aware beforehand, then maybe we can manage things in such a way that it does not happen. That is one possibility.

The other possibility is that because we are afraid that it may become an organization or a cult, we won't do anything at all. That is the other danger, that nothing is done – and then the message that has to be spread cannot be spread. Then it will be left on my shoulders alone to run around as much as I can to take the message to people. I will continue to do that anyway – it makes no difference to me – but the same message could reach many more people.

The greater the number of friends who cooperate, the further the message can reach, the more easily it can reach. And today science is developing so much technology – society is modernizing. We would be foolish not to make use of it; we would be making a mistake if we did not make use of it. For instance, if I was speaking here without using a microphone, it would be adequate. Even if my voice did not reach you very clearly, it would still be heard. When there are a few people they can hear me, but when there are more people my voice will not carry far enough. When we use a microphone, my voice can reach a long way.

Today so much technology is available that if it is all made use of, one person can do more work in his lifetime than Buddha and Mahavira would have been able to manage in twenty lives – had they wanted to. Buddha and Mahavira were at a disadvantage. Making use of whatever means were available to them, the work they did was more than enough. But if someone was asked to work in the same way today, it would be sheer foolishness. A lot of new technology is available today. It can all be made use of. Today, one person can do so much more work in one lifetime than he could have managed even if he were to have lived for four hundred years without this modern technology.

So we must make use of all of this technology. It is important to think about this. It is not possible for me to do it alone. For that, many more friends are needed, many types of friends are needed. Someone can do manual work, someone can use his intellect, someone can take care of the money, someone can help in some other way. Whatever one's understanding, whatever one's disposition, one can help accordingly. It is also important to remember that the wider the variety of friends the better it is, because the more different the types of people who come – contributing in different ways, doing different types of work, offering different types of help – the richer the work will become.

It often happens that friends are afraid of strangers within their own circles. They are afraid that once a stranger comes in, he will cause all kinds of trouble. So what generally happens is that whenever a group of friends gathers together somewhere, they make their circle and then become afraid of new friends joining them. The fear is that a newcomer may create a disturbance. And this fear is natural too; this protective feeling is not altogether bad.

But twenty-five old friends fearing one newcomer is a sign of great weakness. Their thinking should rather be that we twenty-five people will transform the newcomer, not that the newcomer will change twenty-five people! And if we twenty-five are so weak that one newcomer can change us, then we *should* be changed. What harm is there in it? What is so bad about it?

It always happens that whenever any group gathers together, it starts forming a circle. Then a distance is created between the people in the circle and the people outside it. It happens unknowingly; no one does it consciously. These are natural characteristics of the mind.

If you go to some unknown village with a few friends with you, then perhaps you will not make any new friends in that village. You will remain surrounded by your circle of old friends and will not step out of it. But in a situation where you find yourself unavoidably alone, it will be a different matter – you may have to make a friend. But otherwise you would not.

So every group has the tendency to remain confined; there is a tendency to become confined. And in being confined there is a sort of security: everything is known, everything is good, whatever we like the others like too. Some stranger coming in may say new things and disturb everything. We need to drop this fear. If the work is to become widespread and vast, then this fear must be dropped. The emphasis should be on remaining so accommodating – with our hearts so spacious and open, our arms opened so wide – that we are able to assimilate even people of the very opposite nature. Not a single person must be left out. We must make space within ourselves even for someone who is totally different from us, and we must find out what skills he has that can be useful to us.

In connection with this, in the recent past in India, Mahatma Gandhi did a great experiment. He gathered together many people of different and even antagonistic views. Totally dissimilar people, people between whom no consensus of opinion could ever be achieved, came together under the same umbrella and became instrumental in an epic undertaking.

Whenever someone thinks that people of different views, ideas, and personalities should not be included in a particular endeavor, then that endeavor cannot become great. It will remain very limited. It will remain like a small river thinking, "Not every river and stream coming from other distant places should join me. Who knows what sort of mud and rubbish, what sorts of substances and minerals they may bring with them, and how good or bad their water is?" If a river starts thinking along these lines then it will remain only a rivulet; it cannot become a great river, a Ganges. And if it is to become a Ganges, it will have to receive them all. So this capacity to receive everything needs to be there.

It is necessary to reflect on how to assimilate as many people as possible. We will have to create space. Slowly, we will have to see how we can provide people with the opportunity to join in, how we can find work for them, and also how we can help them to participate.

So many people from all over the country come and say to me that they want to help in the work. So many people write me letters asking me what they can do to help with the work. It is your responsibility to make room for all these friends to contribute. Completely drop and let go of the notion that there could be someone who may not be useful for anything. Such a person does not exist on this earth. What to say about people – even animals and birds can be a help. Even their help becomes… There is absolutely no one who is of no use; no person on this earth is useless.

So we need to look at how best to employ someone who is interested. If we concern ourselves with ideas about this man being like this and that man being like that, then it will be very difficult. So if we attempt to sit down and judge people before deciding… In the first place no one has the right to sit in judgment over others. And if we try to judge other people, you cannot imagine how much the work will be set back.

A man used to come to Gandhi's ashram. People complained that he was really immoral, that he was a drunkard – that he did this and he did that. Gandhi simply went on listening to all of it. All the friends became very disturbed that Gandhi was not banning the man from coming to the ashram. On the contrary, Gandhi went on including him more and more until finally, once the man's fears had vanished, he began to enter rather arrogantly.

One day some of Gandhi's closest people told him that the situation had gone too far. That day they had seen this man with their own eyes sitting in a bar, and they said it was absolutely disgraceful and defamatory that this man should be drinking wine there, dressed in khadi – Gandhi-style cotton clothes. They said that it was very unfortunate that such a man should come to the ashram, that it would bring disgrace to the ashram.

Gandhi said, "For whom have I opened this ashram? For good people? Then where will bad people go? And what is the need for those who are good to come here? For what and for whom am I here in the first place?

"The second thing is that you say that he is sitting in a bar dressed in khadi, so what will people think? If I were to see him there I would hold him close to my heart, because the first thought that would arise in my mind would be, 'It is amazing! It seems my words have started reaching the masses. Even drinkers have started wearing khadi!' You are seeing that someone wearing khadi is drinking wine. I would see that someone who drinks wine has started wearing khadi.

"And in such a case, the day is not too far away when this man may drop drinking wine. Transformation has begun in this man. He has shown courage. At least he is wearing khadi! Love has taken birth in his heart, transformation has begun in him.

"So this man can be looked at from either side: that he is drinking wine while dressed in khadi – then your mind will want to throw him out of the ashram. But it can also be seen from the other side: that a man who is a drunkard is wearing khadi. Then you will feel like welcoming him into the ashram and celebrating."

If this gathering is to expand and if it is to reach out to everyone, then you will have to take the second perspective, not the first. Then whosoever comes close to us will only be seen for the good that is in him and for the way in which he can be helpful. And I would also like to say to you that we are giving a great deal of incalculable and priceless energy and an impetus toward being good to the man whom we start looking upon with love.

If twenty good people start to accept a bad man as good, it becomes difficult for him to continue being bad. But when the whole world starts calling someone bad, it becomes easy for him to become or continue being bad. If someone is a thief and another man shows trust in him – as though he were not a thief – his ability to steal and the likelihood that he will steal weakens. There is no one, anywhere, who does not respect the good feelings of another heart.

If a thief were to come among us here, and we all trusted him as though he were a good man, he would not be able to steal. Stealing would be against all the norms, would be impossible, because when so many people give him respect, stealing would be at the cost of throwing it all away. And nothing can be more valuable than having this respect.

Each and every individual has the feeling to be good, but the problem is that nobody is ready to accept them. And when they meet someone who is ready to accept them as good, you cannot imagine what awakens and arises in them.

You may have heard the name of an American actress, Greta Garbo. She was born into a poor family in a small country in

Europe. And until the age of nineteen, she was working as an assistant in a barber's shop, for next to nothing.

An American tourist, whose face she was lathering, saw Greta Garbo's face in the mirror and said, "Very beautiful, your face is very beautiful!"

Greta Garbo said to him, "What are you talking about? I have been doing this job for six years, and no one has ever told me that I am beautiful. What are you talking about? Am I really beautiful?"

The American said, "You are very beautiful. I have rarely seen such a beautiful woman."

And Greta Garbo has written in her autobiography: "On that very day I became beautiful for the first time. One man called me beautiful. I myself was unaware of it. That day when I came back home and stood in front of the mirror, I realized that I had become an altogether different woman."

This girl who was an assistant in a barber's shop until the age of nineteen, later proved to be America's greatest film actress. And she only had that American, who told her for the first time that she was beautiful, to thank for it.

She said, "If this man had not said those few words to me that day, I would probably have remained a barber's assistant my whole life. I had no idea at all that I was beautiful. It is possible that he just said it very casually. It is possible that he was simply being polite. And it is possible that this man had not even been aware of what he was saying. It may just have been a passing comment. And he may not have even realized that a simple statement from him had given birth to an image of beauty in a woman, that he had somehow awakened in me something that had been asleep."

It is necessary to awaken that which is asleep in the people you want to do something for. Hence it is necessary to focus less on what they are and more on what they can be. If you have a big job that needs to be done, and without help you will not get any work done, and I have told you to get so-and-so to help, you may say, "But this man is bad, he is dishonest, he cannot be trusted."

It is okay that this man is bad or dishonest – who isn't? It is not a question of what he is, but rather of what he could be. If you are to get him to do any great work, you will have to call on that within him which he could become.

Kripalani, a famous professor, used to work as a cook in Gandhi's ashram. An American journalist was staying in the ashram and he said to Gandhi, "This man who cooks your food seems to be J. B. Kripalani."

At the time Kripalani was washing the dishes and he said, "This old man, Gandhi, is amazing! In fact, I was best suited to being just a cook, and this man has awakened in me something that is beyond description."

Awakening can happen even in the most insignificant person. Once we call him, once we draw out what is asleep in his soul and trust him; once we call to him and challenge that which is asleep in him, much can come out of him. And you can also demoralize even the greatest man. If you tell the greatest man that he is nothing, and if he hears this several times from all around, you can rest assured he will become nothing.

So if a spiritual revolution is to be carried out on a vast scale in this country… And it is absolutely necessary that this should happen. If we can do no more than pave the way for it, that will be enough, because someone else will complete it. What difference does it make whom it happens through? The point is not that it can only happen through us. No, if we can even pave the way for it so that later, some day, a revolution can come to pass, then that is more than enough, the matter is already taken care of.

So if this is to be done, a very comprehensive group has to be formed. An organization can never be comprehensive. A group of friends can be very comprehensive, very extensive, because within it there is an acceptance of diversity. No one is forced or controlled. Within the group everyone is free and nobody is being controlled – because whenever an intelligent person starts to feel that he is being controlled, he becomes troubled by it.

No intelligent person enjoys being in bondage. Only people with an inferiority complex want to be controlled; only those who are full of inferiority would rather be in fetters. No one else is going to want that.

Hence the group has to be kept so open that whenever someone joins in, he doesn't even feel that he has joined somewhere, that he has been tied down somewhere. He should feel free. Whether he is coming in or going out should not feel any different to him, should not make any difference.

I would like such a group to happen, such a comprehensive group of friends to happen, because the people who initially gather for a revolution are not aware how big the revolution is going to be. The companions of Lenin had no idea that what happened in 1917 would become such a universal phenomenon. Voltaire and his friends had no idea of what the French Revolution would bring. Gandhi and his friends also had no idea of what would or would not happen. Jesus couldn't have known at all what was being started. He had just twelve friends, and they too were not very educated people – just rustics. Someone was a carpenter, another was a fisherman… not educated people. Jesus had no way of even imagining that it would become such a widespread revolution, that one day half the world would recognize his message. He could not have even imagined that.

No one who sows seeds has ever imagined how big the trees they have planted will become. We cannot even imagine how much more beautiful their work would have become had they known.

Meeting with more people across the country, I have begun to feel that this work could become an enormous banyan tree. Thousands of people could find shade under it. It could become such a huge spring that it could quench the thirst of millions. But this is not yet clear to those friends who are the first to gather here. If they can be aware of this, then perhaps they will begin to work in an organized fashion.

Recently I was reading a scientific book. In Russia, when they are building roads, they project how many people will be using those roads in one hundred years' time, and then build them accordingly. And here we are, also building roads in our country, but we don't even take into consideration how many people will be traveling on them in two years' time! So every two years the roads have to be dug up again to make them wider. And every five years we realize that the traffic has increased and the roads are no longer adequate. Are we blind or what – that we can't even estimate how many people will be using the roads?

These people – who can project how many people there will be in a certain town after one hundred years, how many people will be using the roads in one hundred years, how wide the roads will need to be in one hundred years, and who can decide that it is better to build them now – are amazing.

Right now the group of friends is small, but in ten years' time it may be bigger than you could possibly imagine. And we have to work with that in mind: the road has to be made wide enough to accommodate that possibility. In ten years' time, unknown strangers will be walking down this road. You may not be here, I may not be here, none of us may be here, but someone will be walking on this road. So we must keep this in mind while we are working.

And we should remember too that we are not precious, it is the path which we are creating and to which we dedicate our lives that is precious. If it is large enough and wide enough, many people will be able to walk on it.

We need to consider these points in detail. I have just mentioned a few things around the issue which we will be considering over the next days. And it is necessary to contemplate each of these points in detail to see what can be done about them. My understanding of the details is very limited. You have more understanding than I do about these things.

I can tell you some of the pivotal points around which some thinking needs to be done, but I have almost no understanding of the details: how things are to be done, how many people will be required to do them, how much money will be needed, how much work will be needed. About all of these things you probably know more than I do. How to give it a practical form and how far to take it – you certainly know more about all this than I do. I don't know even the *ABC* of it.

That is why I thought I would tell you my ideas, and also listen to your ideas. And between the two sets of ideas – in their meeting, their merger – perhaps something will be possible. I can tell you some things about the sky, but I don't know much about the things of the earth. And talks about the sky alone do not have much value. The roots have to go into the earth; they have to take water and nourishment from the earth. So I will talk about how a tree can spread across the sky and how it can flower, but you will have to think a little about the roots. And remember, flowers are not as important as the roots are. Flowers depend on the roots.

So what roots can we provide this work with, so that this tree can grow? I will give my whole effort and energy to it. I am giving it, whether it grows bigger or not. It is not work for me; it is my joy, my bliss. It doesn't make any difference whether I have fellow travelers or not, it will continue in the same way. But if there were to be fellow travelers, this work could become vast and reach out to many people.

I have said some things to you about these few points. Now you must give some thought to it, to the details: what can be done; how it can be done. Give some thought to it with a very open mind and then we will discuss it here. All your opinions are invited tomorrow morning; express them, consider them, and then come to a decision.

The camp that I am doing here is a small camp. But then the idea will be to arrange a camp for all my friends from all over the country who have become interested in this work. This one is experimental because fewer people will be able to come to a conclusion more easily. It may perhaps not be as easy with larger numbers of people.

So we should reflect and then again have a camp in which people from all over the country can gather. It is also necessary for them to meet each other; it is necessary that they become acquainted with one another. They are doing the work in their areas. Your cooperation and encouragement are necessary for their work. They shouldn't feel alone there. They should feel that there are also more friends all over the country – that they are not standing all alone somewhere, that they have fellow travelers – and that if there is ever a need, they will all be with them to give advice, or if there is work to be done, that they will come and help.

Recently, friends in Rajkot told me that they want to take my message to those cities and places where I have not yet been. And they want to create a base there so that I can go there. It has become necessary. When I go to a new city, a few hundred or a few thousand people get to hear me. If some preparatory work is done beforehand, ten thousand people, fifty thousand people can hear me.

Friends from different places come up with different suggestions. Their suggestions are very significant, very useful. All those friends can meet to consider these things. This meeting will become the basis for these things to happen.

So right now I will not say anything more. From tomorrow morning we will begin to discuss the details. And bear in mind that you have not come here to listen to me. This is not a gathering for my discourses. I have talked as much as I have so that you can also speak. I have not been giving a speech; it has been just to encourage you to think and discuss.

The idea is that in these two days we will come to some conclusions through thinking and contemplating collectively, so that we can move ahead based on firm decisions, which will in turn get some work done.

Enough for today.

2
A New Vision of Sannyas

For many days the thought has been coming into my mind that in the future it is probable that sannyasins will disappear from the world. Within the next fifty years it will no longer be possible for the sannyasin to survive. The organization is already disappearing; the building blocks of that organization have shifted. Soon its building will collapse.

But sannyas is such an invaluable thing that the day it disappears from the world will be a very inauspicious day. In my vision, the sannyasin should go but sannyas should remain. And for that to happen I am thinking of periodical sannyas, periodical renunciation. In one year there should not be a single person who cannot take sannyas for a month. In life, there should not be a single person who has not taken sannyas two to four times.

Permanent sannyas – that some person becomes a sannyasin for his entire life – has proved dangerous. It has two dangers. One is that the person moves far away from life – and the attainment of godliness, love, bliss are experiences that happen in the thick of life, not outside it. The second point is when a person moves away from life, his peace, his bliss are not shared, disseminated, in the world. The world cannot partake of them.

And the third thing is that people start thinking that the people living in the world and the people who are sannyasins are separate from one another. So when people are doing something unconscious they think behaving like that is because of their limitation, because they are worldly people: "When we become sannyasins, we will not do that!" A distance has been created between religion and life.

In my vision sannyas should become part of life. Sannyas should become a tool for understanding and getting acquainted with life. The life of someone who cannot become a sannyasin for a few days every year should be considered incomplete – and also his education should be considered incomplete. A person who leads the life of a sannyasin with totality for even one or two months out of twelve will find unimaginable doors of bliss opening in his life.

For those two months he will become a complete, a total, sannyasin. For those two months he will have no dealings with the outside world; he will not even have the relationship a sannyasin normally has with the world.

You will be surprised to know that the person who becomes a sannyasin for his entire life becomes dependent on the people who live normal lives in the world, on householders. It seems that he is far away from the world but in reality he has to stay close to the world. But a person who becomes a sannyasin for two months is not dependent on anyone: he is dependent on his own earnings which he has made during the remaining ten months of the year. He is not dependent on the world. That is why he is not afraid of anybody and he is not beholden to anyone.

If someone becomes a sannyasin for his entire life, he will become dependent on somebody. He cannot escape it. The end result is that even though a sannyasin appears to be the leader, in reality he becomes the disciple of his disciples. He has to follow his disciples. Worldly people give him orders: "You should do this, not do that." The worldly person becomes the sannyasin's master because he gives him his bread. The sannyasin becomes a slave.

This slavery of the sannyasin can be broken in only one way, and that is if a person becomes an occasional sannyasin. For eleven months of the year he remains in the world and for one month he becomes a sannyasin. Then he is not dependent on anybody. He is only dependent on his own earnings from those eleven months. He does not have anything to do with anyone else. And in this one month he can enjoy his freedom without being beholden to anyone. So in this month he will have the experience of total sannyas, which a sannyasin – a permanent one – can never experience. In this month he can live in total freedom.

In this one month the way in which he lives, the bliss and peace he experiences, and the freedom into which he will enter... After one month he will return to his routine life. He will return, and again in the thick of life will experiment with what he has learned in aloneness. Can he use it in the crowd?

Learning happens in aloneness but the test occurs in the marketplace. One who escapes from the crowd escapes from this test; his education remains incomplete. If you cannot use what you have learned in your aloneness in the marketplace, then that learning is false; it has not much value. The marketplace is the touchstone because the challenges lie there. The circumstances are not favorable; they are unfavorable. Can I remain peaceful there too – or not? Can I still keep the sannyas that I have been practicing within me for a month and the bliss that I have found while sitting in my house or in my shop?

For eleven months a person should keep an eye on himself, observe himself. After one year he should again return for a month, so that he can make all that he has experienced within that one year – in that test – go deeper. He can then climb to a higher place than he had reached the year before.

If from the ages of twenty to seventy a person becomes a sannyasin for fifty months out of those fifty years of his life, no truth in this world will remain unfamiliar to him, and no experience will remain unknown.

This periodical renunciation, this sannyas taken for a period of time, will not distance the person from life. Our traditional sannyasins have become life negative. Wives and children are scared of them, parents are scared of them – because their lives are devastated by their by going away, leaving them.

The person I am talking about will only be a sannyasin for a period of time. There is no need to be afraid of him. When he returns, his wife will find that he has returned a more loving husband; his children will find that he has returned a better father; his mother will find that her son has returned a more trusting person, more loving and filled with more respect. After this month away, during the remaining eleven months – when he is living at home sharing this newfound fragrance in all his relationships – he will refresh the world anew. He will be helpful to life: creating and befriending it. Until now the sannyasin has plundered the world and spoiled it. He has not made it more beautiful.

So according to me periodical sannyas is essential. In this manner, the sannyasin will disappear from the world – which is not a problem – and sannyas will remain. In this way, sannyas will spread extensively on a much larger scale – because then each person will have the right to become a sannyasin. Right now everyone does not have that right – because if every person were to become a sannyasin right now, life would become a graveyard, a death.

If something is not available for every single person to experience, then there is something fundamentally wrong with it. There is something fundamentally wrong with anything that cannot become everyone's right.

Right now, if everyone were to become a full-time sannyasin, then life would be a disaster. Then even those who are sannyasins would have to return to the world. So this lifetime sannyas is an illusion, it is wrong. Because of this it has become very necessary to make some profound experiments so that sannyas can survive in the world. The suggestion made by this friend is very much in tune with my heart. It can make this possible.

Another friend here has said:

> **Osho,**
> ***We understand what you are saying and it reaches our intellects, but still it doesn't change our personalities.***

What he is saying is correct, because the making of a personality takes so many years of one's life. And those who know say that it is a creation of many lives.

You are listening to what I am saying. It is heard by the little corner of the personality called the intellect, and the intellect thinks it is right. But the personality is much bigger than the intellect. The mind is only a small part of the personality. The whole personality is much bigger than the intellect. The intellect is like a door. It is as though there is a palace and it has a door. The palace is very big, but the palace is not the door. The door is also not the palace. The only function of the door is that it gives someone entry to the palace. Besides that it has no other value.

Intellect is just a door into one's personality. Personality is a very big thing, and it is constructed on the basis of many things. Many things, which you cannot even imagine, build up a personality. So if something new enters your mind, it does not have any effect, because your whole personality is built up of so many things which are basically against the thing that has just entered. It will make no difference to the personality; the personality will remain as it is, and then you will start becoming anxious: "What to do now?"

So if it is possible for you to come and stay with me for a month, for two or three months, then I can give you suggestions about all the changes that need to be made in your entire personality. Staying close to me, you can experiment with what can be changed. If only you could understand this just once! You may not even be aware that the personality is linked to such strange things...

You may have heard the name of Hari Singh Gaur; he built Sagar University. In India he was possibly one of the biggest lawyers of his time. He also practiced law in the Privy Council in London.

I was talking with him about personality. Then he said, "I remember one of the experiences I had. I used to have a habit which I was unaware of. Whenever I used to argue and there was a problem – if a difficulty arose and my mind was not working – then unknowingly I used to twist my coat button. I was not even aware of this; it had become part of an unconscious habit. And as soon as I started twisting my coat button, I would immediately get an answer to the problem."

Just as one person may scratch his head and another do something else, he used to twist his coat button.

He was the lawyer in one big case. It was a business affair of the state. The opposition lawyer observed that whenever there was a difficulty with an argument Hari Singh Gaur would twist his top coat button. The opposition lawyer conspired with Hari Singh Gaur's driver to break that button off his coat. When Hari Singh Gaur arrived at court his driver was carrying the coat over his arm. As the opposition lawyer had given some money to the driver, he had broken the top button off the coat.

Once in court, Hari Singh Gaur put his coat on. As he was arguing and a difficulty arose, his hand automatically went to the button – and there was no button there! Suddenly his brain stopped functioning. He became very nervous.

That was the first case he lost. He told me, "I lost because of that button – but at that time I could not understand it. With no button, it seemed everything was finished for me. There was an association, a relationship. It was a conditioned reflex of the mind that if the button turned, the mind would function; if the button did not turn, the mind would not function."

Such a small thing as a button can relate to the functioning of the mind, yet we cannot imagine such a thing. Such a small thing like that button runs our personalities and we are totally unaware of it. So in order to transform the whole personality, there are many things to be understood – things that one cannot even imagine are important to know. By changing a few things in a certain way, real change can happen.

A person wants to become peaceful and that person is wearing tight clothes. He cannot even imagine that wearing tight clothes is inimical to peace. It is not obvious, or else we could have stopped military people from wearing tight clothes long back. It is very essential to wear tight clothes in the military: tight clothes support the tendency to fight. Loose clothes are not supportive of fighting. Clans who wear loose clothes are not fighters.

So small, seemingly insignificant things like clothes can affect the personality as far as fighting or remaining peaceful are concerned. This is not easily understood. You may not be aware that if you are wearing tight clothes and you are climbing steps, you climb two steps at a time. And if you are wearing loose clothes, then you will only climb one step at a time, not two. Servants are made to wear tight clothes on purpose so that they can work efficiently. Their masters have been wearing loose clothes because the question of working does not arise for them.

Throughout the world sannyasins choose to wear loose clothes. There is a reason behind this: they do not have to do any work. The people who have to work need to wear tight clothes. Tight clothes bring a kind of alertness to the mind; they bring intensity, create a force. Loose clothes bring coolness, create a relaxed mind. Everything on the inside relaxes.

I am talking about this just as an example. The personality has many parts and these parts make up a person. From your shoes to your hat, from your food to your sleep, from the words you speak to your dreams, everything makes up your personality – everything!

But all this will stay. If you think that now, just by listening to my talk, everything will change, then you must be mad! Does change happen in this way? This is only an indication that can help change. And if you can understand this indication, then you will have to search through your entire personality and look in every nook and corner for whatever is there that goes against this indication. If you can see that something is against it, then you should change it. To change, one does not have to do much, but one must be able to see it at least once. One should at least understand where the hurdle may be.

Our minds get stuck in such small things. If you think that they are stuck in something great, something big, there you are wrong. In life there are no great things. In life there are only small things. We keep thinking about great things and wasting our time unnecessarily. In life there are many small things which no one either thinks about, is concerned with or takes account of. These small things constitute a personality.

So change is not possible when you are by yourself. But it is possible that if you come and stay close to me for some days, I can see small things in you from being close to you. I can give you some suggestions, I can tell you to change certain things – to try changing a few things and see what happens. Sometimes very minute changes can bring about a transformation which we are unable to comprehend. We cannot explain how such a small thing can have such a big impact.

But a personality is very complex indeed. The intellect is incomplete; the intellect is too small. Intellect is the beginning, not the end. So listening to me, only a beginning happens. It is not the end. It is only an invitation to you: now you can do something about it. So it is appropriate that you stay for more time. Then much significant work can be carried out in any meditation centers that you create.

Many friends that I have in this country tell me that I should do something for their children; that it is essential to think about their children. If someone creates a center, then for one to two months a separate camp could be run for children. For two months children could come, the children of all my friends could come and stay with me. Then I could work with them – because the real work is with them, the real work is not with you. And if you can understand what I am saying, then you will worry less about yourselves and think more about your children. If you can understand what I am saying, be concerned about your children. What can happen very easily with them has become very difficult for you. Your whole stratagem is almost fixed. If you have courage, let your children become part of this revolution.

Children could gather there. If not today, then maybe tomorrow; it is possible there could be a university there, a new place. It is possible that there could be a hostel there. Children would study in the city, but could stay in the center, could stay the night there: then they could experiment with their lives. But they could study anywhere. There would be a big hostel there, and the children of the city who wished to stay there could stay there, whereas they could study anywhere. The organization would have no connection with education, but their lives and the way they lived – how they lived, how they woke up, what they would do – as far as these things are concerned some experiments could be done for them. If there were a center, then such a thing would be possible.

The third thing is, in many places throughout the country millions of people have told me that if a meditation technique could be relayed on the radio for ten minutes every night, then hundreds of thousands of people in this country could switch on their radios and experiment with that technique in their homes. If not today, then perhaps tomorrow, when you have a big enough meditation center, it is possible that you will have a radio station of your own. Then I could be present in the whole country. As Agarwal-ji said just now, it is only appropriate that I move into the mainstream. That is correct. It is good if I can.

But once I go to a place, I cannot go back to that place before one, or sometimes even two years have passed. Something that has been created always seems to disappear during that year. When I return to a place after a year it seems that the whole group is new. Everything seems to have disappeared in the space of that one year. Hence it is essential that there are arrangements for a follow-up during the year. Several people have told me that it would be very appropriate if every night at ten o'clock they could listen to suggestions for meditation for fifteen minutes, and then, following those suggestions, they could go to bed.

If not today, then perhaps tomorrow, when you have a center and have a big plan, then all this can become possible there.

If you start a center in one place in India, there is no need to force me to live there. If not now then later, you can make four such places around the country, and then I can stay for three months in each of them. It is not essential for me to live in the place where you make a center. I will be coming and going. People will be living there, and in one month I will stay there for fifteen days, and for fifteen days I will go away. For fifteen days they will stay with me, for fifteen days they will stay without me. This also has an advantage, because if in the fifteen days that they are without me, they can do what they do when they are with me, in my presence. Doing it in my absence will have some value: after a month they will be going back to their homes, and there I will not be present.

So this will continue – that I go away for a few days and then stay for a few days. This will not make any difference; there is no reason for my travels to discontinue.

These days I get numerous letters saying that people would like to come and stay with me. I do not have anywhere for them. And if I do not have any provision for myself, how can I make arrangements for others to stay? I am absolutely without a base; I do not have any home. If I myself am somebody's guest, then how can I make arrangements for anyone else?

So many letters come! Some people would like to stay permanently. Just three days before I came here, I received a letter from an elderly man who is seventy years of age saying, "Whatever two to four remaining years of life I have, I would not like to lose them. Since I have heard your talks, I am in difficulty. All that I have been doing until now seems worthless. And now death seems so close, I wish I could come and stay close to you and really only do that which is worth doing. So I would like to come and stay close to you. I can take care of myself financially and do whatever is needed."

But I do not have any provision for this. We can agree on an age limit: if a person over fifty-five or sixty years of age wishes to come and stay for longer or permanently, they would be allowed to stay. We would not be willing to take people below sixty years for a longer stay; they would have to go for periodical sannyas. After reaching sixty, if someone wishes to stay for longer, he would be allowed to stay long-term. For such people it would be a permanent or longer term sannyas.

It is not known how many people are eager for this. I also feel that some of my friends are thinking, "Enough is enough! We have earned enough for the last fifty to fifty-five years; we have made all the arrangements. Now we wish..."

I have a friend. He heard me talking – he was fifty years of age – and he said, "This year, when my birthday comes, I shall finish with all my work. Enough is enough! I have been earning, I have enough to eat and I do not have anything else to take care of. For whom am I earning money now?"

So on his fifty-first birthday he closed down his business. He shut down his shop and closed all his accounts. He told his wife, "We have so much that even if we live for a hundred, two hundred years there is enough for both of us. Now what shall we do?" So he closed everything down.

Now again he is writing to me saying, "I have closed down everything and now I wish to come and stay close to you. What is there to do here?"

But I do not have anything organized. I am continuously on the move. So in such a situation, whom should I tell about such people? It would be better if there were a place for people who would like to come and stay permanently. And people who would like to come and go could also do so.

In Thailand, Burma and in Japan there is an arrangement for periodical sannyas. Right from the prime minister to the common man, everyone can avail himself of the opportunity to become a sannyasin for some time during his life if he so wishes.

We keep running in this manner – someone goes away for one month to Mussoorie, someone goes to Lonavala, someone goes somewhere else. But what difference does going away make? Only the place changes, nothing else changes. There is some change in the weather but mentally there is no change.

In a month, it is possible that mental change can happen – and a change of place also happens. And especially with children I can do something. You should be aware of this.

The second thing: the meditation camps that are happening now are taking place for three days, so it is not possible to go deeply into all aspects of life. If there were a permanent center, then we could have different camps for specialized subjects.

My vision is for all subjects. I do not feel that it is only important to talk about the divine. I feel that it is equally important to talk about sex. I do not feel that it is only important to talk about meditation. I feel that it is equally important to talk about love. I do not feel it is only important to talk about yoga. It is equally important to talk about the experience of pleasure or pain. The whole of life can be touched upon.

There are many friends who have written to me that there should be a camp for couples, where both husband and wife can participate together. There could also be a family camp, where a person could participate with his entire family. I could tell you my views regarding the family, about the internal relations within the family, the way the family thinks; my views regarding homes – how a family can live, how a home can become one unit, what can constitute a family.

So much wrong is happening. The family is so wrong, so false, and so ugly you cannot believe it. Houses are good, good houses are being made, but the family is absolutely ugly, is becoming more and more ugly. The family has become rotten: it has no love in it, no respect, and no inner relationships. The whole of life is resting on this structure. We come here, from somewhere outside, and search for peace, but if the style of our families does not change, then peace cannot be found.

What revolution is possible in the inner life of a family? We could have a separate camp to look at this subject. And there could be another camp concerned with marriage, love and sex – this is the biggest problem for the youth of today. If there is no solution to it, then the entire society will collapse. There is no point in criticizing the joys of sensuality. Physical enjoyment is an essential part of life. The person who becomes capable of enjoying it in a balanced way attains to meditation. There is no opposition between yoga and *bhoga*, between meditation and sensual enjoyment, but opposition to it has been upheld until now. This has created a loss; this has not created a gain.

So how can a normal life of physical, sensual enjoyment continue and move into meditation? What can constitute a bridge between the two, not an opposition, but rather what can be the way of joining the two? It is essential to work on this, to think about it and about all questions regarding life – the organization of society, the arrangement of finance... The thing is, you do not realize that all around you, if not today then tomorrow, the things which you are not thinking about at all are going to present themselves as problems to you. If not today, then maybe tomorrow, the problem of communism will face this country. You cannot escape it; you cannot run away from it. And if you do not think about it, then communism will spread like an avenging angel in here, it will spread like a bloody revolution. But if we think about it and prepare the intelligentsia of the country, then communism can come in a very peaceful way. That will be one way. But our religious people do not think about this.

In my vision, the whole of life is worth thinking about. Soon questions to do with the economy will arise. The politics of the entire nation have become rotten. In this, we are all in a fix. Everyone is shouting, but there is no solution, no way out. People are standing by like blind people and enduring it. They can see what is happening. It is almost as though a house is on fire and they are standing outside and criticizing the person who set the house alight: "What happened? How will the fire be put out?" And the house keeps burning away – and while the house is burning we are all thinking!

In ten to fifty years' time our children will blame us, thinking, "What sort of people were around then? When this whole country was on fire and stupidity was on the rise, in spite of all of this, these people just kept sitting down discussing things – and nothing was done about it."

So it is important to think about politics. What should the politics of the country be? How should the religion of the country be? How should the social structure of the country be? How should the families in the country be? How should the financial arrangement of the country be? On all these issues…

In this country people in different places ask me what I do. Just now, here in Matheran, I did not reply to that question, because to give an answer an entire meditation camp would have been needed!

A friend has asked a question:

> **Osho,**
> ***Will you be devoting all your energy toward only a few people becoming peaceful and silent? Will you not be using your energy for society at large? Will you not be doing anything so that this big country, the entire life of this country, can be influenced?***

His asking is perfectly right. I also feel the pain of it in my heart. Something should be done for them – because not doing anything means that we are agreeing with whatever is happening.

Not doing anything does not really mean non-doing. In some ways not doing is also a way of agreeing with the prevalent doing. If someone is killing a person, and if I say I do not want to do anything about it, then I am associated with the killer – because I am standing there, watching the murder happening. I could have stopped it, but I am not stopping it, so I am helping it happen.

So do not think that certain people are not participating in politics. Your so-called saints and sages are not interested in politics, but don't think that they are not part of the politics. They are part of it because whatever is happening has their agreement; they are not opposing all that is happening. So whosoever is part of life is part and parcel of each and every thing. One cannot run away. Even if someone runs away, then too he is part of it, because if he says he does not want anything to do with it, this means he is agreeing to whatever status quo is present: "Whatever is happening is fine."

No, we cannot escape from life. The whole spectrum of life, all the different aspects of life, can be touched. It is important to touch all its aspects because the whole of life is interrelated; everything is connected with everything else. If the politics of the country is wrong, then the education of the country cannot be right. If the education of the country is not right, then the religion of the country cannot be right. If the religion of the country is not right, then the education of the country cannot be right. If the education is not right, then the politics cannot be right. Everything is interconnected. For all these interconnected things to be integrated, we can develop a vision and a lifestyle, a practical lifestyle. For this it is essential that we convene conferences, seminars, camps, for many days to address many issues. These should be in secluded places where we will be able to stay peacefully.

Right now we are staying in a hotel. After all, a hotel is a hotel: a hotel does not have a psychic atmosphere, a hotel does not have a mental atmosphere. We come and stay here, and arrangements for food and lodging are taken care of. But if tomorrow we are going to build a place, then my vision is that we will build it with a psychic atmosphere and surroundings. The trees there should say something to you, the buildings should also say something to you, the pathways, the air should also speak to you. And the people staying there, their presence, should also say something to you. There should be a complete psychic atmosphere in that place so that just by entering it a person feels that not only has he changed location, but that the currents and waves in his mind have also changed.

All this can be accomplished in this new place. And very small things make the whole difference.

When Hitler came to power he ordered that children should not be allowed to play with dolls. Playing with dolls and arranging doll marriages should all stop. All children's toys were changed. They were to have only tanks, guns, and swords.

When a small child was put in his cradle on the first day, there would not be a toy hanging over the cradle, but a tank instead. The first thing that he would see would be a tank. That would be the first thing impressed on his mind: a tank.

Hitler said that dolls were no longer acceptable. Such things would make children weak and impotent. Such things did not make children strong and did not prepare them for war. If one wants to prepare a child for war, right from the first day he should be given a tank.

All children's toys are colored red. This is absolutely wrong. Children who play with red toys will be restless. The color red is the main cause of restlessness in the mind. But by seeing green colored doors you become happy. You do not know how much there is in those green doors! When you go into a jungle, you become happy, you feel peaceful. It is only because of the color green, nothing else. The only reason is that the expansion of the color green cools the cells of the eyes, makes them relaxed. The color red sharpens them, the cells become tense. If you look at the color red for a long time, you will become filled with anger. If all the people here wear red clothes, then in a short time you will become agitated, you will suddenly feel suffocated: something is wrong, you will have to move away from the place. It is not soothing at all. But children's toys are colored red. They should be colored green if children are to live in a silent world in the future; otherwise they will become restless.

What I am saying is that life is composed of so many small things, tied up with so many different things, that we have to think and reflect on them – and that should include buildings. So we should build the center with a scientific vision. The color of the place, the buildings, the plants, the flowers, the roads, the air and the people in that place – whenever someone enters we will be providing him with every facility for his inner transformation.

It is not going to be an ordinary ashram. It is going to be a completely scientific laboratory. It will be totally scientific, based on the present day experiences of human beings. It will be a completely scientific laboratory, so that we can transform a person. Within one month a person can be totally transformed into a new being before he returns home. And whatever he learns there, whatever he takes from there, he will try to bring those changes into his own home.

So according to me, this is good. Now you can all think about it in detail, and organize it. Whatever I am able to do can be done more easily if everything is arranged well.

And right now this friend is saying that his personality has not changed. But his personality could change so much that he will start saying, "Now please don't change it any more. Please let me go home!" This much he could say. There is no problem with this, absolutely no problem at all because we have created the personality of a man, so we can also transform it. We are whatever we have created so far, and we will become whatever we change. To change one's personality is not difficult, not a problem at all, because there is a straightforward science to changing a personality. There is a science behind its making; we have made it in a specific way. Now all the bricks that we have laid will have to be moved; then that personality will become totally different, an absolutely changed personality.

So think in this direction. And other suggestions that have come from some friends are also of importance. Think how the publications can reach as many people as possible. Also think how the talks can reach many people. This needs to be thought through. If you think, then many ways will occur. If you think, then you will find many friends who can give their energy and put in their efforts. We have friends, but today we do not have work. In many places people ask me, "What shall we do? We would like to do something." We do not have any work right now that we can give them to do. If you have work, then you will not have a shortage of workers. Many good people will be coming. Every day more and even better people will be coming.

If someone starts digging a well, then initially he encounters only pebbles and stones. Then slowly he finds good soil. Then he reaches to the source of the water. We should think of ourselves right now as the pebbles and stones – as we have only just started digging the well. Far better people than us will be coming. And we should be ready, so that whenever a more dedicated person than us comes, we can give up our place, and we tell them, "Please come! You will be able to look after this place in a better way than I can."

This is the quality of love in a group of friends: that we are always willing to leave a place, that whenever a better person arrives we will give up our place to them. I am only here until a better person arrives; otherwise I shall immediately tell him and leave – because every day better people will be coming.

It is such a big country; this country has so much energy and people here are so good. The day we start calling them, many people will be coming. Up to now we have not even called, we have not even made a sound. Up to now I have not said anything to anyone in this country about all of this.

Whenever you are ready, I will start speaking. Within a few days you will become afraid because we have found so many people for the work!

I have not made an appeal to anyone yet to come and help with the work. But people have started talking about it by themselves. The day I start to appeal and invite people to come and work, you will find it difficult to find enough work.

So decide on the work, think of the directions, and I will bring the people. Don't worry about the people; there will be no difficulty as far as that is concerned.

Enough for today.

3
Work Will Bring Its Own Wealth

Some two hundred years ago a war broke out between two kingdoms in Japan. The smaller kingdom was very frightened; their defeat was certain. They had fewer soldiers. They not only had fewer soldiers, they were highly outnumbered. If the enemy had ten soldiers, they had only one.

The army commanders of that kingdom refused to go to war. They said, "Obviously it would be absolutely foolish, when defeat is so certain, to take our men into battle just to be needlessly butchered and killed."

So the commanders refused to fight. They said, "Defeat is certain. We are not ready to have our faces painted black with defeat, and for our soldiers to be killed for no purpose whatsoever. We will not agree to do this. It is wiser to accept defeat than to get every single person butchered, when that will simply mean the same outcome: defeat. There is no possibility of victory."

The king could not say anything to them. What the commanders had said was true; the numbers were as unequal as they had said. So the king went to see a mystic living in a village and asked him, "Would you become the commander of my army?"

His commanders were not able to understand why he was talking with the mystic. At a time when the commanders themselves were refusing to go, then to ask a mystic – someone who has no experience of war, one who has never been to a war, one who has never fought a war, who has never talked about war – what was the purpose of taking this impractical man to the battlefront?

But the mystic agreed. In situations when most practical people are not ready, impractical people become ready. In situations where people who understand the matter take a step back, people who do not have any experience step to the front. The mystic agreed to the king's proposal. The king became a little frightened inside, but there again, it seemed all right. It was better to be defeated by fighting and getting killed.

The soldiers became very scared to go with the mystic: this man did not know anything! But the mystic was filled with such enthusiasm, the soldiers had to go. Even the commanders started to follow the soldiers; they were curious to see what was going to happen.

Just a little distance from the enemy camp the mystic halted all the soldiers at a small temple and said, "Before we go on, we should at least tell God that we are going to fight, and ask him what his wishes are. If we are going to lose, then we will return home, and if we are going to win, then everything is fine."

The soldiers waited with great hope outside the temple. The mystic folded his hands, closed his eyes and prayed. He then took out a one rupee coin from his pocket and said, "I am tossing this one rupee coin. If it falls with its head up, we will understand that victory is ours and we will proceed accordingly. And if it falls showing its tail, then we will assume that we would have lost. We will return and tell the king, 'Don't arrange for our deaths. Our defeat would certainly happen. It is the wish of God.'"

The soldiers watched carefully while the mystic tossed the rupee coin. In the glaring sunlight, the coin shone and fell. It fell with its head facing upward. The mystic told the soldiers, "Forget your worries. Forget about defeat. Now there is no one in this land who can defeat you." The rupee coin had fallen heads up. God was with them.

The soldiers started fighting. Within days they had defeated the enemy. They came back victorious. When they were close to the temple the mystic said, "Now that we have returned, at least we should express our gratitude."

All the soldiers stopped, they folded their hands, prayed to God and said, "We are very thankful to you. If you had not given us an indication we would have surely lost. We have won because of a sign from you."

The mystic said, "Before you thank God, please look carefully at the coin which is in my pocket." He took out the coin and showed it to them. On both sides of the coin there were heads; it did not have a tail side! It was a false coin: on both sides it had heads, so it could never fall with the tail side up.

He said, "Do not thank God. You were filled with the hope of winning; that is why you have won. If you had had no hope – if you had been filled with the desire to lose and had been certain that you were going to lose – you would have lost."

In life all the success of our work is based on whether we are filled with the hope of winning or we are scared by the idea of losing. And people who are filled with great hope and with little ability can do so much, whereas people who have great ability but who are filled with hopelessness cannot achieve anything. Ability is valuable, but ability is not the real wealth. The real wealth is hope – and the idea that some work which has to be done *will* happen, and that no stone will be left unturned.

The talk about ten million rupees could seem great to some people. For friends who have limited wealth it may seem a big amount. It seems like a big thing because we immediately count ten million as a very big amount. The figure ten million is very big to us!

I remember one incident...

There was a very beautiful mountain near a village. There was a temple on that beautiful mountain which was ten miles away from the village. It could be seen from the village. People used to come from far away to worship in that temple and visit the mountain.

A young man lived in the village. He thought that he should go to see the temple sometime. But it was close by, so he could go at any time.

One day he decided, "How long should I wait? Tonight I should get up and go." In the day the heat would increase, so he got up early – at two o'clock in the morning – lit a lantern and went out into the village. It was a very dark night; he became very afraid. He thought, "This is a small lantern; it lights up only two or three steps ahead of me, and the distance to be covered is ten miles. How can this long and dark distance of ten miles be covered by this small lantern? It is so dark, the darkness is vast. What use will this little lantern of mine be? It cannot light up ten miles. It will be better to wait for the sun to rise; then it will be all right to proceed." So he sat down outside the village.

It seemed right, his arithmetic seemed correct. Generally most people use similar arithmetic. The light only reaches three feet ahead and the journey is ten miles long. If three feet are divided into ten miles, then how can this small lantern serve the purpose? A hundred thousand lanterns will be needed. Only then can the distance be covered.

He sat there afraid, waiting for the morning to come. Then he saw an old man coming with a small lamp in his hand. He asked the old man, "Have you gone mad? Don't you know any arithmetic? The journey is ten miles long and the light from your lamp is not enough to light even one step!"

The old man said, "Fool! Can anyone ever walk more than one step at a time? I cannot walk more than one step at a time even if the way is lit for a thousand miles. And by the time I walk one step, the light also moves one step ahead. What is ten miles? I can cover ten thousand miles! Get up! Why are you sitting down? You have a very good lantern. If you take one step forward, the light will move forward that same distance."

In life, if we keep calculating beforehand about the whole of the life that lies ahead of us, we will not be able to move. We will become afraid and will be finished there and then. In life, the people who count one step at a time move thousands of miles, and the people who count thousands of miles do not move one single step forward; they are afraid and they stay where they are.

I say do not worry too much about this ten million rupees; the sum is too big, there is no point worrying about it. One should not think that ten million is a huge amount. And also please do not think – as Durlabh-ji bhai has said – that one hundred thousand rupees can be given by one hundred people. It is difficult to find a hundred people who will give one hundred thousand rupees each, but even today it will be easy to find ten million people who would give one rupee each. Don't think of one hundred thousand rupees. Think of one rupee. Think step by step. Why think about a distance of ten miles?

So this is not something to worry about. It is so easy to find ten million people who will give one rupee each – it is very easy – but if it is not possible for you, please let me know. If it is possible for you to arrange for the rupees, it is fine, otherwise tell me and I will manage that too. You need not worry about it; you need not become afraid of it. I cannot promise you a hundred thousand rupees, but I can promise you one rupee. Where is the problem with that? So please do not worry how this will be done. It is not so difficult.

In this land, which has a big tradition of beggars, if you cannot do it, I am prepared to become a beggar. There is no problem. Here, Mahavira is a beggar, Buddha is a beggar, Gandhi is a beggar. Here, there is no problem in becoming a beggar, there is a problem in becoming a king! Here, to become a king is contemptible, is very sinful. To become a beggar is a thing of great respect!

Once Gandhi was at a meeting in Dehradun, and when it was over he said, "No one should leave without giving a donation. Everyone must give at least something." He spread out his hands and went into the crowd saying, "Wherever my hands point, the person facing them should give me something. So whatever they could give they gave, whatever they had they gave. When his hands were full, Gandhi emptied their contents onto the floor and again opened them, saying, "Everyone, please remember to take care that no one takes my wealth which is lying on the floor."

There, in that crowd, his hands were filled several times and everything was emptied onto the floor. He walked away after emptying his hands for the last time, and told the workers to collect the donations from the floor.

Mahavir Tyagi was one of those workers. He collected everything and took it to Gandhi. There were many rupees, many ornaments. By the time they had collected everything it was one o'clock in the morning. Things had been scattered between people's feet; everything had been thrown onto the floor in among the crowd.

They counted everything in the middle of the night. When they went to Gandhi, they found that he was still awake. He asked, "Did you count everything?"

They had counted everything: so many thousand rupees had been collected and so many other things. But among all this, there was only one woman's earring. Gandhi asked, "Where is the other earring? Can you imagine why any woman would give me only one earring? Go back! There should be another earring somewhere." Then he said, "Can you conceive that there is such a woman in our country who would give one earring and take the other one back home? That is impossible. It must be your fault. Go! There should be another earring lying there somewhere."

Later Tyagi said, "We became very shaky. How strange this old man was! First he throws everything down on the ground, creates a big commotion, and then when we have collected everything so late in the night, in the dark, he says that one earring is missing!"

But when they went back they were surprised: not only did they find the earring they also found some other ornaments.

Gandhi said, "I could not believe that in this land I would beg and someone would give only one earring. They would give both. So it was missing. And now you have brought some more things. Tomorrow morning go back and look properly. Perhaps even more things will be found."

This country has a big tradition of begging. This country also has another interesting thing, which is that here, the beggar is not considered inferior to the donor. Here, the person who begs is not inferior to the giver, he is considered superior to the giver. And the beggar does not give thanks, saying "Thank you for giving me so much. I am so grateful to you." The beggar does not say this. Here, the giver says, "Thank you." He says,

"I am grateful to you for accepting. If you had not been willing to receive, what would I have done?"

I was in Jaipur – just last night I was telling you about it. An old man came and put a big bundle of rupee notes in front of me and bowed down.

I said, "I accept your *namaste*, but I do not need these rupees right now. Sometime, when I am in need, I will come and ask you. At that time I will come and ask you. For now, please keep your rupees. Right now I have no need of them."

I told him this casually, but then I saw tears in his eyes. He was a seventy-year-old man. He asked me, "What are you saying? I have not given it to you because you need it! I have it, now what will I do with it? I give it to good people so something can be done. In any case I am not doing anything with it. Your needing it is not the reason I have given it, so the question of your need does not arise. I have it, but what will I do with it? It is essential for me to give, and I give money to good people so something worthwhile can come out of it."

The old man then said, "You do not know that by saying no you are hurting me very much. I am such a poor man. Except for money, I do not have anything. I am so poor that except for money, I have absolutely nothing! If someone refuses to accept my money, then I will be in difficulty. What will I do with it? When I want to do something, except for money, I don't have anything to give. So please don't say no to this offer. You can throw it away, burn it, but I will not let you say no, because then I will not have anything to give – and this idea of giving has come into my mind. I would be very grateful if you would accept it."

So please don't worry too much about money. And the day you feel you need money and you cannot manage it, please let me know. Money will be arranged. Money is not a concern. That I do not ask for money is a different matter, but the day I have to ask for it, money will come. There is nothing cheaper than money in this world. Anybody can give it. As far as giving money is concerned, there is no one who is so weak that he cannot give something. People give their hearts, their lives – giving money is nothing!

So there is no reason to worry too much about it. If you get started with some work, full of courage, you will find that the work will bring its own wealth, will bring its own money.

In various places, people have come and said to me that they want to give ten thousand rupees to the work. Now what am I supposed to tell them? Which area should this money be offered to? I do not need it. How am I to carry it? What will I do with these rupees? They say, "Okay, if some day you need it, if some work arises..."

You may think that people do not give because they do not want to give, but you would be surprised. My experience is that people hesitate to say, "We want to give money." My own experience is that people hesitate; they think, "How can we say this, how can we dare to say this? A poor thing like money – how can we say that we want to give money?"

The day they know that money is needed, it will start flowing. There will be no problem. If you worry about it a lot, then there is nothing worse than money. That worry is born because you calculate in terms of lakhs, in terms of hundreds of thousands of rupees. A person with lakhs of rupees has little capacity to give money, while the capacity to give of a person who has one rupee is enormous.

There was once a mystic, a Mohammedan mystic called Hassan. He used to live in a small hut. The hut was so small that only he and his wife could sleep in it.

One dark and rainy night they were sleeping. It must have been around midnight when a stranger came and knocked at the door. Hassan said to his wife, "Open the door! It seems that a traveler is lost."

His wife replied, "Can't you see there isn't room for more than two people in here!"

The mystic said, "Mad woman! This is not a rich man's palace, where there is no room. This is a poor man's hut. The palaces of the rich are small; the huts of the poor are big. This is not a rich man's palace, where there is no space; this is the hut of a poor man. Right now we two are lying down. Soon we three will be sitting up. There will be lots of room then. Open the door! Do you want the person who is at the door to go away?"

The door was opened. A man came and sat inside. The two of them got out of bed and sat down, and as all three were sitting, they started to chat. The door was closed.

Two more people came and started knocking at the door. Hassan said to the guest, who had just arrived and was sitting by the door, "My friend, please open the door!"

The man said, "What are you saying? There is not enough room in here."

Hassan said, "Not enough room? If this room had been too small, how would you have been able to come inside? There is plenty of room in here."

The man said, "Can't you see that we three are sitting with great difficulty?"

Hassan replied, "Now we are sitting, but soon we will all be standing. This is the hut of a poor man; here there is never a shortage of space."

The door had to be opened, and the two men came in. All five people stood up and started talking.

And then a donkey came. A donkey, who had got wet in the rain, came and knocked at the door. He banged on it with his head. Hassan told the man standing opposite him, "Friend please open the door! A guest has come."

The man said, "It is not a guest. It is a donkey."

Hassan said, "You do not understand. This is the hut of a poor man. Here we treat donkeys like human beings. It is a different story with the houses of the rich: there, even human beings are treated like donkeys. Open the door! Now we are all standing a little far apart from one another. Soon we will be standing close to each other. But this poor hut can never become less accommodating. If necessary, I will leave, my wife will go outside, but as long as we can manage it, we will make room for you."

If you think in terms of hundreds of thousands, then you become worried. The person with hundreds of thousands of rupees does not have a heart. He has a small heart. So please don't worry about this. If a man with hundreds of thousands of rupees grows a big heart, then hundreds of thousands of rupees will come from him. Otherwise, the man with one rupee has still got a big heart. There is no problem with all this. It will be possible.

If you engage in any work with courage, there is no barrier to its success.

Right now I do not have anything more to say to you. In the night I will listen to what you have to say, and then if there is something more to say, I will say it.

4
Collecting Friends, Not Funds

All day long we have been discussing the means by which we can make it possible for a total revolution to take place in people's lives – and particularly in the life of this country. But means are very lifeless, very peripheral things. More important and significant are the friends who will take such a revolution, such a movement to the people. It is essential to talk a little about these friends.

Firstly, whenever some new idea, some new wind of change has to be taken to people at large, a psychological preparation of those who want to do this is essential and much needed. If they are not psychologically prepared, not only will they not be able to offer what they intended to, on the contrary, all their efforts may well have exactly the opposite outcome.

What do I mean, what is intended, when I say "psychological preparation?"

Firstly, in this world the driving force behind anyone who has brought the seeds of some new vision to the hearts of mankind, who has tried to grow some new crop in its heart, has always been deep love, deep kindness, and compassion.

There are two things. One is that when we find our ideas appeal to us, we feel like taking them to other people. And along with that, we also feel such love for those with whom we want to share these ideas that we won't stop until we have done so.

But respect just for an idea can be dangerous. More necessary and central should be our love for those to whom we want to bring these ideas. More necessary and central should be our concern for the fact that these people are in a situation that warrants the ideas being brought to them. If we do not love them and there is only an intensity and urgency to convey a vision, then knowingly or unknowingly we will start doing violence to them. This is what has been happening throughout the history of mankind.

Mohammedans went and destroyed people's shrines and statues all over the world – just obsessed with wanting to bring people the vision that "statues are obstacles to experiencing the divine." They became so obsessed with spreading this idea that they didn't even bother anymore to ask: "Can it be right that the people we are taking this idea to are being butchered, oppressed, exposed to violence?" The vision became so important to them that the very people they wanted to share it with became less important.

To this day, the world over, those who proclaim visions are committing much violence. Violence has come about because the idea has become the most important thing, and the people to whom the idea is being brought are not even considered.

We most certainly need to remember that no matter how important an idea or a thought may be, more important is the one to whom we are offering it. The person is not secondary. In fact, he is the one who is valuable – that is why we want to offer him the thought, the idea, in the first place. It is like when someone is hungry and we bring him food: the important point is not the food; the important point is the fact that the man is hungry. Because he is hungry we want to bring him food. But if the food becomes important to us, and if that man doesn't want to eat anything, and if because of this we start misbehaving with him – we hold him down and start forcing the food down his throat – then clearly we are giving the food more importance than the man. So far, this is what has been happening in the world. Visions and ideas become important to us and the person to whom we want to offer them – the hungry person – becomes less important.

We have to remember that, for us, ideas are less important. It is *people* who are important – today's people who are surrounded by pain and misery. Only they are important. If something can be of use to a person, we are ready to serve him, but nothing should be imposed. We should not have the fanatical idea that it has to be imposed. But this is what often happens – unintentionally and unconsciously – before we even know it.

So we have to keep this in our awareness. Now the idea has arisen to expand the work, we need to keep all the basic fundamentals in our awareness: how it will truly grow, how it can remain free. So this is the first thing to remain aware of.

The second thing to be aware of is that we – the friends who will be working toward this – will need to do much self-introspection and much self-inquiry. As long as you are alone, it is all right: you are okay as you are. But the day you want to take a message to others, intensive self-analysis and self-examination become necessary. From that day it becomes very necessary to pay attention to what you are saying and how you are saying it; to what your behavior is like – because when I am bringing an idea, a vision, to others they will respect it only to the extent that my own personality and behavior have a depth. People will come to know about my vision only later on; first they will see me. First they will see me. My message will follow me. Only through seeing me will they become interested in my vision, in my philosophy of life.

So whenever someone takes on the task of bringing a message to others, the very act of sharing it will inevitably begin an inner transformation. The man's behavior – the way he sits, the way he stands, the way he talks, the way he relates – everything becomes significant. And its significance is in exact proportion to the greatness of the vision he is eager to spread. He becomes a carrier, a vehicle, for some great message, so he needs to adjust his behavior in accordance with that great message. Otherwise what often happens is that because the impact of the message is so great we start spreading it, but we forget to create the worth, the merit, within ourselves that such a task requires. This is what we need to pay attention to.

A seeker's work is not as big a task as that of a worker. The seeker is alone, he lives inside himself; he is doing something for himself. A worker has taken on a greater responsibility. He too is a seeker, but he also becomes a medium for spreading what has appealed to him so much.

So this is about the medium. How should this medium be? How will he be able to take the message to people? Very small things can make a difference. Every single word makes a difference.

I see it here. A small thing, when it is said in a slightly different way, reaches straight to the heart of a person. Say the same thing in another way and the person is ready to fight.

An astrologer came to the court of King Bhoj. He looked at the king's palm and said, "You are the most unfortunate man. You will put your sons into their coffins with your own hands. You will also put your wife into her coffin with those same hands. You will take all your sons and daughters to the graveyard."

Bhoj was enraged. He had the man handcuffed and put behind bars: "This man doesn't even know how to speak! What is this madman talking about?"

Kalidasa, the king's favorite courtier, was sitting in the court and saw and heard all of this. Once the astrologer had been taken away, Kalidasa said to the king, "You should reward the astrologer and release him with honor."

The king retorted, "Reward that man? Did you hear what he said?"

Kalidasa said, "May I see your palm?"

Kalidasa looked at the king's palm and said, "You are very fortunate. You will live to be more than a hundred years old; you are blessed with a very long life. You are so fortunate that even your sons will not have as long a life as you will have. You will leave them far behind."

The king asked, "Is this what that man was saying?"

Kalidasa said, "Yes, he was saying the same thing, but the way he was saying it was absolutely wrong."

Bhoj rewarded the man with a hundred thousand gold coins and saw him off with respect. As he departed the king said, "My friend, if this is what you wanted to convey, then why didn't you say it like this? What a strange way you chose to speak!"

There once was a Jewish thinker and rabbi called Joshua Liebmann. In his memoir he writes, "When I was young and I first went to my master's seminary to learn, a friend of mine went with me. We were both in the habit of smoking cigarettes, and we were both worried what to do about this, how to deal with the situation.

We were allowed to go into the garden outside the seminary for just an hour, to contemplate the divine. That was the only time we could possibly smoke. There was no other opportunity at all. Still, we thought it was only right to ask the head rabbi before going ahead.

So my friend and I both went to ask him. When I came out from seeing him I was very angry, because he had denied me permission to smoke. And as I came into the garden my anger multiplied – because there was my friend, sitting on a bench smoking! It seems the rabbi had said yes to him. It was the ultimate injustice!

I told my friend that the rabbi had denied me permission to smoke and asked if he had been told he could, or whether he was just smoking without permission.

My friend wanted to know what I had said to the rabbi.

I told him, "I asked if I could smoke a cigarette while contemplating the divine, and he said, 'No, absolutely not.' What did you ask?"

My friend said, "I asked if I could contemplate the divine while smoking a cigarette, and he said, 'Yes, certainly.'"

Now in essence both these things are exactly the same. "Can one smoke while contemplating the divine?" and "Can one contemplate the divine while smoking?" are in essence the same activity – and yet they are completely different. The same man said no in response to one, and yes in response to the other.

Certainly, who would accept the idea of smoking, while you contemplate the divine? And who would say no to contemplating the divine while smoking? Anyone would say, "This is very good. If you contemplate the divine even while smoking, what is bad about it? In fact it is very good."

That second young man said that he, too, had first thought of phrasing his question the same way, because that was the straightforward thing to do. But then he immediately realized that it would be a mistake, that the answer to that approach was bound to be no.

Liebmann wrote that he experimented with this many times in his life. And slowly he got a very clear understanding that to get a yes or a no from someone is not in that person's hands, but in our own. The other doesn't even realize when you have got him to say yes, or when you got him to say no. And if the other says no to you, know well that somewhere you must have made a mistake. Maybe your intention was right, maybe you had the right idea, but your way of presenting it must have been wrong. Otherwise no one on this earth would like to say no. Everyone wants to say yes. But the preparation, understanding, and the awareness of the people who get others to say yes, are all part of it. It all depends on how we present something.

How can a revolutionary vision be brought to a society that is so tied up in traditions and conventions that are thousands of years old? If a great vision is to be put into motion, if a world center is to be created to launch this vision for the transformation of living human beings, then how is this to be accomplished? Money is not that important here – because even if the money comes, if there are a few wrong people standing at the doors to the center, then all that money will come in vain, it will be of no use. And the question is not about you going out and arranging for money because the money can be brought in.

The real question is that the heart of the donor should come along with the money – otherwise do not bring it. Many times people give money just to get rid of the person who is asking for it, so that the person moves on, goes away. That kind of money should not be brought here at all, because that kind of money is very expensive. It comes at the cost of the loss of a person. We should be able to create such a climate that the giver feels joy in giving; that he feels he didn't give enough.

And it is not just about money. Other things too, such as work, intelligence, friendship, help – whatsoever we might accept from someone – the donor should feel that in relation to the person who came to ask, the work he is contributing, his own contribution, is too small: "I was not able to give as much as I wanted to." In his heart he should keep feeling that he would like to contribute again the next day.

So a heartful milieu is needed for all of this. The people who become messengers of this work – of any work – their whole state of mind, their qualities, their whole training, their whole approach, their thinking, their everything... Relating is an art, relating with another person is a great art.

It appears difficult to us: ten million rupees looks like a big target. That is not the reason why it seems difficult. The reason is that we do not understand the art of relating. That's why things appear very difficult.

Relating is a question of great perception and understanding. We find breaking off with someone very easy, and becoming connected very difficult. We easily learn how to hate, but not how to love. It is utterly easy to create an enemy. The question is how to create a friend. And a person lives his life successfully and artfully only to the extent that his number of friends grows daily, so that by the time of his death he can say that he has a great number of friends on this earth.

But usually the opposite happens. As a child, one has many friends but as one goes on getting older, the number keeps decreasing. You remember childhood so well: there were so many friends, everything was so wonderful. But as people grow older their number of friends slowly keeps diminishing. Something must be missing in the way they live their lives, in their art of relating in life. Otherwise the number should have grown – whosoever they met should have become a friend.

Roosevelt was fighting his first presidential election. He wrote personal letters to ten thousand people. Personal letters! The list even included taxi drivers, railway station porters, hotel waiters;

all kinds of people were on it. People were simply amazed: a waiter, a porter, a driver, receiving letters personally addressed to them by Roosevelt, saying, "I was worried whether to run for office or not, but when I remembered you, I thought, 'One vote is certain.' So, I *am* running."

"How is your wife's health now? When I came to your village she was ill. Your son must have grown up by now; did he find a job? Let me know if you need me for anything."

When these letters reached ten thousand very ordinary people, they forgot all about which party Roosevelt may or may not have belonged to. The man had remembered them!

He would arrive at a railway station and refer to a taxi driver by name – someone whose taxi he had used on some earlier occasion. He would ask, "Where is so-and-so? He is an old friend of mine; I would like to take his taxi."

He might travel in a taxi for five minutes, but he wouldn't let those five minutes go to waste. In those five minutes he would make friends with the taxi driver. He would ask him how his wife and children were, and who was doing what.

Roosevelt's friends would say, "Why do you unnecessarily get into these conversations?"

He would say, "You must be crazy. Here I have this five-minute opportunity to make friends with a human being, and you say it is unnecessary chitchat! What else is meaningful in life besides the richness of friendship? For five minutes I have the gift of this living human being, and I can either continue to sit quietly in the back seat, or else get close to this man's heart. So there is no reason to let these five minutes go to waste; I am using them."

The number of Roosevelt's friends grew to tens of thousands, and he never gave them anything. One doesn't have to *give* anything while creating friendships. Just a loving and open heart, just a hand extended in friendship, and all is accomplished.

Perhaps in ordinary life we don't actually need to make too many friends. But those who have become enthusiastic about bringing some message to people need to keep it in mind to expand their circle of friends continuously. Anyone who comes into contact with someone like him even once should end up as a friend.

So those upon whom we pin our hopes – friends of the center, our companions, this gathering of friends – these friends should keep growing in number. And whosoever comes near has to become a friend.

I am amazed to see to what extent even the closest friends of the people in whose homes and families I stay have remained unacquainted with me – because none of the family ever bothers to bring their friends to meet me. In the homes where I stay, guests, acquaintances, relatives will come by, and my hosts bring them to meet me saying, "This is my brother."

I tell them, "I have been visiting you for two years now and you have never introduced this brother to me before!"

They reply, "No, it just didn't occur to us."

When I ask, "You never invited him here?" they reply, "No, we didn't get a chance to inform him."

It is simply amazing!

In one lifetime, a person can relate with such a huge world of friends. It is just a matter of becoming aware, alert, conscious of this just once in your heart, and then within ten years... You are talking of raising ten million rupees, you can also raise ten million friends! This is not difficult at all; there isn't any obstacle to this happening. The question is of your remembering this.

I would like to remind you not to bother about money as much as about friends – because as far as money is concerned, it will come with the friends. And what is so great about money?

What use does it have? But if we don't bother about friends and we do bother about money, then everything will go wrong. Or similarly, if you bother about a friend just because you want to get money out of him, then, too, everything will go wrong. You are not aware that whenever you go to get money from someone, you are insulting that person.

Recently, the daughter of a friend of mine got married. He is very rich and this girl is his only child. He has no son. The girl kept rejecting every suitor that came to see her. Her father got fed up; he came to me and brought the girl along, saying, "I am in great difficulty. She rejects every boy that comes as a suitor. What does she really want?"

The girl said to me, "So far I haven't come across a single suitor who might be coming because of me. They are all coming because of my father's money. I can't be insulted more deeply than that: someone wants to marry me for my father's wealth. The very fact that they have come because of his money negates everything else for me. When someone comes for me, I am ready. But first let someone come for me!"

So whenever you go to someone for money, you don't understand the fact that you are insulting that person. And when, because of this insult, the person refuses to oblige you with money, you feel puzzled: "This is an extremely miserly person, very tightfisted. He cannot part with a paisa!"

You have no understanding whatsoever. How can that person give you money? You have come to him for money. There is no greater insult to a human being than approaching him in this way.

Go for the human being. Money comes as a shadow of man; power comes as a shadow of man. If friends come, their shadows will accompany them – you don't have to go and fetch their shadows. But if you go to someone's house and say, "I invite your shadow to come to a meeting," the invitation will end there and then. Neither the shadow nor the person is going to come to that meeting! Wealth is the shadow of man. As long as we do not understand this, we are mistaken. The one who comes is the person. Behind him follows his power, his love, his strength – his shadow. And then the shadow comes dancing with joy. You don't have to go anywhere to fetch it or send it.

So I hope and pray that you don't catch on to the idea of going and collecting ten million rupees directly. It is not about going directly. It is a question of increasing the number of friends. It is a question of bringing a maximum number of friends closer together. It is not a question of money at all. This is not an economic matter. So the name you have given it – some fund or other. What did you call it? What are you calling it in Gujarati?

Osho,
Bhandor – a collection of funds.

No, don't call it "A Collection of Funds." Call it "A Collection of Friends." It is a fund for collecting friends. So no *bhandor* at all! That very approach is wrong. It makes no sense. For example, Maya bhai is the organizer of the fund, so he needs to remember that he has become the organizer of collecting *friends*. It is not so much a question of money and all that.

He readily agrees!

Yes, so he should – because it will be awkward for the one giving money as well as for the one asking for it. The number of our friends should go on increasing. Money is secondary; it will come, it is not a big thing. Increasing our number of friends, that is what all the friends have to remember. And whosoever is our friend... You all have to make sure that each and every person who comes close becomes one of us; that he becomes one of us because of our behavior, because of our way of relating, because of the way we talk. You have to make sure that not a single word we utter becomes something to put him off, but rather something that brings him closer. If you keep this in mind – and it is not difficult – within two years many friends will have gathered.

But normally we are not aware that we need to keep increasing our number of friends, that our circle of friends has to keep growing, that whosoever comes near us must end up becoming a friend. You should not miss the opportunity. A person has come, so he should be fully respected – and full respect lies in the fact that we make him a friend.

Osho,
It means making four hundred thousand friends a month!

Yes, this is absolutely possible. We simply have no idea about this, no idea at all. In the course of a day, how many people meet how many other people? How many people does one approach? With how many people does one relate? No, we are just busy with our work; we are only involved with our job. We have nothing to do with friendship, we are not aware of direct and simple friendship.

And whenever someone becomes alert to direct and simple friendship, then even those people we would have called weak, incapable and without talent start becoming such a force. They start becoming very powerful.

So as I see it – this is one thing that I wanted to say to you – money is important, but it should not become so important that our whole mind starts thinking about it exclusively. It has always to be placed below people, after friends. If you are gaining a friend but losing money, then gain the friend and let the money go. And if by giving money, a person wants to let go of the friendship, do not accept the money, just save the friend. That will be more farsighted, more meaningful, deeper and more profitable. We have to pay some attention to this.

And if there is any fear in the hearts of our worker friends, if anyone feels hesitation coming from within, this will bring in hesitation from the back door. The hindrance that comes to the work from the outside is not as great as the fear that comes from inside a person. So we should clear up completely whatever inner fears we may have. As we gather here, if you have any inner fear, you should not keep it hidden inside you – because hidden inside it will always be there, and it will keep pulling you back from behind. It will create fear about going forward: "This danger may come, that danger may come," and so on.

We should clear up all those fears so that our hearts are completely free from fear. The more fearless a heart is, the faster it gets things done. But if there is fear inside, then you will keep pulling yourself back with your own hands. Then you will remain afraid. On the one hand you go on saying that you want to get this or that work done, and on the other hand, you keep being afraid of impending fears and dangers.

So I feel that the biggest hindrance to becoming active in this direction arises from inner fears. There can be many kinds of fears. All fears should be considered; we should get a thorough understanding of all of these fears – and having understood them, become totally fearless. If they go on working deep within you, you will find that you are keeping self-made chains inside you that continually hold you back.

Let us talk about a few of these fears to see what they might be.

The greatest fear, for example, is that there are so many friends gathered here, and the moment thoughts like: "We have to collect so much money" or "So much work has to be done" or "So many arrangements have to be made" arise, then suddenly a direct question arises: "Will I have to give money? Will I have to do all this?" This first fear naturally arises from within: "Where do I stand in all this?" Yes, this will bring fear.

But this fear is totally groundless; groundless, because not a single person needs to contribute to this work out of embarrassment. If any friend feels that he has this fear, he should stand up and just speak out – just like Khetan-ji did just now. His statement was right. A person should say, "I won't give any money toward it, but I *do* want this work to grow. So whatever else I can do I will do, but I cannot contribute any money." One should say this and become free from fear. Then such a person gets engaged in the work without fear; then for him no concern, no question, remains. Someone like this should not feed his embarrassment, because if he does that, then just to hide the fear he will do dozens of other things, and he will go on brooding – and through that, difficulties will arise.

This is a straightforward, clear-cut thing. Here there is no question whatsoever of someone contributing out of embarrassment. If it comes as a joyous act of friendship, then that is another thing. If it is beyond his capacity, over his limit – if he is in a dilemma – then he should simply drop the very idea. He should clearly state: "I agree with this, it is good work and I will be a part of it, but what I cannot do is this and this." Then he will become free from fear. And if there are fifty such friends, free of fear, great power will gather around them. Or if the person says, "I can give this much, and I will," then too he will become fearless. So there is no question of worrying and thinking about it.

In the same way, and from various nooks and corners, many similar fears start taking hold of the mind. So whenever our group of workers meets – when we meet the next time – you should speak very clearly about all of these things.

Some friends carry grudges against other friends. They tell me about them confidentially. This I don't like. Whatever the complaints, we should express them when all of us, all of the friends, meet together. After all, this is the meaning of friendship: that if one has a grievance one can say to the person, "I have this complaint, and it will harm the work or will create hindrances to the work." Then we should be able to talk about all those grievances so that they can be cleared up. It is possible I may be mistaken; my complaint may be without grounds. It is possible the friend I have a grudge against is wrong, and then it gets cleared up. But if certain things keep on lying there within our hearts and minds, they create walls. And where we need to stand united we fail to do so.

So this one thing has to be kept in mind: if we are to complete a momentous task which will require vast cooperation, then we should find a way to dissolve each and every thing that can become a hindrance to this cooperation. Next time we meet we should be ready for much self-analysis; and we should also be ready to criticize our friends. And we should also develop an understanding about what we can do to remove those barriers. But we need to stop talking behind other people's backs.

Everyone should remain aware that the work is more important than he is, and that if any obstacle arises in the work because of him, then he should be ready to change. If he happens to make some mistake, he should immediately be ready and willing to change.

If we keep these few things in mind, then there is no reason why we should not be able to go full steam ahead, why we should not be able to accomplish what we want to, and why it should not only succeed but also bear good fruit. Success can come in many ways, but getting the right fruit is a difficult thing. Just succeeding can come about in many ways. There are thousands of ways of doing things whereby the means as such are wrong but the end result would be successful. We don't want that kind of success at all. We shouldn't even think of it.

So then, how to achieve the right fruits? How to ensure that the fruits that come are indeed good? Mere fruition is not enough. To create a center, to create an ashram, to create a university is not enough. They should be created while fulfilling our true intentions. In my view good work, even if incomplete, is right, and bad work, even if complete, is wrong. Bad work – even if successful – is not good, and good work – even when the outcome remains only a dream – is still good. Other people will come and take that work forward. We haven't signed a contract that says we must realize a dream. But if the dream is beautiful and good, we must strive toward it.

And one should be prepared not to compromise in any way.

Paramanand bhai said just now that he is happy because I am tied to an anchor. He is mistaken. He is utterly mistaken. I never get tied to any anchor, anywhere. There is no reason and no need to get tied to anything. If I had the slightest fear of getting tied to something, I would simply not have brought this issue up. It is because I have no fear whatsoever of getting tied up that I agreed. If I had had the slightest concern that this might create some bondage for me, I simply would not have agreed to it. I have no such fear. That's why there is no question of any bondage, why bondage simply cannot arise for me. I do not compromise at all.

If tomorrow you tell me, "This man is contributing a hundred thousand rupees, so please don't speak against his religion," I will not be ready to listen to you. If tomorrow you tell me, "All these people have done this or that work so please don't say a certain thing," then I won't agree to it. I am not ready to compromise on any point. There is just no question of compromise.

So I don't get attached anywhere; no bondage arises out of anything. Nor am I ready for any compromise. What I am saying, I will go on saying – and I will say it loudly! And all these arrangements are so that I can say it loudly, so that I can do what I am doing more intensely, so that I can hit harder than I am hitting today, so that I can punch more intensely than I am punching today, and so that more strength can gather to make these hits more intense, more powerful.

My very vision of a sannyasin is of someone who stands in the midst of all sorts of bondage and yet is not in any bondage. I call him a sannyasin. Someone who isn't in bondage because he is escaping from bondage is not yet a sannyasin. His heart is afraid of falling into bondage – that is why he runs around escaping. He is already bound, that's why he is running. Somewhere, his mind is fearful; somewhere, it is stuck. For the one whose mind is not stuck anywhere, no fear remains, no cause for fear remains.

So you need not keep any thought in your minds that I am getting tied to something somewhere. And what I am saying today is just the logical outcome of what I was saying yesterday. Tomorrow I will discuss even more things with you, the day after tomorrow still more. The more you prepare the foundations, the more I will speak to you of the things that are further ahead. Once you are prepared up to a certain point, I will speak of things a little beyond that point, so that you can go a little further ahead.

Had I said these same things to you two years ago, perhaps you would not have been ready to commit to them. I didn't say them then, not because I wasn't ready to commit, but because two years ago you would not have agreed. That's why I did not say them then. And whatever I have said now, in two years time I will say even more. The more you continue to prepare yourselves, the more I will continue to point to further things.

I have the whole vision in my sights, but it can be spoken of only as far as those aspects that you are ready for are concerned. Otherwise there will be no point speaking about it, no reason to talk about it. I am getting ready to take your minds into many more revolutions. Perhaps many friends will become afraid of those revolutions and will be left behind. Perhaps many will find, "I had no idea it was going to be a revolution of this enormity; otherwise I would have stopped long ago."

But the greater the challenges that come, the greater the inner forces that also keep on arising. And if one friend is lost, ten others will arrive if the challenge is true – if it is indeed going to be for the benefit of the life of mankind.

So I am not showing you a path strewn with roses. More thorns are yet to come on this path, and I am fully aware of this. But if the idea has arisen in your heart that now it is necessary to transform the country's consciousness and man's consciousness; if you have realized this through your own anguish and pain – seeing the trouble all around, the chaos all around; that all around, life is falling to pieces, its roots have been shaken and are withering away in every sense – if you feel that this country's consciousness and man's consciousness can be infused with some new life, then courageous steps need to be taken.

The more you prepare yourselves, the more I will talk of things that require greater courage. I have a complete vision for how a revolution can be brought about in the whole of life.

I have started by talking about religion because religion is the most central element. And my understanding is that the person who agrees to bring revolution to religion will agree to bring revolution into any other aspect of life – because that is the core attachment of one's very being. If someone has agreed to bring about a revolution in religion, then he won't be afraid to do so in *any* other areas of life. That is why I have begun to speak from there. My understanding is that the people who are ready for that will become ready for other things too.

Finally one more thing – and we will also be discussing this again tomorrow morning. Our whole discussion has been about the functional, business side. In this whole matter, as I said to you yesterday evening, it is a mistake and it is dangerous to become completely self-centered. But that does not mean that we should get totally caught up in the work and forget who we are. The very work exists so that others can be reminded of the self that is within us all. So if we ourselves forget this, it is dangerous.

Hundreds of very sincere people joined in Vinoba's work. But out of the experience of ten, twelve, fifteen years, they slowly started coming back – filled with only pain and anguish. Many of them have told me that the vision they had gone there for was pushed aside and Vinoba just put them to work: "We had come for our self-realization, for self-knowledge and inner peace. All that was left aside and he just put us to work. Fifteen years of our lives have gone. And we feel, 'Okay, so what? We used to run a shop, and now this was another kind of shop that we were running – but what was the outcome? What did it do for us?"

So tomorrow morning I have some things to say to you about this. You have to remember that no matter how involved you become in this work, it is secondary; it is not the most important thing. The most important thing is that bliss and light descend in your life. If you have that, you will be able to share. If you don't have that, you will not be able to share.

So we do not want a functionary who isn't a seeker. We don't need such functionaries, because if not today, then tomorrow, that functionary will start suffering. He will get into trouble and he will throw the whole responsibility onto us: "They got me entangled in some work and I lost everything."

A friend, Manik Prabhu, who is himself from Pune, went to Vinoba. He first went to the Ramakrishna Mission and they placed him in a hospital – so for three or four years he served in a hospital. Then he felt, "This is okay, I could have done this work in any hospital, but what has it accomplished? It has not taken me anywhere. I am still where I was before."

He left and went to Vinoba. Vinoba said, "For ten years, walk around the whole country taking my literature to every village."

The poor man started going from village to village with his bag of publications. He has been traveling around for two years now. And about three days ago he came to Jabalpur and came to see me.

So I said to him, "Now a second hospital round has started!"

It is good that he has realized this after just a few years: "This is a hospital, all fine and good, but what has this changed within me?"

What will he get by selling *Gita Pravachan* – Vinoba's book? Or if I take *Gita Pravachan* away from him and instead give him our *Perfect Way* or *Seeds of Wisdom* and ask him to go around selling them from village to village for ten years, what will that do for him?

So I told him, "If you have no idea that this is secondary and that something else, which is not to be forgotten, is central, then just as those hospital days went to waste, so will these ten years. Otherwise what will you bring to people? And from where does this question of 'bringing to people' even arise?"

So the seeker comes first, his being a worker is absolutely secondary. And if you have to lose one of the two, let go of being a worker, not of being a seeker.

I will talk to you about this in the morning because before we leave, we need to discuss this as the final point. Otherwise, if you return home from here, having become a perfect worker after these three or four sessions, tremendous harm will have been done. So tomorrow morning we will gather and talk a little about this.

But you should always remember this: you are a seeker; being a worker is utterly secondary. If being a worker is to be lost, let it be lost, but being a seeker cannot be lost – cannot be lost at any cost. If while remaining a seeker some work is possible for you, certainly do it, certainly get it done.

If the soul remains, the body will. If only the body is left, it has no value whatsoever.

In India, this mistake has happened many times. It happens every day. And you can become a functionary, a worker, immediately. This I know. This is not difficult; it is a very simple thing. The difficult thing is becoming a seeker. It is very easy to become a worker. What difficulty could there be? Instead of doing some other kind of work you do this work – but it won't be any different.

You will find many people ready to work immediately, but remember: only if doing takes place from the center of non-doing is it meaningful, only then is it spiritual; otherwise not. The center that we are going to create is for teaching non-doing. So don't let it happen that you become just a worker. Then the whole point is lost. What would we accomplish through building such a center? It would be futile, it would have no value.

All this we will discuss tomorrow morning.

5
Four Things to Remember

My beloved ones,

A religious leader had a dream one night. In the dream he saw that he had reached the gates of heaven. During his whole life he had talked about heaven and during his whole life he had shown people how to find the way to heaven. He was sure that when he reached the gates of heaven, God himself would be there to welcome him.

But at the gates of heaven there was nobody. The gates were not even open; they were closed. And the gates were so vast that even to see them from one end to the other was not possible. Standing in front of those huge gates he looked like a tiny ant – he looked that small.

He knocked on the gate again and again, but it was difficult to be certain whether the sounds made by such a tiny man's knocking could even be heard. He became afraid. He had always said that God created man in his own image, but that day, standing in front of those huge gates, he felt very small.

After a lot of shouting and knocking on the gate, a tiny window in it opened and someone peeped out. The person who peeped out had one thousand eyes and his eyes were shining so brightly that the religious leader backed away into a small niche in the wall.

He became very scared and he shouted, "Please, don't show me your face. Oh God, please keep your face inside. I am very scared."

The person with one thousand eyes said, "I am not God. I am just the guard here, the gatekeeper. Where are you? I cannot see you – you are so small. Where are you hiding?"

The religious leader shouted and said "I would like to see God and enter heaven."

The gatekeeper asked, "Who are you and from where have you come?"

He said, "You don't know? I am a religious leader and I have come from Earth."

The one-thousand-eyed man said, "Earth? Where is this 'Earth'?"

The religious leader was surprised and said "You don't know about Earth?"

The one-thousand-eyed man asked, "Of which world system, of which universe, are you talking? There are millions of universes, millions of world systems. Each world system has millions of suns. Each sun has its own planets. Which one are you talking about? What is the index number of your 'Earth'? What number does it have?"

The religious leader did not know anything about all this. He said, "We only know of one world and one sun. That is why we have not given any name or any index number to them."

The gatekeeper said, "Then it will be very difficult to find out where you come from. This is the first time the name 'Earth' has been heard at this gate. And *human being* – this too is the first time I hear those words."

The religious leader's heart sank. He had thought that God would welcome him at the gates, yet here no one even knew which world he had come from!

The gatekeeper then said, "Relax, I will get someone to inquire, but for that some time will certainly be needed. I will get the inquiry started at the big complex where we keep all the records – the maps and index numbers of all the worlds of all the universes – but this will take a few months and until then it is very difficult to determine where you have come from, what species you belong to, and what is the purpose of your coming here."

The religious leader said, "I would like to see God."

The gatekeeper said, "I have been at this gate for countless years and so far I have never seen God. And until now I have never come across any person at these gates of heaven who has seen God either. Even to know the whole creation of God is already difficult enough, to know God himself is even more so, because that is the name of totality itself."

Greatly perplexed, the religious leader awoke from his sleep. He was perspiring profusely. He was at his wits' end. He could not sleep for the rest of the night. He kept thinking, again and again, "Could it be that because man is under the influence of his own ego, he has come up with all these ideas of God creating man in his own image, of God being equally eager to meet man and of calling him? And the gates of heaven, and nirvana, could it be that all these are creations of man's own imagination?"

The reason I am starting my talk with this story, with the dream of this religious leader, is because man lives in an immensely vast world of misconceptions. He does not know what he himself is. In this vast universe he does not occupy a significant place. If we experience the vastness of this universe, and then we look at ourselves in comparison to it, where do we stand? Where are we? This earth of ours is very small. The mass of our sun is three hundred and thirty thousand times bigger than that of this earth. And this sun is the smallest among all the suns we know of. Some two billion suns are known, and each sun has its own vastness and expanse. And these two billion suns are not the end, there must be universes beyond them, there must be expanses beyond them. In this endless universe, in a tiny corner of this small earth, is a tiny creature called man. Then too mankind does not comprise a huge number. The total number is about six and three quarter billion. If we consider this in the context of the number of all the other creatures, man stands nowhere. There are very small living creatures and their number is infinite. Among them is this small number of human beings.

Man has a tiny corner, his own tiny corner in this vast universe, yet who knows how great he thinks himself to be? We are not what we think we are.

Man lives only for a short while, some seventy or eighty years, at the most one hundred years. In the expanse of this endless, timeless universe one hundred years does not count for anything, has no value, no place. Our earth itself came into existence some four billion years ago. And this earth is a very new arrival in the universe. Billions and trillions of years have gone before – there is no end to the number – and there is a similar amount of time on the other side, an infinity, an eternity. There is no end to that side either. Within this eternity man lives for a few moments and who knows what he thinks of himself! From the point of view of space, man is nothing, and from the point of view of time, he is also nothing.

I call that man religious who attains to this experience of his nothingness. But so far the story of the so-called religious man has been just the contrary. He declares: "I am the ultimate, I am God, I am the soul, I am the eternal soul, I am the inheritor of nirvana, I am this, I am that!" This so-called religious man proclaims all of these things.

I do not call such a person religious. A religious man is one who experiences his nothingness, his being nothing. The day this nothingness is experienced, some closed doors of life open, and the way to being everything – the whole – is cleared. The experience of nothingness is very basic to this: the very first step is to realize that we are nothing. But to come to realize this becomes extremely difficult for us because we live among other human beings whose illusions are similar to ours. So our illusions are never questioned or criticized. On the contrary, we go on feeding each others' illusions.

When Galileo and his colleagues were the first people to say that the sun does not go around the earth – it is the earth that goes around the sun – it hurt man's ego very much. The religious leaders said, "How can this be so? God has created man to be special, and he has created the whole of the rest of the world for him to use. So how can the earth, on which man lives, go around the sun? It is the sun that goes around the earth."

Galileo was summoned to the court and told to ask for forgiveness and not to say such foolish things. How could the earth on which man lives go around the sun? Surely the sun must go around the earth?

Slowly, as our understanding grew, we found out that this earth is not the center of the universe; that the whole universe does not revolve around it. So why was the idea of the earth being the center born? – because we liked the idea that we were the center, that we were the center of the universe and the whole universe revolved around us. We liked the idea that we were the most important, at the center: that the human being, humanity, is at the center, and all the rest revolves around him.

For thousands of years the religious man has been saying that man is the supreme-most creature. It is very surprising that, without asking any of the other creatures, we have been declaring that man is the most supreme. We have asked neither the ants, nor the birds; we have simply accepted this one-sided testimony. We have been praising ourselves, saying that man is the supreme-most creature, that he is the crown of creation. We have proclaimed this without consulting with any other creatures in the universe. And because no other creature knows about this proclamation, no refutation comes from anywhere, no denial comes from anywhere. We human beings go on making proclamations as we sit in our corner: "We are this, we are that."

If animals and birds were to be asked, if some day we could know what they were thinking, perhaps there would not be a single species that did not think in its heart of hearts that they were the most important creatures. The ants must be thinking: "We are!" The monkeys must be thinking: "We are!"

Darwin simply said that man has evolved from monkeys. But if the monkeys were asked, they would never be willing to accept that man has evolved from them. They must believe that man has *fallen* from them: "We jump and swing from tree to tree. Man simply moves on the ground. This is his downfall! Some from our species have fallen and become human beings. This is not evolution!" If there were a Darwin among the monkeys, he would never be ready to believe that this is evolution or progress, or that man has progressed.

But man has believed it. Man is immediately ready to believe in whatsoever feeds his ego. So the earth was seen to be the center and man the supreme-most creation! But slowly, day after day, man has been robbed of all these ideas. Science has been knocking them over day by day.

The first hit was that the earth was no longer at the center. The day this happened it was a big hit to man's ego. Then he believed that the deeper he entered into himself, the more he would encounter the divine, the more he would encounter the soul. Then came Freud who said, "However deeply man enters into himself, he will not find anything there except sex." This caused great agitation the world over. People denied this, saying, "All this talk is rubbish! Inside us all there is God. This Freud, saying that inside us there is only sex! All this talk is patently wrong." But as our understanding grew more profound, it was discovered that at man's center, basically there is only sex. He is born out of it, he lives in it, he lives for it, and he dies in it. This was another big hit. Another center of the ego was broken down.

And the third big hit came when investigations into this huge universe began and it was found that the universe is boundless and endless. There is just no end to it; it simply goes on expanding and expanding. There is no place where we can say: "This is the end, the boundary."

We used to think that the stars are very close to us – they are so easily visible at night – but as our understanding grew, we discovered that the stars are very far away from us. They are so far away that even to count them is impossible. It takes four years for the light of the star which is nearest to us, to reach us. The speed of light is not ordinary; it is one hundred and eighty-six thousand miles per second. In one second, light travels one hundred and eighty-six thousand miles. If the light starts traveling today from the nearest star, it will reach here, to Lonavala, in four years' time. And this is talking about the nearest star. The light from some of the farthest stars started to travel the day this earth came into being, four billion years ago, and it has still not reached the earth. There are stars beyond this too; their light will never be seen by us, because their light will never reach us.

The stars that we see in the night are not actually where we see them. No star is where we see it to be. The night is completely deceptive; no star is actually where it seems to be. It was there once. Its light took so long to reach us that in the meantime it traveled across immense distances. It is no longer where it was. In four years it must have traveled billions of miles. It is also possible that in four years it has disintegrated and no longer exists. Still we can see it because it existed there four years ago when its light – which has reached our eyes now – started to travel toward us. So we are seeing it as if it is still there.

The whole night is deceptive. No star is where we are seeing it now. One star was where it appears to be now seven years ago, another one a thousand years ago, another one a hundred thousand years ago, another one tens of million of years ago, and another one a billion years ago. The light from stars that were there four billion years ago has still to reach us.

This whole night is deceptive. These stars are so far away that the distances perplex man. These expanses and this expanding world have made man very small. He is not worth anything anymore, he has no value. The so-called religious man has been immensely hurt.

As I see it, a religious man should not have been hurt, instead his insight should have increased with this knowledge, because from all this information the realization has come that we are nothing. The old illusion that we are everything has been broken. That illusion has received a big jolt – and the jolt has shaken the entire religious world. It is trembling. And if there is this feeling that man is nothing, then what about our proclamations – proclamations of our immortality, of our soul, of the *brahman*, of godliness, of the attainment of enlightenment – what will happen to all of these?

But as I see it, the past three hundred years' scientific research has created grounds for the genuinely religious man to be born. The first characteristic of a genuinely religious man is his awareness that he is nothing. The day someone realizes his nothingness in its totality he attains to *shunya*, to nothingness.

So this morning I would like to talk to you about a few things in this context.

Our realization that we are nothing should keep growing more deeply. Our realization that we are nothing should keep becoming more and more intense in us. And this doesn't mean just thinking that we are nothing – if you just look at life, it will become clear that we *are* nothing. Where is the difficulty in becoming clear about this? Every day death brings the message that we are nothing, but we never look attentively at the message that death brings. We have hidden death away. We build our crematoriums on the outskirts of our towns so that we do not have to see them.

Some day, when mankind is wiser, when mankind is religious, we will build them inside the towns, at the crossroads, so that we pass them ten times in one day, so that we see them as we come and go, so that we remember death – that it exists. Now, when a funeral procession passes by, we call our children inside the house saying, "A dead body is passing by. Come inside the house!" If we had some understanding, then as a dead body was passing by we would call all the children outside and tell them to come and see the dead person, and tell them this is the way we are all going to die one day.

Whatsoever deepens, whatsoever intensifies our realization of our nothingness – all of these processes help the birth of true religiousness, the birth of truth, and the birth of light in our life.

What are the things that deepen our understanding of our nothingness? This very process – as our nothingness keeps being revealed to us – is what meditation is. But our situation is just the opposite. Throughout our lives we keep trying to prove that we are something.

Bodhidharma was a monk who went to China fourteen hundred years ago. Emperor Wu of China welcomed him.

Wu had spent tens of millions of rupees on spreading Buddhism. Thousands of monks received meals every day; he had made thousands of temples; he had made millions of statues of Buddha. One temple alone that he had made had ten thousand statues of Buddha in it. That temple with ten thousand statues of Buddha is there even today.

So when Bodhidharma came to China, Wu came to meet him and said, "Can I ask you a few things? I have built so many temples, I have given so much charity to so many monks, I have helped to spread the influence of Buddhism, I have distributed religious books publicizing the religion far and wide. So what will be my reward for all of this?"

Bodhidharma said "Nothing!"

The emperor was very puzzled. The monks had explained to him that he would be rewarded, that he would attain to nirvana, and would go to heaven. All of this had been explained to the emperor, and Bodhidharma was saying, "Nothing! There will be no reward, but you have certainly committed a sin."

Wu said, "What are you saying? By doing all this I have committed a sin?"

Bodhidharma said, "All this has strengthened your idea that you are something: 'I have done so much work, I have built so many temples, I have printed so many religious books, I have helped spread this religion so much' – all this has made your idea stronger that you are something. There is only one sin in this world: the idea that 'I am something.' And there is only one virtue: to experience that 'I am nothing.'"

Wu became very angry. He had done so much work and this monk was telling him that there was no reward for it, that, on the contrary, all that he has done was a sin. He became angry and left, and declared that Bodhidharma would not be able to stay in his kingdom.

When Bodhidharma was told that Wu had said he could not stay in his kingdom, he replied, "Wu is mistaken. Even if he had wished for me to stay in his kingdom, I was not going to. How could I stay in such a sinner's kingdom? Tell Wu," he said, "that even if he had wanted me to stay, I was not going to stay any longer. There was no need for his order. I was going anyway."

Bodhidharma left Wu's kingdom and went across the river into another kingdom.

Some ten years later, when the time of Wu's death was approaching, he kept thinking about Bodhidharma's statement. Every day it kept piercing his being, that Bodhidharma had said there was no reward for his work, on the contrary it was a sin because it had given birth to the idea that he was something. He kept thinking about it every day. As death came closer to Wu, he started feeling "I will become nothing. Tomorrow when death makes me nothing, then this idea that I was something – I did so much work, I was this, I was that – what value will it have? What meaning will all this have?"

As the emperor was dying, he sent a messenger saying: "Go and bring Bodhidharma back! I am realizing that perhaps what he was saying was right. I am sinking, everything is disappearing."

When the news reached Bodhidharma he said, "I will come, but the person whose message you have brought me has missed. It is too late now. If he had realized that he was nothing at the time that I told him, he could have had the experience of eternal life."

At the time of death everyone realizes that he is nothing, but the one who come to know this while still living is blessed. Those who realize this truth of being nothing while still alive... At the time of death everyone has to realize this, but by then it is too late, by then there is no time for a revolution. If someone realizes this during his lifetime instead, if he comes to know during his lifetime that he is nothing…

You may have heard the name of Chuang Tzu. He was a remarkable mystic. He was just outside a village. It was evening and getting dark. He was just outside the village when his foot hit a person's skull. He was walking through a crematorium. He picked up the skull and touched it with his own head. Then he took the skull to his hut and kept it there.

His friends and disciples asked him, "Why have you brought this skull here?"

Chuang Tzu said, "I have committed a big mistake. I was passing through a crematorium and it was no ordinary crematorium for common people. It was an upper-class crematorium."

There are different types of crematoriums, different ones for lower-class people and different ones for upper-class people. In life there are separate lower and upper classes, and even in death we make such separations: this is a crematorium for the emperors and this is one for the poor people.

Chuang Tzu then said, "It was a crematorium for upper-class people. This skull must be from some big shot. It is possible that it is the skull of an emperor. If that person were still alive today, I would have been in trouble: his skull was hit by my foot. So although he is dead it is better to ask for forgiveness; it is the skull of someone important! That is why I have brought it home with me. I will keep it with respect in my house and every day I will ask for its forgiveness."

"Moreover," said Chuang Tzu, "if this skull remains here near me, I will be reminded that if not today, then tomorrow, my skull will also be in the same situation. If not today, then tomorrow, my skull will also be lying in some crematorium and it will be receiving kicks from people's shoes and feet. This skull of mine, for which I expect so much respect, will be lying in the dust tomorrow, and to help me remember this truth, I am keeping this other skull near me. Since the day I started keeping it near me, even if someone comes and kicks my head while I am alive, I will ask for his forgiveness and inquire if his foot is not hurt – because such a kick is inevitable, it is going to happen tomorrow. How long can I prevent it from happening? This skull is going to be kicked tomorrow."

A revolution takes place in the life of anyone who, while still alive, becomes capable of knowing the simple truth that life will be scattered into nothingness. I call this revolution religion. Unhappiness comes to an end in such a person's life because the roots of unhappiness lie in the idea that "I am something" – and the stronger one's idea of that is, the deeper the misery one keeps falling into.

There is no other spiritual meaning of unhappiness than this idea that "I am something." The more intense the knot of "I am something" is in the mind, the more it hurts. And it becomes impossible to make a person who forgets this idea unhappy. He cannot be made unhappy. The day that all possibilities of unhappiness disappear from inside you, is the day when bliss begins to shower on you.

No one can seek out bliss, nor is it available somewhere so that you can simply go and fill yourself up with it, nor can anyone give it to someone else. We can seek out unhappiness, we can accumulate unhappiness, we can tie a knot of unhappiness inside ourselves and keep accumulating it. But if we want, we can also do away with unhappiness, we can say goodbye to it. And when unhappiness disappears, what remains is bliss.

What is the knot upon which unhappiness accumulates? It accumulates upon no other knot than the knot of "I," the knot of the ego. Yet the efforts of our lives only serve to accumulate this unhappiness, gather this unhappiness Even if we build a temple it is just to nourish our ego: "I have built this temple." If we give something to charity that, too, is in the service of our ego: "I have done this charity work." Even when we love, that too is only a proclamation of our ego: "I am loving." But then even love brings unhappiness, even charity brings unhappiness, even religion brings unhappiness, even temples and mosques bring unhappiness. Wherever there is "I," unhappiness is inevitable. Unhappiness is the shadow of "I."

We all want to be free from unhappiness, but a person who does not want to be free from "I" cannot be free from unhappiness. We want to avoid unhappiness but want to go on feeding our egos. These two desires are so contradictory, such opposites, that they can never both be met.

Is it not possible for us to come to know that "I am nothing"? If this is looked at from many dimensions, then mankind can succeed in this.

Firstly I have said that one should repeatedly remember the dimension of space. Every connection with the dimension of space has been broken. In the settlements made by man, there is no way of feeling, of perceiving, space. In a place like Mumbai, one does not even know when the moon rises or when it sets. Man's houses are so huge that even the sky is hidden by them.

If someone lies on the ground for a little while and gazes at the vastness of the sky, he will realize, "I am nothing. Where am I?" This realization of the vastness of the infinite, this experience of the boundlessness that spreads all around – this awareness of it, this awakening to it – will kindle the feeling that "I am nothing."

One dimension is of space and the other is of time. There is no boundary to either time or space: infinity is behind, infinity is ahead: "Where do I stand in all of this? In this infinite stream of time, where am I? In this infinite Ganges of time where does my dewdrop exist? It is nothing more than a dream."

There are two dimensions: that of time and that of space. By looking into these two dimensions in all their depth, the experience of "I am nothing" begins to arise. So we need to deepen our meditation on these two every day. Standing, sitting, walking, sleeping, it is important to keep full remembrance of this realization: "Where am I in this vast infinity? I can only exist where these two dimensions exist. The point where time and space meet is the only place where I can exist, and if both are infinite, then how can my existence matter? What is the value of that tiny period of time in which I live? And what is the value of this tiny space that I occupy? Tomorrow death will come, and then I will occupy neither space nor time. Both will end."

Meditating constantly on these two dimensions – having a constant remembrance of both, a constant awareness of the two – takes you into wondrous depths, into peace and silence. But only if you do so will you be able to understand this, otherwise not.

I would like you to pay attention to these two dimensions. It is not right to forget them at any moment. The infinite expanse on every side should become a constant remembrance in us. If the awareness of these two dimensions becomes clear to you, then you will find that a revolution is happening within you. You may not even notice that someone has begun to change inside you and another person is beginning to grow. So, on a deeper level the awareness of these two dimensions is to be maintained, but many other realizations around them can also be helpful.

Buddha used to say to his monks to go and sit sometimes at the crematorium.

One monk asked him, "Why at the crematorium?"

Buddha replied, "There, life comes to its completion. You too are walking toward it every day. Maybe sitting there you will remember this. In the crematorium, when a body is burning on the funeral pyre, sit and watch it. Maybe some day you may be able to see that on the funeral pyre there is no one else but you. There may be some delay – today someone else is on the pyre, tomorrow I will be on the pyre, the day after another person will be on the pyre. Perhaps one day seeing the burning body, you will remember it is none other than yourself on that pyre."

Essentially, he was telling his monks to meditate on death.

The second thing is the constant changes of life. Yesterday I was one thing, today I am something else. The day before yesterday I was a child, today I am young, tomorrow I will become old; one day I was not here and one day again I shall not be here. Life is a flux, a constant stream of changes.

Heraclitus has said: You cannot step into the same river twice. By the time we step in again, the river has flowed on, by the time we step in again, we have changed. You cannot step into the same river twice.

When someone would meet Heraclitus, before the person left, Heraclitus would say, "My friend, remember the person who came is not the same as the one who is going back. And also the person you have met is not the same as the one you are saying goodbye to. You have changed and I have also changed."

For twenty-four hours everything is changing continuously. Nothing is stationary here, nothing is.

Edington once jokingly said, "In language, some words are completely false." He was speaking at Oxford. Someone asked him to give an example. He said, "For example *rest*. *Rest* is a totally false word. Nothing stops. Everything is changing. Nothing is stationary and nothing is standing still. The thing you perceive to be standing still is not standing still; deep inside everything is moving. It is a totally false perception that the walls and doors of houses are standing still, are stationary. This door is not stationary. If it were, it would never become old. It is moving inside and it is becoming old. This wall is not stationary, inside it keeps on changing; otherwise this house would never fall down. Everything is changing."

If one has a total understanding of this change, then one will not know that feeling of "I" because, when everything is changing, where is there a place for "I" to stand? When nothing is stationary, when everything is a flux, when everything is a flow, where is "I"?

Buddha started saying a very amazing thing. He said that there is no soul – because where is the place for a soul to exist? People could not understand what he was saying. But Buddha used to take the same meaning for both the soul and the ego. He used to say that the feeling of "I am" is the ego, and it is the soul. If everything is changing, where will "I" find a place to stand? Where is it possible for "me" to be stationary?

In the evening we light a lamp and in the morning we say, "The lamp is still burning. Please blow it out." We are not speaking correctly. The lamp which was lit in the evening faded away a long time ago. The flame keeps on changing every moment. A second flame comes, the first one dies away, then a third one comes, then a fourth comes... With such speed the flame is fading away, is turning into smoke, and a new flame is being lit. The flame we lit in the evening is not the same flame that we blow out in the morning. Through the whole night the flame has kept on changing, changing, changing... During the whole night the flame has kept on changing. The flame that we see in the morning is not the same one.

The person who was born is not the same person as the one who dies. Everything keeps changing, everything keeps changing. Just like the flame, from birth until death everything keeps on changing. The very understanding of this total change allows a person to know that "I" does not exist.

So the awareness of these four: the dimension of time, the dimension of space, moment-to-moment change, and finally, death. One who meditates on these four attains to that ultimate state where he comes to know the reality which is even more infinite than time, which is even more expansive than space, which does not die and which is beyond change. But it is only through awareness of these four that one comes to know that which is different and separate from these four.

Why does one become aware of this by understanding these four things? In reality, to know about anything, to understand anything properly, one needs to have knowledge of its opposite.

In schools, we make black colored boards for children. On the white wall one could write with white chalk, but then the children would not be able to see anything. And if a teacher were to write with white chalk on a white wall, we would call him mad! We make black colored boards and we write with white chalk on them because on a blackboard white lines can be seen very clearly.

If we are to search for that which is infinite and boundless, if we are to search for that in which no change ever happens, if we are to search for that which never dies, if we are to search for that which is eternal, if we are to search for that which is divine, which is truth, then we will have to create an awareness of it, and a background for it which is constantly changing, which is constantly dying. Against this blackboard of change, the distinct white lines of that which is a complete contrast – which is totally different – will emerge and can be seen.

The darker the night is, the brighter the intensity of the stars. The stars are there even in the daytime, but they cannot be seen. To see the stars one has to wait for the night, because in the daylight there is no background against which the stars can be seen. But in the darkness of the night they start shining, they appear as separate entities.

So the deeper these four remembrances become, in the same proportion the reality which is distinct from these four – which is non-temporal, non-spatial; which is in neither time nor space, which is unchanging, unmoving, which neither changes nor transforms, which is undying, which never dies – can be experienced, realized, seen.

For this experience, it is essential to make preparations. And the day this experience happens is the day when life really becomes life in the truest sense. It is only on this day that life becomes filled with splendor. It is only on this day that life becomes free from all bondages. We only come to know this experience on the day that we understand there is nothing left to know or to attain. And this alone is an attainment. It is in this direction, in searching for this very ocean, that the rivers of our lives go on flowing. But if someone comes to think that these rivers are all there is, he will miss the experience of reaching the ocean.

An understanding of these four things will create a deeper sense of nothingness, of non-being, of "I am nothing" in you. The day this feeling that "I am nothing" becomes total, the explosion happens and one comes to know that which one is – which is everything. It is through nothingness that the door to the experience of the whole opens. One who is settled in this nothingness, in this emptiness, is blessed. The longing and the thirst to be settled in this nothingness is called the spiritual search.

Last night I told you that being a seeker should be at the center of our lives. Being a seeker means this sense of being nothing.

Kabir used to say: "I am a hollow bamboo. The music is flowing through me but 'I' am not the music itself. I can stop the music by becoming a block but I am not the creator of this music." If there is something wrong with the flute, the music cannot be born, but the flute itself does not give birth to the music.

The day someone realizes "I am nothing," he becomes a hollow bamboo, and then the music of existence starts flowing spontaneously through him. Then from our side there is no hurdle; then we are just hollow bamboos. That nothingness is the hollowness; that being nothing has given way to the hollowness. Now existence can flow through us.

Rabindranath Tagore was dying. Two days before a friend had said to him, "You have sung so many songs, you are so lucky, you have had your desires fulfilled, and you have attained that which is worth attaining."

Rabindranath said, "My friend, the songs that I have sung have no value at all. But the songs that I was singing when 'I' was not present at all have some value. I have sung two types of songs. Firstly, the songs that 'I' have sung have no value. The others, the songs that 'I' did not sing – when I became a flute, an instrument; when someone else was singing them through me, when they came flowing through me – those songs have value. The songs which people have thanked me for are the songs that 'I' did not sing at all. The songs that 'I' have sung have mistakes in them. They do not have that quality, they do not have that timeless melody in them."

The meaning of being a spiritual seeker is to become so empty that one becomes a medium for the whole; one becomes a flute through which all music can flow. The meaning of being a spiritual seeker is to become so empty, so hollow, that existence can flow through you – you can become a passage. The meaning of being a spiritual seeker is to become the way, the medium, a bridge, so that existence can manifest through you. You become a flute for the whole, for the music of the very being that is hidden within everything.

I pray to existence so that you may also become this flute. And I also pray to you too because if you make a little effort with those four things I have told you about – the four remembrances and the meditations I have told you to do – then there is no reason why you cannot become a hollow bamboo. We are essentially what we want to become; it is only that we do not remember, we are not aware, we do not know.

We are like a man with closed eyes, who is standing in front of the sun shouting, "It is very dark! What shall I do? Shall I light a lamp?" But what will happen to a man with closed eyes even if he lights a lamp? If someone tells a person who is shouting, "What should I do? What should I not do? I am standing in the dark!" to just open his eyes, he will be surprised. "How will this vast darkness disappear just by opening my eyes? Such a small thing as an eye, a small curtain like an eyelid, how can it make the darkness which is surrounding me disappear? He will say, "I cannot trust what you are saying, that such a vast darkness can disappear just by opening my eyes. What does opening my eyes have to do with the darkness disappearing?"

Even if we try to explain, he will not be able to understand because what he is saying seems right, seems logical. Such a small eye, such small eyelids, what can they have to do with such vast darkness? And will such vast darkness disappear just by opening such tiny eyelids? But he only has to open his eyes to find that the darkness definitely disappears. A curtain of tiny eyelids creates such vast darkness.

The tiny sense of ego creates all our darkness. If this curtain of the ego is removed, if the eyes open, then there is only splendor, then there is only light. The sun is always present but we are standing with eyes closed. Besides that there is no other hurdle.

May existence help our eyes to open.

I am very, very grateful that you listened to me with such love and silence. Now to end, I bow down to the godliness dwelling within each of you. Please accept my *pranams*, my offering of respect.

6
An Organism Built on Foundations of Love

This morning I was listening to your discussions. In this connection, the first thing you have to understand is that religion never has any organization – it can never have. And the only outcome of any effort to create an organized religion will be to destroy religiousness.

Religion, religiousness, is an absolutely personal matter. It can only happen within each individual's life. It has nothing to do with any organization or crowd.

This does not mean that there cannot be other kinds of organizations. There can be social organizations, there can be educational organizations, there can be moral and cultural organizations, there can be political organizations. There just cannot be any religious organization.

It is important to remember that if friends who have gathered around me want to create an organization, it will not be a religious organization, and that a person will not become religious simply by joining that organization. By becoming a member of *Jeevan Jagruti Kendra* – the Life Awakening Center – no one will become religious in the way we think that we are "religious" just because we are a Hindu or a Mohammedan.

Becoming religious is an altogether different matter. For that, it is not necessary to become a member of any organization. Rather, the reality is that anyone who is a member of some religious organization will find that their very membership is creating hindrances on their way to becoming religious. A person who is a Hindu cannot be religious, a person who is a Jaina cannot be religious, a person who is a Mohammedan cannot be religious either…because to be in an organization is to be in a sect.

Sect and *religion* are contradictory terms. A sect divides and religion unites.

So, the first thing it is necessary to understand is that if any organization is formed around me, it is not a religious organization. To form one, thinking it is a religious organization, would be wrong. So the friends who have said that there cannot be a religious organization have said absolutely the right thing. There can never be. But perhaps they have the misunderstanding that there cannot be any other kind of organization either.

There can be other kinds of organization. The Life Awakening Center is another kind of organization, not a religious organization. There are so many diseases, so many sicknesses, so many troubles and so much ugliness in this society that a religious person cannot be ready to quietly tolerate all this ugliness, stench and stupidity. A religious person will not be ready to tolerate this ugly society continuing. A person in whose life even a ray of religion has entered would like to transform this society from its very roots.

The Life Awakening Center is not a religious organization. It is an organization of religious people for social transformation and revolution. Nobody will become religious by becoming a member, but those who want this society, this life, this morality, this current system, this tradition to change can become members and strengthen the organization. This will be an organization for social, not religious, revolution. It will be for social reform; not for spiritual peace but for social revolution. This should be made clear: it is a movement for social revolution.

It is violent for any person who is even slightly aware, peaceful and able to see and understand life to allow this society to go on as it is. No religious person can tolerate the present situation in society. Only the irreligious person can. Only those who have no compassion in their hearts can stand by and watch the ugliness that prevails in this society. Only those who have no ray of love in their lives can bear so much dark hatred; only those whose humanity has died can agree to live, surrounded by such a dead kind of humanity. The religious man will either change this society – will at least try to change this society – or he will perish. But he cannot be ready to live in this society as it is.

So, the Life Awakening Center will be an organization, not a religious organization but an organization for social revolution and upheaval. It will be an organization, but not in the sense that Mohammed's organization is an organization – when you become a Mohammedan everything is achieved: those who are Mohammedans reach the gates of paradise, but those who are not will find the gates closed. It will not be that kind of organization; it will have nothing to do with spiritual liberation or the gates of paradise.

An organization never has anything to do with spiritual liberation. That is the personal matter of each individual. But will anyone who has experienced even one iota of peace, even a tiny fraction of the light of existence in his life, go on tolerating this society just as it is? He will find it intolerable.

A religious person will be fundamentally rebellious. And if a religious person has not been rebellious in this world up until now, there is only one reason: that person must not have been religious in the first place. A religious person will have to be rebellious; there will have to be revolution in his life.

But a revolution cannot be brought about by itself. For it to take place an organization is needed – because when we start the revolution, the forces that oppose it will be organized. What can one person do against them? The reactionary forces that are against revolution are all organized. What chance does a single person have against them, what possibility?

In life, the wrong people are organized, and the good man – thinking "What is the need for an organization?" – only supports and encourages those wrong people. Always remember this: in life, all the thieves and hooligans are organized, all the politicians are organized, all the people who spoil life are organized. Meanwhile, the good man is thinking, "What is the need for an organization?" This will have only one outcome: the good man, knowingly or unknowingly, will end up being the agent for those bad people. To bring about any change in the organized set-ups of bad people, good people need to organize themselves.

Always remember that our organization is not religious and that it will have no direct relationship with religion. Religious people can be in the organization, but no one will become religious simply by becoming a member of it.

An organization has become extremely necessary, but keeping the focus on social revolution. It has always been a tragedy that the bad people are organized and the good individual stands alone. That is why the good people never win, are defeated. And in the future too, the good man will not win unless he becomes organized. The forces of evil are united. It is necessary to raise equivalent forces against them.

So, I am completely against religious organizations, but not against organization. You need to take note of the difference.

The second thing is: what are the aims of our organization? What does it want to achieve? What will it do?

If we look at the needs of society, the activities of this organization can be understood. The whole way society is organized is sick. There is a need for a radical change; there is a need to change its very foundations. The way we have been molding, conditioning, man up until now, has proved to be wrong. The mold inevitably gives birth to diseases. Then we fix the responsibility onto the person – "You are responsible!" – whereas, in fact, he is just a victim, not the cause. And we have been making him responsible for the past five thousand years. This has been absolutely unjust toward mankind.

If a man is poor, it is possible that he will become a thief. If a man is wretched, it is very possible that he will become a sinner. As long as there is poverty in the world, wretchedness in the world, we will not succeed in making people moral in the truest sense. When there is such great poverty that one's very being is being drowned beneath it, it is very difficult to remember morality. On the one hand, all the money in society accumulates in a few people's hands – leaving most of its people poor – and on the other hand, we tell those poor people not to fall victim to greed, not to become attached to money, not to look at anyone else's riches with envy.

The teaching goes something like this: There is a load of delicious food in one corner of the house and hungry people have gathered all around it. The aroma of the food is reaching their nostrils, they can see the food there, they are hungry and their whole being is asking for food. Yet we are teaching them: "Look! Never ever think of food; never ever look at the food belonging to others because that is the greatest sin."

The whole system of society is such that it gives birth to immorality. If we wish to develop a moral life within society to any extent – and I am not saying *religious* life – we will have to think and reconsider the whole concept of this society from its very roots. We will have to look at it in every dimension.

So, the Life Awakening Center will want to adopt a very clear point of view regarding society's economic system as well. And that point of view will have to be carried to each and every village, to every nook and corner.

Society's education is contaminated; the whole educational system is contaminated. Only fraud is carried out in the name of education. A person does not develop through it, nor does his soul grow. Nothing happens in his being that we could call essential to life, to the art of living. Without knowing anything he returns home with degrees in his hands. Without being anything he returns home, and the most precious period of his life has been wasted in the name of education. The time when something could have really happened is totally and meaninglessly wasted. The Life Awakening Center will have to develop a clear vision on a new system of education, on how it should be.

Our family system is also totally rotten, but we have been living in it for so long that we don't even realize how rotten things have become. No couple is happy, no father is happy with his son, no son is happy with his father, no mother is happy with her children, no teacher is happy with his pupils, and no pupil is happy with his teachers. It seems as if the whole of society has been created only in order to cause suffering to one another, to hurt one another.

The entire concept of the family needs to change from its very roots. A new kind of family needs to develop where the father and the sons, the mother and the children, and the wife and the husband are all content, can reach the greatest contentment in life. And such a society can be created; such a family can be created. We just haven't given it any thought, any consideration.

I have said that the Life Awakening Center would like to create a movement that concerns every area of our lives. I have a vision for it all. I have a vision about religion, but that does not mean that I do not think about every other aspect of life. My own understanding is that a person in whose life even a little ray of the light of religiousness enters becomes capable – with the help of that light – of seeing, of understanding, every aspect of life. With the lamp of religiousness in our hands, we become capable of looking at all the problems of life.

I have a vision for every aspect of life. I want to tell you about this, I want to share it with the whole society. The Life Awakening Center will take care of bringing this to everyone.

There is not a single aspect of life that is not facing a need for change. The reality is that our lives have just developed and grown out of historical necessity. Human society has not grown out of any proactive and conscious choices. The society that has been created so far has simply developed out of unconscious and historical processes. Nothing belonging to society has been created proactively, through conscious thinking and understanding.

Now there is a need to create society proactively. By rethinking about each and every aspect of life, *everything* can be transformed.

In Israel, they have done a small experiment for the last fifteen years. They are called kibbutzim. It is a revolutionary experiment regarding family. I want that experiment to be done in each and every village of India. In the coming two hundred years, the children that will have grown out of this experiment of kibbutzim will be of an entirely different kind.

The kibbutz is a system in which the child is handed over to the village commune after he is three months of age – just a three-month-old baby. The baby is raised away from the parents.

Parents can meet the child: once a month, once in a fortnight, every week, daily – whenever it is convenient for them they can go and give their love to the child – but the entire upbringing of the child has become collective.

There have been amazing results from this collective raising. Generally it had been thought that if children were brought up in this way, the love of the children toward their parents would diminish. But the result has been that the kibbutz children love their parents in a way no other child in the whole world does. The reason for this is that these children have been able to witness only their parents' love. They don't get the chance to see any of the other things in them. Whenever the parents come to see them, they only hug and love their children, and when the children go to the family home for a couple of hours they only receive love. The parents don't get a chance to get angry with the children – to become annoyed and shout at them – and the children don't get the chance to see how their father misbehaves with their mother or what sort of language their mother uses against their father. They have no idea whatsoever about all of this.

Their parents appear like gods and goddesses to them because whenever they go home that is how they find them. They go for just an hour or half an hour, or the parents go for an hour or half an hour to see their children. And when the children return home at the age of twenty, having completed their education, there cannot be any hatred, any anger, any reaction, any rebellion in their hearts against their parents. The amount of love that they have received from them…

Until now it had been thought that keeping a child away from his parents would mean that his love for them would diminish, but the experiment of the kibbutzim has proved that the love between the parents and the children grows in an amazing way. The children who lived there collectively, communally…

We have simply no understanding at all that to raise a child with older people is completely immoral. The mind of the small child is that of a small child, and the mind of an older person is that of an older person. Older people have had a lifelong experience of things. They think in one way and children think in another. And right now we bring up our children alongside much older people. It is very difficult to calculate how bad this process is for children. Older people cannot understand children, nor can children understand them. Older people become sad when children harass them, but they have no idea how much they are harassing their children.

The kibbutzim say that raising children with older people is a way to drive them crazy from their very childhood because children have a different way of thinking. It is not that the adults' way is wrong, but they have had their own experiences of life, they have their own way of thinking, people of their age have their own way of looking at things – what can all this have to do with the child?

So the kibbutzim say that to raise people of the same age group together is psychologically more correct. Children of a certain age should be raised with the other children from the same age group. And the result is that the children coming out of the kibbutzim have a freshness, a newness; they have a different joy and aura around them.

Our children become sad because they are living with older people. Before they can learn to be cheerful and joyous, sadness grips them from all around. They become completely fearful because in everything they feel they are wrong. Their father is reading his book, his Gita, and the child feels he is doing something wrong if he is noisy. Now a child can never understand how reading the Gita can be so meaningful and his noisiness so meaningless. To the child, jumping around and making noises is so meaningful that it is beyond his imagination to comprehend how sitting down reading a book can be something so great that he is not supposed to make any noise.

Slowly, slowly the child discovers that everything he does is wrong. In this way we make every child feel guilty. From his very childhood he starts feeling that everything he is doing is wrong. If he makes a noise, that is wrong; if he is playing, that is wrong; if he runs around, that is wrong; if he climbs a tree, that is wrong; if he jumps into the river, that is wrong; if he stands out in the rain with his clothes on, that is wrong... Whatsoever he does is wrong. The cumulative effect of all of this upon him becomes that *he* is wrong. We are creating guilty people from their very childhood.

And the sole reason for this is that children are being raised with people from an altogether different age group than their own. In the kibbutzim they have organized it so that children are raised with their own age group. Even their caretakers are only slightly older children from among them all, not adults. Adults remain at a distance, to the side. They are only there to ensure that no child harms or hurts himself by mistake. That is more than enough. More attention than this is not needed from them.

A friend of mine went to a kibbutz school and he was amazed. The children were having their meals, and he said that for the first time in his life he experienced that this is how children should have their meals. There were fifty children there. Some were dancing on the tables – on the same tables they were eating on – some children were playing guitars, another child was dancing the twist and a girl was singing. All this playfulness was going on, and in the midst of it all dinner was taking place.

He said the dinner continued for two to two and a half hours – the music, the dancing and the meal. He asked if this was how it happens every day and he was asked, "How can there be meals without dancing and singing?" He said he was mesmerized for those two hours; the children were so joyous and happy.

But this cannot happen while eating with adults. This would be impossible. Our children lose their happiness even before they can know it. They have never been raised like children.

So my vision is to transform the whole spectrum: children, old people, the economic system, the political system, education, society, the family – everything. And for that an organization is needed, but not a religious organization. I won't be able to discuss all of this in detail now. To do so I am thinking of making a separate camp where I can discuss the whole thing with you – about how we can change every part of society.

Secondly, as we move ahead, we should understand a few things. For example, the society we are living in is sick. If we make it a condition of the organization that only healthy people can become members, then the organization will never take off. It is like a hospital putting up a notice in the entrance saying that only healthy people will be admitted. Then no one will come to that hospital, firstly, because then there will be no need for a hospital, and secondly, because people only go to a hospital when they are ill.

So if we impose this kind of condition – that only non-egotistical people should join the organization, that only those not hungry for respectability, position and status should join the organization; that only those who make no discrimination between rich and poor should become part of the organization – we are making the wrong kind of conditions. I believe that people will become like this after having been part of the organization, but this cannot be a precondition of entry into the organization. A person who has been a part of the organization should end up being like this, but to say that this should already be the case before we form the organization is madness. Then there would be no need to form the organization in the first place!

This we will have to accept: that when the organization begins, it will begin along with the sicknesses of man. We will have to move with this understanding: that man has his sicknesses. Of course it will be necessary to keep an eye on how far those sicknesses can be avoided, on how far they can be removed; it will be necessary to make arrangements for that. And the final aim should be that they are eradicated.

How will these sicknesses be eradicated? Everything the common man does is initiated by his ego. The state of no ego is only found when ultimate religiousness is experienced; then all activities become non-egoistic. But before this happens, how to proceed?

An egoist can do good things as well as bad things. His ego can be associated with good acts as well as bad acts. Certainly good acts – in the ultimate sense – only happen when the ego is annihilated, but this cannot be the precondition for any organization. Whenever a society or organization is beginning, it has to be from this basic premise: "We accept the sicknesses of man. We will try to make the maximum use of those sicknesses in the service of good."

For example, this issue that some people are staying in fifty rupee accommodation and some in thirty-rupee accommodation. There can be many reasons for this. And as society is divided into classes it is impossible to create an oasis without there being class divisions as a part of it – because the people who are coming will be coming from that same divided society. The whole structure of their lifelong thinking is one of class division. They will come here for three days, bringing that class structure along with them. So if we make it a condition that in order to come here people have first to drop their ideas of different classes, no one will ever come.

Society is divided into classes. A person who is coming here is coming from such a society. Division has taken deep roots in his heart. This division has to be removed, an effort has to be made to remove it, but "No class divisions, please!" cannot be made a qualification for entry.

If there is a man from the fifty-rupee class, he will demand the fifty-rupee amenities – he is used to that. If he is not given them, he will not come here. I have come to know that three to four hundred more people were going to come from Mumbai, but the fifty-rupee accommodation was full so they couldn't come. A man like this only stays in that class of place.

I am not saying that these differences should be abolished. What I am saying is that the differences should be made a little bigger. There should also be a one-hundred-rupee category, an eighty-rupee category, a seventy-, a ten-, a five- and a zero-rupee category – because as one friend mentioned, there are some people who cannot pay anything at all.

The only way to bring those who cannot pay anything at all here is to also have a one hundred-and-fifty-rupee category for those who are only happy when they can pay one hundred and fifty rupees. There is no other way than this. Only then can the man with no rupees also be included.

Some people only feel happy when they pay one hundred and fifty rupees, when they are staying in one-hundred-and-fifty-rupee accommodation. They should be allowed to have this much joy. This will be something for later, that through the way we set it up, through our thinking, through our philosophy and our actions they will come to understand that they were fools; that they were mistaken. People who are paying nothing and people who are paying one hundred and fifty rupees will be treated in exactly the same way by the people running the center.

I am saying "actions." I am not talking about the beds and pillows. Because it is only appropriate that you will have to provide the person in the one-hundred-and-fifty-rupee category with two good pillows – and you should. But as far as the way the center workers behave is concerned, if a center worker speaks to the person staying in the one-hundred-and-fifty-rupee category more respectfully, then that will be a mistake, then he is mistaken. If he speaks disrespectfully to a person who has not given a rupee, then that is a mistake. Then we will be recreating classes.

These classes – the one-hundred-rupee class, the one-hundred-and fifty-rupee class – already exist; we are not creating them. Society is rooted in them. We want to create a new society and get rid of all classes. On the level of the way people act here, there should not be one iota of discrimination.

There will be a difference in that the person paying one hundred and fifty rupees will stay near my bungalow. This is not discrimination. If he pays one hundred and fifty rupees and he stays out there in the village, how can that be justified? Let him stay here. His staying here makes no difference, because when he comes to see me he will realize that, from my side, there is no difference in how I meet the person who has had to walk a hundred yards to come to see me and the person who has only had to take a few steps.

What is more, we should develop a new kind of understanding: that the people staying in the bungalows costing one hundred and fifty rupees are not healthy enough to stay in a place costing only ten rupees. We should develop that kind of understanding. The one staying in the fifty rupee facility is less healthy, the one staying in the thirty rupee facility is healthier – he can live on thirty rupees! We have to change our understanding, our values.

You will not get rid of the one hundred and fifty and one hundred rupee categories that easily. You will have to develop the concept that a person staying in the thirty rupee category is healthier. Someone staying in the fifty rupee category is unwell; the one who is staying in the one hundred and fifty rupee category is even more ill – he needs more facilities. And there should be kindness, compassion, for a sick person, not hatred. Naturally, one is always kind to a sick person – what cause can be there for hatred?

We should change concepts and values. A difference should be brought into our thinking and values. Hence, it comes to me that the classifications that the friends at the center have made... Perhaps make the thirty rupee category "A" and call the fifty rupee category "C." Then the person in the fifty rupee category will be in the third class; he will not be in the first class. This is actually how it should be.

This is actually how it should be – and we should be able to change the way this is seen so that the person staying in the fifty rupee category also realizes that staying there is a little bit of a humbling experience, is a little bit like becoming an object of sympathy, and the person staying in the thirty rupee category realizes that he is a healthier person. One who can stay with a hundred other people is a more social person. A person who says he will stay alone, that he cannot fall asleep together with others around, is sick. We will have to do something about this person, and we will, so that slowly, this person is able to stay with a hundred others. But if we put a condition that here there will be only one category, we are hindering this man.

And the most interesting thing is that the very person we will be hindering is the one who would have supported those who have little or no means to come. Perhaps you have no idea that the thirty-rupee facility is actually costing more than that: it comes to some thirty-five or thirty-seven rupees. Those seven or so rupees are coming from the man using the fifty-rupee facility. The actual cost there is not fifty rupees; it is something around forty. Those extra ten rupees from the fifty-rupee person are there to reduce the forty-rupee class down to thirty. But man's mind is strange. If you try to arrange things for him, he suffers because he has been made part of the thirty-rupee class. If you do not make arrangements, he will not be able to come because he is not in a position to pay forty rupees. And on top of all that, the person who is paying his extra ten rupees is becoming an object of hatred for him.

This society of yours! The Life Awakening Center is not responsible for it, nor am I. The responsibility goes to your forefathers. The society that they founded five thousand years ago is full of stupidities. Today, one has to start by accepting that society – even if one's purpose is to change it.

It is certainly necessary for the friends at the meditation center here to be very careful about the way they act. At that level there should be no consideration about money in their hearts – none at all. This does not mean that money should be insulted. Our minds usually function in this way: either we respect money or we insult it. We just keep swinging between the two. There should be a natural acceptance of money. Money is valuable, money has power – and those people who think money has no value and no power are mistaken. Money has tremendous value and tremendous power, but a person does not become respectable because of it. To be human is something much bigger than money. A bed is obtained with money, a pillow is obtained with money, a house is obtained with money, food is obtained with money, but the status of being human is not obtained with money. So there will be differences in beds, in pillows and mattresses, but there should be no difference in the respect for a person as such.

And slowly as the friends here at this center manage to create a milieu where there is no differentiation between people, we will reach a point where a person pays what he can: "Between thirty and one hundred rupees or between ten and a hundred rupees – pay whatever you can." Everyone will pay what he can and will say where he or she would like to stay. I am talking about a gradual evolution, that in five years from now we will be able to do this. A person will pay whatever he can between ten and a hundred rupees and can ask for any facility – according to his need. Maybe the person paying ten rupees is not well and needs the one-hundred-rupee facilities, which he cannot afford. And it is also possible that someone paying one hundred rupees can afford it but as he is not ill and does not have any other reason to stay there, he will be capable of living in the ten-rupee facility.

We can gradually give birth to such a loving milieu, but it cannot be made a basic condition from the start, or the first qualification to participating. Everything depends on the milieu and our creation of it.

Similarly, the friends and workers at the Life Awakening Center will not immediately become free from competitiveness. But they *can* become free from competitiveness, and this will be kept as a goal. There is no need even to make this a direct goal. As I see it, one should never have negative goals. The focus should be that love grows. The more love grows, the less competition there will be.

Perhaps you may not be aware that it is the person who is deprived of love in life who joins the race to become number one – because in love, everybody becomes number one right away. Whomsoever I give love to becomes number one; if you give me love, I become number one – then I am no longer second in this world. The person who does not receive love in life, who is unable to give or receive love, compensates for this by competing. Competition is a substitute. One who has not received love becomes a competitor. He says, "Somehow, in this way or that, I have to become number one."

If I love a girl, she unknowingly starts experiencing that there is no other woman on this earth who is more beautiful than she is. Just my love will induce this feeling in her – that there is no other woman more beautiful, more significant than she is. If someone loves me, that will induce this same feeling in me: because of her love, because of the way she looks at me, because of the way she touches me, there is no other man like me in this world. Love makes everyone first. On whomsoever the look of love falls, that person becomes first.

The poor people in whose life there is no love try to become number one. The question is not of competition, the question is always about love. A person in whose life love is happening forgets all about becoming first. The very question of becoming first no longer exists. Love makes everyone first.

So, the question is not of dropping competition. That is not how I see things. My vision is how the friends at the center can become more loving. That is the direction we are to make efforts in. The more loving they become, in that same proportion the competition will keep diminishing. Competition is simply a disease; it is born out of a lack of love. Therefore the idea of eradicating competition is wrong. Competition is never eradicated until love grows.

There is so much competition in this world because there is no love at all. And this competition will remain. If you demolish it in one place, it will appear in another. If you suppress it here, it will start manifesting there – because the basic question is not competition; what needs to be emphasized is how love may grow. And our entire organism is to be built on foundations of love.

There are keys to love – that I gently discuss with you many times – about how love can grow. In the same connection, a few small things have been talked about in the morning that I would like to share with you now…

This happens every day. A group of workers is bound to grow around me. It is also necessary that it grows. If it doesn't, it will become difficult for me even to survive. I wake up in the morning, and from getting up in the morning to late in the night there is not a single moment's rest for me. There cannot be – I know that this is not a time for me to rest. Man is in such misery: what time is there for me to rest? It is just that in order to continue the work, for the very sake of the work, one needs rest – not in any other sense. But the friends that come to see me have no idea about all of this.

Recently in Varanasi, I came back at around ten in the night after having spoken, and there were eight to ten people gathered in the house, waiting. I had been speaking from the morning, had returned at ten in the night and I was going to go straight to bed – but there were eight or ten people sitting in the room. They had no idea and they cannot be blamed. They just wanted to ask me a few things. They had come to see me out of great love. They began talking about their things. They were still asking things at half past twelve at night.

Now my host, the owner of the house, became restless and started pacing up and down. He started gesturing to me again and again seeking my permission, asking whether he should get rid of them now. But these people were so absorbed in their discussions, and the discussions were useful, meaningful. These were the problems of their lives. How could they be expected to be bothered whether I should now go to bed?

At last, they had to be told at one o'clock in the morning. And when they were told, they became sad. They said, "We have been waiting for your arrival for the last six months. And tomorrow morning you will be gone. Is it not possible that, for our sake, you don't sleep for just one night?"

I said, "It can be done. But how long can things go on like this? I can forgo sleeping tonight, and I can forgo sleeping tomorrow night, but how long can this go on?"

Recently, there was to be a meeting at eight o'clock in the evening. I returned home, very tired, at seven and went to sleep so that I could go fresh to the meeting at eight.

A friend came to see me – that friend is present here – so my younger brother said to him, "No. He won't be able to see you now. Come to the eight o'clock meeting."

The poor man must have been thinking of coming to see me for months. He was very hurt. He went back home weeping.

I came to know of it only yesterday.

There was no mistake on his part. He had no idea about anything. Mustering courage for six months, he came to see me with such love. He must have come full of tremendous feelings; no one can say how precious, how meaningful the things he must have come to discuss were. And someone says, "No. Right now you cannot meet him."

Now who is at fault here?

I believe it is always the worker who is at fault, because the person who has come cannot be at fault. It is always the worker who is at fault; because the same thing could have been said slightly differently, could have been said with more love. In saying "He cannot be seen right now; come to the eight o'clock meeting," I was taken care of but not the man who had come to see me. That was a mistake. That was an utter mistake.

The person who comes to see me is to be cared for even more than I am, because there is no way to measure with how much longing, with how many ideas, with what cherished thoughts he has come.

The same thing could have been said in this way: "He has returned home, tired from the whole day, and has just gone to bed to rest. If you say so, I will wake him up. It is up to you. You decide."

I don't think that a man who returned home weeping because he was not able to see me would have been ready to wake me up. This could not happen; this would be impossible. Had the man been told how tired I was – that I had come home from a long day, had just gone to sleep, and had to go to another meeting at eight that evening, so waking me up would be inconvenient... But that if he insisted, I could be woken up – it is impossible that this friend who went home weeping, who had come to see me so full of such feelings, would not have shown any kindness toward me. I cannot believe that. But then he would not have returned home crying; then he would have gone home joyfully.

A worker slowly gets into a routine state. He doesn't even remember the notion of persuasion. He has his own problems. If the worker were dealing with just one person, he could persuade him, but he has to say the same things to many people every day.

The very meaning of doing the work is that we are relating with human society at large, that we are relating with many people. And if we can be loving toward many people every time, only then is there skill, art, and success in our working.

So of course the friends at the Life Awakening Center are to take care of me, but more than me they are to take care of those friends who will be coming to see me. Even if sometimes you have to stop someone, in that stopping find a way to leave it up to him or her. And if the person is not ready to let go, then you should let go of your concern about me. I may go through a little hardship – no need to worry about that – but for someone to go away hurt is utterly wrong. If you can manage it so that the person goes away happily, great, but if you cannot, then don't send him away. My inconvenience is not that much of a question; their happiness is more important. After all, the whole effort that I am making is that people become happy. So if the person becomes unhappy, there is no point in all my efforts.

Even if a single person returns unsatisfied from being around me, then the fault lies with me. My friends ought to be aware of this. I understand their difficulty; I understand their troubles. Every person wants to arrive and just go in and see me; every person wants to talk to me – wants to take hours of time – and from where can you find that much time? Time is limited. After two minutes they have to ask a person to leave, because fifty others are sitting waiting to meet me – and time is limited. Anyone would feel bad leaving after just a two minute meeting. But my own understanding is that a person can go away happily even after a meeting of just two minutes, and that the workers need to learn the whole science of behavior.

That is why I have been thinking recently of holding a small meditation camp of two or three days just for the workers, where I can talk to them about everything regarding this. A small word makes all the difference. A small change in behavior makes all the difference. A small touch of the hand makes all the difference.

A friend of mine was with me in a certain city. After his departure some friends came and complained to me, "He walked us out holding on to our hands in such a way that it felt we were being thrown out."

We can lead someone out as if we were throwing him out – and this is bound to create hurt. We can talk to someone in another way…

Recently two people came from Mumbai. Just the day before yesterday they came to Jabalpur to see me simply to lodge their complaint. The husband and wife reached Jabalpur from Mumbai to say, "We were not allowed to see you in

Mumbai. We were pushed out saying, 'Go! Go! He cannot be seen right now.'"

"So we were badly shocked. Aren't we human beings? Yet we were pushed out like animals."

Now this is very difficult. I know what a difficult situation a worker is in. Throughout the day, from morning to night, he is overwhelmed, he forgets. But in this very forgetfulness he is no longer a worker. He will have to become extremely humble; he will have to become extremely loving.

One more thing has to be taken note of: that if my comfort is being protected at the cost of someone's happiness, then that comfort is not to be protected. Don't bother about it. Don't bother about it at all. If my convenience can be managed alongside the happiness of others, only then is it to be managed, otherwise not.

If you keep this in mind, it will make a difference. Not a single person... And you have no idea how precious each person is. Each person is unique. An ordinary person comes, a stranger, but you do not know what he is, what he can be, what he can do. When a person leaves with a hurt heart you are sending away a very potential force. That is wrong and it should not happen.

But the number of workers has not yet grown. So far only a few friends have dropped all of their own work to do a little of mine instead. The number of workers will only grow when an extensive organization develops and we can slowly manage every aspect of things. So a new category of workers is certainly to be raised.

Three things to end...

One, I want a youth organization. I want a *Yuvak Kranti Dal* a Revolutionary Youth Force, all over the country – a youth organization called *Yukrand* – which may be organized on military lines. Young people will meet there every day – both boys and girls – and they will play there. And my concept goes on growing that meditation for older people will be about relaxation, and meditation for the young will be active – meditation in action, meditation while playing, meditation while parading, exercising, drilling.

Youth organizations are to be started in every town, city and village. They will play, and along with the games and sports they will also do experiment with meditations, they will also practice fitness and meditation techniques. And then, based on the energy and strength of these young people, we will take the fragrance, the message, the milieu of the things that we want to transform to each and every village. So first, a youth organization is to be started.

Secondly, hundreds of male and female sannyasins – Hindu, Jaina, Mohammedan – continuously meet me and want there to be a new kind of sannyasin in this country who does not belong to any particular religion or community, who only belongs to religiousness. So far this has never happened in the world. Someone is a Jaina sannyasin, someone is a Hindu sannyasin, someone is a Muslim sannyasin. I want to start a new order of sannyasins. And nearly two hundred male and female sannyasins have agreed with me that the day I call them, they will be able to leave their sects and come. This new category of sannyasin – who does not belong to any particular religion but to religiousness – will travel from village to village bringing all the messages of life transformation.

So there will be a new organization of male and female sannyasins. And then too, whenever someone feels that he is now fed up with sannyas, he can immediately go back to being a householder. And this won't be humiliating – there should be no restriction or bondage concerning it. Then any young person coming out of university wanting to be a sannyasin for a couple of years can do so. He can taste the sannyas life for two years, familiarize himself with it, and go back. There will be no obstacle made for him. So the second thing is a new category of sannyasins.

And thirdly, I have plans to establish hostels all around the country where students can stay. Irrespective of where they study, the hostels should be established to transform their daily lives, so their daily life routines can be transformed.

In order to accomplish these three tasks, a vast organization of the Life Awakening Center is needed with branches from village to village, centers from place to place. Then it can accomplish these things.

So think in this direction. And keep in mind that I am not starting this organization as a religious organization. Keep in mind that this is an organization for social revolution. And think about how we can create it, how we can develop it so that a permanent change in the social consciousness of this country can be brought about in ten to fifteen years; so that lives can be influenced and some doors, some windows, can be opened in the direction of transforming life. They *can* be opened.

Regarding this, I would like there to be a three-day camp for workers soon, so that I can share my views on every aspect of this with you and listen to your views. Then we can engage in extensive work to bring it about.

Is there anything else? If there is something to ask, please ask.

Osho,
There are many mistakes in the translations.

The work that has happened so far on the books is better than nothing happening at all. It is not something that has yet become what it ought to be – and it could not have become so yet. Friends who felt love for the work started doing something. They were neither literary people nor writers. Those who came out of love also did some translation work. That translation, too, was only a symbol of their love; it is not that they had some great qualification for doing it. But had they not done it, it would not have happened. Because they did it, this idea can arise today that something better should be done.

This is totally right. Something better should happen. And every center can work in this direction, because I am speaking so much that it is beyond the capacity of the Mumbai center alone to cope with publishing everything. The amount I speak in a month – on various subjects, on various topics – no one center can handle alone. The Mumbai center is coping with it, coping beyond its capacity. And what center? There are just three or four friends there. What can be called a center there? Seeing the word *Mumbai*, everyone thinks the center must be big, but just three or four friends are there running it. And that is why, whatsoever they are doing, I simply don't mention any of the mistakes, because they are doing so much and under such difficult conditions that to mention any mistakes would be unjust. I simply don't talk about them, because it is just a couple of friends who are pulling everything together, devoting their whole time, devoting their whole energy.

This is quite right. There are many mistakes in the translations. Every place should care for this work; every center should care for this work. Wherever you can manage to publish them, publish them. Gujarati publications in Gujarat, that is good; Marathi publications in Maharashtra, that is good; Hindi publications in the Hindi region will be best. There is nothing in the way of this. Whichever friend wants to do something by himself, even privately, should do it.

My idea is that for now and for about the next five years, whosoever can manage to do whatever they can should do it. In five years' time we will take stock of the situation: what has been right and what has been wrong. After that we will consider how to do it right. For now, whosoever can manage whatsoever should go ahead and do it. For now, I believe that even somebody doing something wrong is doing right. At least he is doing something! And because of his doing, at least a few people will be struck by the idea that something has been done wrongly. Then something right can be done.

So I don't stop anybody. To whoever tells me that he wants to do something, I will reply, "Go ahead!" – knowing very well what kind of translation this poor fellow will do!

One friend translated my words into English. His translation could not have been right. Other people also told me that his translation was not right. I said, "But none of the people whose translations can be right ever say to me that they will translate something! This man says he can, so I let him do it. When someone who translates correctly comes and says he wants to translate, I will let him translate. Right now, I let whoever comes do it. Just look at this poor man's courage! He doesn't know much English and yet he is translating."

And he did translate. When the translation was published, many people said it was a bad translation. I asked them to do a correct translation, but then they did nothing. Not one of those people has done a correct translation so far.

Our difficulty is that if some work is done... I remember one thing...

There was a painter in France who did a painting and left it at a crossroads asking for the opinion of the whole village, asking people to tell him if something was lacking in the painting. He left a book in which people could write down their suggestions.

The whole book was filled up. It was beyond his understanding how it could be possible to commit so many mistakes in one single painting. It had to be a very difficult task – a small painting with so many mistakes in it! It would have taken a genius to accomplish such a feat.

He told all this to his master.

The master said, "Now do one more thing. Put the painting there with a note saying, 'Please correct the mistakes that you find in this painting.'"

No one came forward to correct anything. Not a single person in the village picked up the paintbrush to correct a thing.

Our minds, our way of functioning is such that first we see what is wrong. What is right, what it is that needs to be done, doesn't even occur to us.

So what I say to you is, "Good." Do something there in Baroda. The friends in Ahmedabad can do something too. Whatsoever feels right to you, just do it.

And my attitude is that whatever you do, I will say, "Good." Because right now, my view is that something should happen. Later on we can assess what has been done rightly and what is wrong. But first of all something ought to be done!

So in every center, whatever work is possible, just start.

And Mumbai is not a center as yet. What center is there in Mumbai? Just three or four friends! But the idea has run through the whole country that Mumbai is some kind of center; that it is wealthy. There is neither wealth nor money; they are constantly in debt and in trouble – no question of making money. They are losing every time. In any case, with me, there can only be a friendship of losing, not of earning!

So I too feel uncomfortable. And those poor fellows, I am amazed at their patience. When they quietly listen to such stories – that they are making money, and this and that – I am amazed. There is no question of them making money. Recently, they arranged for there to be chairs in the meeting and asked people to leave a few paisa in the box when they left. Even with that not everyone obliged. The organizers had to pay for the chairs themselves. And when they stood up with a donation box, so many letters of complaint came to me afterward: "This is not a good thing to do!" but no one bothered to ask how much they had collected in the box. Nothing was collected, but an endless number of letters were sent to me telling me how bad it was to stand up with a donation box. It is doubtful if those who wrote put even a single rupee into the box.

If the work is to be of a high quality, but people are saying that it is wrong to stand up with a donation box, and meanwhile the organizers cannot even pay for the rental of the chairs, then from where is all this meant to happen?

My own view is that if the center has to do the work, then for five years the very idea of criticism should be forgotten. Just do the work. Then, after five years we will make a comprehensive assessment of what mistakes have been made and we will correct them. But first the work!

And my own understanding is that the work itself goes on correcting the mistakes. As the work progresses, more skillful people will come, more intelligent people will come. They will go on correcting the work. The work is the priority, and every center is to do it. The Mumbai center is not contracted to do all the work! They are doing what they are doing. In fact, I want other centers to start doing something so then their burden is shared a little.

So take care of this. Create centers everywhere. Take the work into your hands in every place and share the work. Only then can the work be done.

Osho,
Tell us something about the center.

The Mumbai center has created some rules. They have a charter, a constitution that can be made available to you. But you can make your own rules for the center that you start in your own village. My view is that, at present, every center should make its own rules and start the work in its own way. Later, when all the centers are functioning, we can amalgamate them – but later, afterward. One center imposing itself from the start on all the others – ordering them around and getting things done – is wrong. Each unit should start working on its own according to its own convenience.

Now if someone starts a center in Mumbai and charges a membership fee of two hundred and fifty rupees, that amount is nothing there. But if you charge a two hundred and fifty rupees fee in a small village, not a single person will become a member. They will charge a fee of a quarter of a rupee. If someone starts a center in Gadarwara with the same constitution as the center in Mumbai, it will be a very difficult proposition.

I was recently in Gadarwara. They have started a center there. They asked me if they should organize it in the same way as the center in Mumbai. I said to them, "Don't even bother to do that. They have patrons who pay one thousand rupees. Your whole life will be gone in just trying to find one patron. You won't find one here. If you look for patrons who will pay fifteen rupees, you can find some."

So take care of your things according to your local requirements.

My own view is that first there should be small units all over the country. They will start their work – under their own arrangements, according to their own convenience, facilities and location. Then later on, we can bring them together, unite them – at any time. There will be no difficulty in that.

So we are not going to open branches of the Life Awakening Center in many places. They are all Life Awakening Centers; they are not branches, they are all independent units. And there is no one superior to order them around. I don't even believe that such a thing should happen – that someone commands from above to do this, to do that – because then hierarchies begin, then all those entanglements begin.

Each and every unit is independent. It can create its own systems and rules and begin its work.

The unit in Mumbai has been functioning for a long period of time. If someone wants some advice, he may take it; if someone wants some guidance, he may take it, but each unit should begin its work in its own way. Later on, when two hundred units have started functioning in the country, then together we will amalgamate them all. How long does that take? No time at all. There will be no problem doing that.

Right now don't look to anyone, start your work yourself. Take a look at the constitution that Mumbai has. If it looks useful, study it well.

7
A World Center

This place should not be lost at any cost. Even if we were to spend five million rupees, we could never build a place like this. It has a ten-acre compound. The walls of the compound are about nine feet high; if we had to build them, that alone would cost at least half a million rupees. It has a nine-feet-high stone wall. And if we can buy this property for about one and a half million rupees, it is as good as free.

None of this is as significant as the fact that even though this place is in Mumbai, the moment you enter it, it feels as if you are in Matheran, not Mumbai. There are such big trees, and the place is so silent, so peaceful.

So as soon as I saw it, I felt this could become a world center. And if we have to build one, a world center can only be built in Mumbai.

Now all over the country there are so many people who have become interested, who would like to come and stay with me for one month, two months, or three months. It has become very important to make this possible for them. So this place could become the center for all our activities. And if the right effort is made, over the next ten years seekers from all around the world will be able to come. It could become a center for meditation and a center for spreading the idea of social revolution.

So from that day it became clear to me that this place should be obtained at any cost. Today one and a half million rupees may seem too much, but looking at the place, one and a half million rupees is nothing.

My idea is that we make a hostel for about two hundred students there. Two hostels are already there – and they are ready. They are completely ready. They must have been built for bachelors, bachelor officers. They are so good that even if a student pays two or three hundred rupees a month, it will be cheap.

So, one thing is that we will make hostels there. I would like the children of our friends to be the two hundred students staying there so that right from their childhood, the individuality I am trying to create can be given a direction in them. All over this country, in the various houses where I stay, my friends keep saying, "Take our children, take our daughters, so that they can come and live close to you." But I am moving around, so what can I possibly do for them? What means do I have to take care of them?

So I would like to make arrangements there for those two hundred children. They could study anywhere in the city, but they would stay with me, so that some experiments could be done to transform their personalities from their very childhood. And if our experiment becomes successful, then I have a promise from friends in different places, that again we could have such hostels in other big cities, in ten to fifteen different cities in the country. They could be organized on a bigger scale. Right now we can accommodate two hundred people. Tomorrow, if needs be and if we feel it would be good, we could make arrangements for two thousand. So much land is available there that any number of hostels could be made.

So the first thing is that experiments can be done with children and their whole lifestyle.

I get hundreds of letters from seekers who come to the meditation camps saying, "In three days our thirst gets awakened but then it is time to leave." Now among them there are many people who, no matter what the cost may be, would like to come and stay with me for a month or two. I know that a revolution would take place in their lives if they could come and stay for two months. So arrangements could be made there for such seekers.

All the publishing work could be done there too. I have a vision for each and every thing. I have a vision for the smallest of matters of life. For instance, I cannot call the way the books are printed "printing"! If we had our own printing press, if we organized it ourselves, then the printing would also be an art. If you look at a Japanese book about meditation, just looking at the book you will enter into meditation. You will read the book afterward, but as you start looking at it and turning the pages you will feel that you have started to become silent.

The books should be this artistic, created in this manner. The moment a book is in someone's hands, it should touch him.

I have several ideas in this area which I would like to experiment with there. For example, as I see it, music can be immensely valuable and helpful for entering the inner life. But right now, throughout the world, music is being used to stimulate desire. Just as music can stimulate desire, music could also help desires to become silent. I have a vision that some musicians would keep coming and staying there, and we could experiment in the direction of a music that makes the being peaceful. Painters could also come and stay. They could make paintings which would take a person inward. Poets could come and stay and I could talk to them about poetry becoming a way of taking their lives toward religiousness.

So all aspects of life can be touched, and for that we need to have a center. And there are people all over the country who would like to come and live with me. They could contribute a lot. There are so many artists, poets and musicians who are interested in me, who would like to come and live with me. For this we will have to find a solution and make arrangements.

Today we may feel that to find these one and a half million rupees is a problem. But once the center is started, many people from this country – and slowly people from all over the world – will start coming.

A few days ago Harikrishnadas-ji was in Amritsar. Thirty Germans were there, touring India. They came to meet me. They became immensely interested. They talked for about two hours and the questions they asked were so authentic and genuine.

The person who had brought them is a sannyasin, who has lived in Germany for a few years. He has some sixty thousand disciples in Germany. The German government has given them a huge area of land in the Black Forest region to make an ashram. The ashram has already been built. So I asked the thirty people he had brought with him, "What has he taught you all? What are you all doing?"

They have been taught "Hare Rama, Jai-jai Rama"! Those Germans are prepared to perform this theater anywhere: to stand up and sing, "Hare Rama Jai-jai Rama." It was taught to them and they say it gives them peace.

I spoke to them and told them that this was nothing. Anybody can do this! But they have learned it all with such enthusiasm – as if they have learned something great. And now they had come to tour India.

Their guru became worried because they were eager to come to Jabalpur to meet me. And they came to Jabalpur. I told them to come on the sixth, but they came on the fifth with their guru.

And by the evening of the fifth they had left with him. They left a message saying, "We wanted to stay for longer, but Swami-ji – our guru – does not want us to meet you, so he is taking us away. We are helpless; he does not want us to stay here."

Friends of mine want me to stay in Pune. Pune is good from the health point of view, and it is good even from other points of view, but I think that from the work point of view only Mumbai will be good. People from all over the country come here and they can meet me. People from outside the country also come here and meet me. We will be able to build an organized center from where we can spread the news faster.

So if they can take this step with courage... Today it may seem like a courageous step; tomorrow we may easily feel that we missed if we didn't buy it. The interesting thing is that if we decide to build instead of buying, it will seem like an almost impossible task. The reality is that it is difficult to build a place. If it takes twenty years to build that much, and meanwhile all that time will be wasted. And this place is so ready. Looking at it, it seems to me that it has been made for us. The compound is big enough for ten thousand people to sit together. There is so much room that three or four different meetings can happen simultaneously and independently there and not disturb one other. The trees are so huge that two to four hundred people can easily be addressed under their shade.

So to me it feels that this place should be bought. One woman was ready. I went to see the place with her, and she was ready to purchase it. But she wanted the building to have her name on it. Then the same story would have started all over again, and this is not the right way to go.

It will be good to buy it in the name of an institution. Any individual can buy it, and if someone buys it as a business investment, then they will certainly do well. If they buy it for one and a half million rupees, they can easily make five million rupees out of it; there is no question about that. That is why I think that if friends come, they should think about this, and if they gather the courage, it will not be difficult for them. Otherwise you may have to think about it again later on; you may have to address the matter again later on, and wait for another place like this to come our way.

Osho,
This work is so vast that if some people could permanently...

Yes, this is possible, but if many people come to stay permanently, their interest should be in meditation, their interest should be in some work; otherwise they will just be staying there, and then, later on, there could be a problem. It is not a problem as far as you are concerned, but if a group of people comes just to stay there, and their only goal is to stay – their whole intention is simply to stay there – then it will create a difficult situation on our campus. Then it will become a disturbing factor for us that they are living there with the sole purpose of just having somewhere to stay.

Then many people will come?

Yes the place is so beautiful that soon it will become crowded. But we will make arrangements for those people who would like to stay for meditation.

Is it something like this, that people could come and stay for one month, and people like us would come and stay for six months?

Yes of course they could stay there. But we should remember that if we make it a place where people can have permanent ownership, we will be making trouble for ourselves, because then, whom do we stop? Then anyone who can afford to build will come and live there. And that will cause us trouble. It is not a question of six months. If someone wants they can stay for six years; there will be no problem about that. But we should not have permanent residents there. That should not happen, because later on that will become a problem for us. If people who have no interest in what the place is set up for come and start living there, it will become painful for us.

I would like to create a very disciplined life there. Even a little nonsense will not be tolerated like it sometimes happens in the meditation camps right now, with some people doing whatever they want. This will not be allowed in the meditation camps there. It will be very strict. The place will only be for those who have come to meditate.

People should understand that this place is to improve the life of society and give money accordingly.

There is no question about people staying if they want to stay, but if we make special arrangements for them to live there, then it will become difficult. And there are so many houses there that you will be absolutely free from any difficulties. Even if two hundred people are staying there at any one time there will be no problem. There are six bungalows.

Two will become hostels.

Yes two will become hostels. If two become hostels, then we will have four bungalows for us. Even in four bungalows fifty people can be easily accommodated at any one time. It should be very easy. The houses are very big; they have big halls in them. We can think about the living arrangements later. That can be thought about later.

One or two acres on the other side could be put aside and made into residential quarters.

No, I would not like that. That will cause trouble right from the start. I don't want that to happen. If we already start thinking in terms of "residential" and "professional" and things like that, and someone says he is donating a certain sum of money so that some special arrangement can be made for him to live there, then right from the start we will have problems.

No, there would no relationship between those two acres and the rest.

No, but the relationship comes along with the idea! If you don't want a relationship, then why even allow those kinds of residences?

No, but if we take off two acres from the ten acres...

Today you take off two acres of land, and tomorrow you will take off another two acres. No, there is no question of cutting even an inch from the land. Whoever wants to can come and stay in *these* houses. Or the organization can build more houses so that whosoever wants to can come and stay there. No houses should be built there for personal ownership.

So there will be no personal or private ownership there?

No, there is no question of personal ownership. That will disturb everything. Arrangements can be made for people to stay for however long. Right now those ten acres seem big to you, but if I stay there for a year, then even those ten acres will seem small. So many people will start coming. There is no question about that. Soon this place will seem very small. Just six houses will not be enough for all of you.

This shouldn't be a problem. Will you people please not make any arrangements for personal ownership?

It should give courage to you, and to other friends, that it's okay, if we can manage half a million rupees, we can manage half a million more. If we can find half a million rupees from among twenty-five friends, we will find one hundred more friends. Where is the problem?

Yes, there is no real problem here. No problem at all. If we feel that it can be done right from the start, then really not much of a problem is left – not much of a problem.

When everything is decided, take all the friends there and show them the place. Then they will have an idea of how amazing it is. It is indeed amazing and not ordinary. It is amazing, really very amazing.

So there should be no question of too much thinking and bargaining about this. Whatsoever is appropriate, give it, donate it. Anyway, bargaining and thinking are what we do in the marketplace. Do it there! What is the big fuss all about?

If a meditation center is to be made, as soon as we start thinking about private ownership and such things, trouble will immediately begin. First of all, whosoever wants to make a donation has to do it in a free and unconditional way.

This will be one of the last things to think about, after the place is bought.

Osho,
So the building, the land will all belong to the society; all of it will belong to the society?

No, no, no. This is not a matter to be thought about now. Once you buy the land, only then will you have to think about all of this. After all, who else has to think about it? It is all of you who will be thinking about what you want to do and what you don't want to do. Nobody else is going to come and think about these things! But right now as soon as you include such ideas, self-interest immediately attaches itself. Giving does not remain clean and unmotivated, without any self-interest. So this means you do not understand what I am trying to say.

No. Isn't what you are saying in itself, selfishness? That in itself becomes the problem.

Self-interest has already begun. Thinking selfishly has begun. That is why you should not think about it now. Tomorrow it will be your organization, it will be your land, it will be your committee; you will be the ones who have to think about what should be done, and will do something accordingly. But right now, to think about this while giving your donation means trying to make an arrangement in advance: "We shall be giving this much money, so please make a certain arrangement for us." That is wrong.

So this is, in a way, an unconditional donation from us?

Yes, at this point it is without any conditions attached – unconditional. Later on it will be up to your committee, and you can think and do what feels right. Do not think about it now. Right now, it is unconditional. Do not think about it now. Make a committee later and think about it then. What is the problem with that?

8
The Art of Living in a Juicy and Blissful Way

Interview One

Osho,
I would like to present something about your life and your philosophy of life in a magazine.

So will you be talking about my life or about my philosophy of life?

Both together!

What is the value of a life? A life has no value, only the philosophy of life has a value.

Only yesterday you said that we should not run away from life.

Yes. So what do you want to write? Tell me, what do you want to tell people about?

I would like to ask you some questions.

All right, ask! Ask me the questions.

Where were you born and when were you born?

In 1931, in Gadarwada, Madhya Pradesh.

Near Jabalpur?

Yes, near Jabalpur.

Are your mother and father still alive?

Yes, they are there, right now, in the village.

Are they Jainas?

They are Jainas.

Are they traditional Jainas?

They are Jainas, but I am not a Jaina. Remember this, or again there will be a misunderstanding, because birth has nothing to do with religion.

All right, between the two of them – your mother and father – whose influence do you feel is greater on you?

No. Nobody has any influence on me.

Nobody influences you?

Nobody. And I do not believe that anyone should have any influence over anyone else. In my understanding everyone should just be himself. One should not be impressed by anyone; one should neither be influenced by anyone nor have influence over anyone. One should not influence anybody.

In your school life do you remember any eventful episodes?

There are many things worth remembering. Right from childhood there were events upon events.

Would you share one or two?

Regarding what would you like to know about these episodes? Because...

Was there someone from whom you may have received some loving impetus in all this growth of yours, or some event which is still vividly in your memory even now? For instance, you told us yesterday about a man who renounced money, but that fact remained in his memory for thirty years.

Yes, I will have to tell you something like that! But I have never renounced anything; so it will be very difficult...

So, the first thing is I have never had any faith in the tradition of the family, or in the education of society, or in any guru's teachings – in none of these things. Right from the very beginning I had no faith, no belief, and I doubted. When I was taken to a temple I said, "I cannot see any God, I can only see a stone idol. If you can see God, then bow down, but I won't bow down until I can see God." And since then I have not been to a temple.

When did this happen? How old were you?

It has been a long time since this happened. I must have been something like eight or nine years old.

Only if there was some rationality in something would I find it meaningful.

In our school, it was compulsory to wear a cap. I did not wear a cap to school. When I went to high school I arrived without wearing a cap. The person who was the headmaster was very strict as far as caps were concerned. It was not possible for anyone to enter the school not wearing a cap. He summoned me, and I told him, "I will wear a cap – not just one but ten at the same time – but first you should explain the reason, the benefit, of wearing a cap to me. And if you cannot explain the reason, then you should not tell me to wear a cap. So think it over and explain the reason to me. And the day you are ready to explain the advantages and benefits of wearing a cap to the body, to the mind, to the soul – to any of these – then I will be ready to wear it; otherwise I am not prepared to wear it. I will not wear it just because it is your rule."

So I did not wear it. And for that he made me stand outside the classroom for two months: "Stand outside!" So I was standing outside. We had to study in school for three full years, so I was prepared to stand outside the window and study, but I would not bend about such a thing for which they did not have any logic.

After two months he felt sorry. He said, "I beg your forgiveness. Sit inside and study. If you want to wear a cap, wear it. If you don't want to wear one, don't wear it."

So it is the same regarding anything. Until my mind is entirely convinced, I am not prepared to accept it. It may concern anything.

In your school life did you have a special interest in any teacher or was there someone whom you respected?

No I cannot say that, I cannot see that.

All right. Any incident in college life?

Many things happened. The question is which ones are of interest to you. At college I was expelled when I was at the intermediate level. At the intermediate level I was sent away from the college.

You were expelled from the college?

I was expelled from the college because my being there was too much for my professor of logic. After all, the subject was logic, and so I would fall into an argument with him about philosophy. After eight months he said in writing: "Either I can stay in this college, or this student stays. We cannot both stay here at the same time."

He was not ready to keep you in his class?

No. The principal told me, "We cannot let him go. He has been our professor for twenty years. And he is a prestigious name, a person famous throughout India. We cannot let him go."

So I said, "I am ready to go, but I would like to know what I have done wrong. If he can say that I was wrong in the things I have argued about, I am prepared to leave. But if you remove me forcibly, then you will repent. One day you will feel sorry."

But the professor stayed at home; he did not come in for three days. So I was expelled from the college.

I was given admission to another college on one condition: I was made to agree in writing that I would not ask any professor any questions in any class.

No questions?

So the principal of the college which was giving me admission made me agree in writing, because in that whole town it was known that I had been expelled from the other college, and the reason was that I was a logical person. Then I told him, "I shall also make you agree in writing that in your college I will not have to attend classes, because if I am not allowed to ask questions then my presence is also not necessary. But please keep giving me attendance marks."

He said, "This will be done."

Then I did not go to the college for two years, because if I was not allowed to ask any questions, there was no need to listen either. And if I was going to listen, then asking questions would have been inevitable! So for those two years he gave me full attendance. I did not go into the college, but he gave me full attendance marks.

And there were many incidents; there was a long series of episodes – of logic, of arguments, of discussions – because if there was something which I did not feel to be right, then to believe in it was a very difficult matter for me.

To believe, just because a professor has said...

That was why there was no question of believing, agreeing.

Did you like anyone's lifestyle in the college – some teacher who thought that your logical ability was a good thing?

Yes, yes, I did meet a few people, some professors there. When I was doing my M.A., I did find some good people because, by then, I had left Jabalpur, as I could not get admission to do an M.A. in Jabalpur. That was why I did my M.A. at Sagar University. There I had four professors. All four were remarkable, were good people. They took me into that university.

Sagar?

Yes. I had gone to Allahabad University to talk in an All India Debating Competition. There, one of my judges was a professor. He gave me ninety-nine marks out of a hundred. He was a professor at Sagar University. He told me to come to Sagar. So I went there because of him.

At Sagar the professor took me to meet the vice-chancellor of the university. He had written to the vice-chancellor saying that such a student had never come to the university before, and it seemed unlikely that such a student would come again soon, and that was why it was essential that he should meet me. So he took me to see the vice-chancellor as he wanted me to get a scholarship and other help.

In those days I used to wear wooden sandals. As soon as the vice-chancellor saw my wooden sandals he said, "You wear wooden sandals? You are studying for an M.A. and you are wearing a *lungi* – a sarong?"

The professor who had taken me to him said, "He is inclined toward a natural lifestyle." So a discussion on natural lifestyles took place with the vice-chancellor. The vice-chancellor was somewhat against lifestyles and such things! For people with scientific minds, all these kind of things… The argument went on to such lengths that the professor, who had brought me there, became afraid that the idea of a scholarship was becoming a far-distant dream, that the argument might be spoiling everything. He started to tug at my clothes.

I said to the vice-chancellor, "This professor, who brought me here, is surreptitiously tugging at my clothes. He is indicating that if I argue with you, then I will not get the scholarship. But I cannot believe that you are such a bad person."

The vice-chancellor couldn't say anything more. He simply wrote a letter and awarded me the scholarship.

The poor professor was perspiring freely. And as soon as we went out he said, "You put me in such difficulty – beyond my imagining. What will the vice-chancellor think?"

I said, "It was necessary for me to say that. You kept pulling at my clothes, and he kept on arguing. I found myself in such a difficult position. What was I to tell him?"

For two years the vice-chancellor gave me everything I could possibly need. He said, "I was very happy that although you had come to get your personal work done, yet you still had the courage to argue with me – and you were not at all sparing in your arguments! You were not ready to compromise even a tiny bit. It was your personal work, so you should have been flattering me. Forget about humoring me, you were ready to argue with me! And you criticized my words in such a way that I was astonished. Now as long as I am here I will give you everything you need." He provided me with everything, with many amenities.

So this professor who had taken me in was a beautiful person, a very wonderful person. Right now he is a professor in Allahabad University. I had just gone...

What is his name?

Professor Roy, S. S. Roy. He is a Reader in Philosophy at Allahabad University.

And then I met Dr. Saxena. Now he is a professor in Hawaii, in America. He was also very concerned about me – too concerned! He was concerned to such an extent that he was never sure whether I would take the examinations or not. So whenever there were university examinations, he would come and wait outside my hostel at seven o' clock in the morning with his car saying, "At seven-thirty I will drop you off outside the examination hall. Only then will I relax."

So he would come regularly every day. Whenever there were examinations he would drop me outside the examination hall – only then would he feel relaxed. I used to say to him, "Why are you so afraid?"

He would say, "You are not reliable. You are studying, that itself is unbelievable. That you will also do an examination seems difficult to comprehend!"

So for two years he took such care of me, it was unbelievable.

Right, so now you have become eager to create an ashram, the purpose of which is to make humanity human. Your college teaching work was also similar, so why did you leave it?

I did not leave it because the work was wrong. I left it because the work was too small. I can do a vast amount of work, so I had to leave. This means I did not leave it because it was not right. With that same amount of energy a vast amount of work can be done, so to use all that energy for ten to fifteen students did not seem appropriate. And I am giving time to those students even now. That was the condition on which I left the college. The boys who were my students asked me to agree that whenever I came to Jabalpur, and whenever they needed my time, I would give it to them. Before, I could not give them the amount of time they are taking from me now. So I left them on that condition.

The question was that in philosophy classes there are sometimes two students, sometimes three, so if I were to spend two years with three students, that would have been a criminal waste. Knowing this, I left. I did not leave because it was wrong. Working at the university was not wrong.

A huge amount of criminal waste was happening. And friends throughout the country were after me: "What are you doing?" So under such compulsion I left the job. I did not leave the university because the work was not valuable.

All right. Now, about the ashram that you would like to make: I have a feeling that, as you have also said, there are so many ashrams in India, this one could be just one more. Might this not become the case?

No. There is no ashram like this one will be.

But everyone says. "Our ashram is very different!"

No, no. If you could understand my vision…

I do understand your vision. That is why I am asking this question, I hear you teaching that there should be no ashrams. Anyway, you can transform mankind through your talks. So what is the need of an ashram?

No, no. What, after all, is the meaning of an ashram? What is the purpose of an ashram? The first thing is, the purpose of an ashram, as I see it, is only that there is a place – a center – where people can come and stay close to me for a longer period of time. During the talks you are with me for one hour and still there is no personal contact with me. If you like my talks, if you find them appealing and you wish to have still more contact, more closeness, then there should be a place where you can sit and be close to me.

Now from all over the country I receive hundreds of letters from people saying that they would like to come and stay with me for a month, for two months, for three months, so that they can integrate everything I am talking about into their lives. Right now I do not have a place for them to stay with me for three months.

So, for me, an ashram does not have any other meaning than this. The meaning of *ashram* that is prevalent in this country is not my meaning at all. For me it is more like an education center, where people can come and stay with me and then return home. There, they will be able to live in totality. And I will be able to talk with them and advise them about their daily routines throughout the day, I will be able to correct any mistakes. I see it from this point of view.

If this ashram were going to be the same as any other ashram, then I would not agree to it. There would be no point in simply increasing the number of ashrams. This ashram will be very different! Its daily activities and entire life vision may well be the complete opposite of all the other ashrams.

The person who comes out of this ashram will not be life-negative. All those other ashrams create a life-negative vision. Here, my vision is to teach the art of making life juicier and more blissful. Other ashrams teach that life is meaningless. We could explain this: that it is the ashrams that are life-negative. It is their approach that is life-negative.

Right now in this country, even outside this country, there is no center where a person can learn how life can be lived totally and blissfully. I am not against beauty, not against women, not against love, not against the world, nor against being a householder. Up to now, there is no ashram in this world which is *for* life. All of them are *against* life. Those ashrams are set up for people who are disappointed with life, who are poor and pitiable, close to death. I want to set up the whole thing for young people so they can think about really living life.

So this ashram is going to be very different. And what you are saying is also right. Everyone says that their ashram is going to be different!

Will it be like Shanti Niketan?

Shanti Niketan was a different thing. The vision of Shanti Niketan was different. The vision of Shanti Niketan was not to transform life in its entirety but to transform the mode of education. My idea is to transform the whole of life; education is just a part of it. In Rabindranath's vision, at his place, education was all there was. So this is the major difference. And because everything there was oriented toward education, things went wrong – because today, modern education has fallen into the hands of the government. And when the university at Shanti Niketan became too big, it was turned into a major university run by the government.

My ashram will not just be concerned with education: the whole of life, everything, will be included – every aspect of life. Education is only a small part of life. In my vision, education is not so important that it should encompass everything else. In fact, I feel there is no harm in a person remaining uneducated. If his life becomes rich in all other aspects, then being uneducated will not make such a big difference. So I am not in great favor of all of that; my vision is not restricted to intellectual training. That is why everything will become clearer when I start to build the ashram. Then the whole picture will emerge more clearly about everything that is possible there and how different it will be.

You will only know the difference when you see all the other ashrams standing there in stark contrast to our ashram.

Then you will understand that our ashram is not like theirs. This will be an entirely different undertaking.

Right now, people even think that I am one among the many saints and sannyasins. When the saints and sannyasins turn against me, it will become clear that I am not one of them!

This is fine, but with the ashram I think that...

It is all right. Thinking is fine. I can understand that.

...now you are here, everything is all right, but later on, what if it becomes like all the others?

One should not worry about the future, the reason being that my idea is that then everything should be disbanded. It has to be disbanded; it should not be carried forward. My thinking is that just as man dies, so too must institutions die; otherwise the institutions become a burden.

The people staying close to you will be influenced by you, but you say that nobody should have any influence on anybody else. So what is the point of staying close to you? Why should someone come and stay?

Yes. If someone can understand this, if by staying close to me a person can learn the art and the science of staying free from anybody's influence so that what is hidden inside him can manifest – then that person has made good use of me. And this will not be about my influence. It will have nothing to do with my influence. If the person becomes like me – if he starts to live the way I live, if he starts saying what I say – then know well that a false man has been created. But if he manages to remove all the hindrances that are preventing what is hidden within him from manifesting – and I could also become one of those hindrances, and if that is the case, he should also get rid of me – then the hidden will manifest.

So the emphasis in the ashram will be less on the positive and more on the negative, on how the hurdles of life can be removed, so that whatever is hidden inside a person can manifest.

One way is to copy someone as far as the outer is concerned, to become like him. We may become like Gandhi, or like so-and-so, but that is not my vision. Many friends say to me that the people who are with me should become like me. I tell them that this is out of the question. They should be themselves. There is no question of them becoming like me or imitating me.

That is what the mind thinks, but I feel that people who come to you will be influenced by you. How is it possible not to be influenced?

My efforts will continue so that this influencing does not happen. My efforts will continue so that they do not become like me. And if they do, then it will be their mistake. What can I do about it?

Interview Two

Osho,
People have been comparing you and Krishnamurti.

Yes, they have written something comparing Krishnamurti and me. The first thing is that comparison should not happen; it is wrong. Secondly, the meaning they have finally derived from what I am saying is also worthless and very strange. They have taken words out of context and made mischief with them.

Please look into that. Please look into it, and if you feel it is necessary to reply, write to them.

When Krishnamurti comes here, it will be the right time to publish what they have written and our reply to them. Both articles can be distributed among his three thousand people, so that they can become a little acquainted with me and some connection can develop with me. Concerning this, publish both, the article written by them – that is necessary – and the article written by you. Both of these articles should be published simultaneously and distributed – only with the idea that the people who love Krishnamurti become a little familiar with me too. They have already started discussing me vigorously, and one outcome of this seems to be that these followers of Krishnamurti have become a little bit afraid. And just to counter this fear they have been doing this kind of thing.

So please look into this. And if you feel to, write an answer, publish their article and your reply and distribute them both. The sole purpose of doing this is that although my name is reaching to a larger number of people who are Krishnamurti's friends, they have not been introduced to me. It is essential that this introduction should happen.

Some of his people have already come.

Yes, some of his people have come. The people who have come have started becoming familiar with me. But those who have not been able to come, even if they can just hear the news... That is why two types of tasks have to be accomplished through your reply.

Unnecessary opposition happens.

Yes, this is unnecessary, it is unnecessary.

The thing is that if only one of the articles is published there will be unnecessary opposition. But if both are published, then we are on equal ground.

Their article was given to Bachchu bhai to publish. But Bachchu bhai is close to me, and he said that he did not think it was okay to publish it. Then he must have shown it to Kishan Singh Chawla who said, "This is foolishness, do not print it" and returned it to this friend. I asked this friend to look into it, and to prepare some reply if he could. I also asked him to print both their article and his reply, and distribute them in Krishnamurti's meeting.

The other point to remember is that there should be a list of all our literature at the end of our printed reply…

But Kishan Singh would be a more appropriate person for this.

Who? Who?

Kishan Singh-ji.

No. You see, it is not a question of whose name it is. You look into it. If some ideas come to you to write, you should write. The question is not under whose name it is printed – and it makes no difference either. Do you understand?

Kishan Singh was saying he spent a lot of time with you in Ahmedabad.

Yes, yes, in Ahmedabad. Then recently I was staying at his house for three days in Vadodara.

All right. Yesterday there was something that I did not agree with, did not like.

What was it? Tell me!

Bhula-ji bhai said that the names of those who give a substantial amount of money will be engraved on a marble plate, that there will be boards bearing their names. To me, in a place where uprooting the ego is being taught, why should its very foundations have something that enhances the ego? I feel this is putting our egos into the very foundations. Just as you were saying yesterday – that if we give money, you will not thank us for it – in the same way he should say that however much money a person gives, their name will not be inscribed anywhere, because the money is not being given for the sake of having one's name written on a board. To give people's names is, in a way, to perpetuate the ego. That is why for the name...

But that is my emphasis, no? His emphasis is not that strong. There is a difference between what I emphasize and what the people who work with me emphasize. Their understanding has to be gradually increased. But we will bring it to his attention. We will bring it to his attention.

Because it has to start with authenticity right from the beginning, so that nothing wrong comes in.

That is right.

Are you going to Jabalpur now?

Yes, today I am going to Jabalpur.

So the first thing: look into that paper. Then, if you feel like writing, write. Yes, do write it. And it should be written to serve as an introduction, so that even Krishnamurti's friends can become acquainted with me, and can connect with me.

Interview Three

Osho,
You have mentioned two points regarding your talks. One is to make a compilation for the press. And the other is that there should be a book about your philosophy, your thinking. And if some translation is still remaining then...

Yes, some translation work still remains.

All three things are useful. One is that there should be a compilation representing my whole philosophy, so that just by reading one book my entire vision can be understood. Secondly, Madhu can pull out material for the press. And at the same time, there is great demand for all the books throughout the country, and if some translation could also reach people in English... All these three approaches will be useful.

Recently one friend translated something, but I didn't like it. He had translated *The Perfect Way*, but it was not a good translation. One thing was that he translated it in an Eastern way – just like Eastern scholars would, just as one would translate ancient scriptures like the Puranas. He translated it into archaic English. It did not feel good. And then he also made some fundamental mistakes. In many places the meaning became completely the opposite of what I had said. So that translation had to be stopped, it was not allowed to be sold. But the book had already reached some places.

It had not been shown to you beforehand?

It has become very difficult for me to see everything. I do not get so much time, because day and night I am traveling.

But it is important that at least you have a glance at it before it goes into print.

Yes, I was sent a small part of it, some eight or ten pages. What happened was that those few pages that were sent to me in the beginning seemed to be all right. After seeing them, I returned them. Then what happened was that the person who had translated those eight or so pages did not carry on with the work, and he got someone else to carry on translating it. And then everything went wrong. But now, if you or someone else can look into this area a little, do so. Then it will be good.

I will try.

Yes, yes. Do try.

Right now I am busy with one or two books of my own. They are going to print now. I will have to manage things a little. After that I will surely see to it.

Yes. Do look at the translations. All of them will be sent to you. Just have a glance at them.

I will look at the compilation and also have a look at the translations that have been done.

So have a look at them. Translating can only be enjoyable if you like it.

I think that the translations should not be done in such a way that they look like translations.

They should not be like that, you are absolutely right. Otherwise they will not be enjoyable to read.

The meaning should come correctly, and the language of the translation should be similar to the way you speak in English.

All right, good. That is it. That is right.

If the translation appears to be a translation, then the readers do not enjoy it.

They do not.

So it is good if the person who is translating reads your books, listens to you...

Yes, here there are many recordings. You could listen to some tapes...

One is in the way of a philosophical exposition, which means saying what you are trying to say and giving the logic behind it. If someone could present it in that manner, then it could be very influential in foreign countries too, because there, people prefer analysis.

Just look through it once, and then think about it in these two or three ways – about how it can be done. But it has become very necessary.

There is a lot of demand, and there is only one book available in English, up to now. So our problem is that when we give people this book, they ask for more. So we need to work from the point of view of how this demand can be fulfilled.

So you do something!

Yes, of course. *Whatever you have said we have all liked very much. And the book, which has been produced from your talks, all the beautiful words you say, are liked by all the readers including women and children. Everyone enjoys the book. Once you start reading it, you want to finish it and only then put it down. You feel that once you start it you have to finish it. People like the book a lot. All the students are reading it. No one wants to put it down. Just now I have returned from the college.*

That is good. Please also make some effort, write something in Hindi. For example, what I was speaking about with the women yesterday, you could write an article about it – that will be good in Hindi – and then send it to some good magazine here. And it could also be printed in the form of a booklet. People are already doing this in Gujarati. You could take some trouble and do it in Hindi too.

Interview Four

Yes, speak.

Osho,
To reach the ultimate goal, is it essential to start from meditation?

It is essential to start from meditation.

Then how to meditate?.

For that you come to a three-day meditation camp, where I am teaching meditation for three days.

Where will the meditation camp take place?

Now there is a camp in Aajol, which is near Ahmedabad. Come to Aajol for three days, otherwise there is a camp in Indore after that – come there. If you do the whole process with me for three days, you will get the idea, the understanding. You will really understand.

Interview Five

Talks with the *Times of India* reporter

Osho,
Where were you born?

I was born in Gadarwada, Madhya Pradesh.

In which year?

In 1931.

How many brothers are you?

Six brothers.

Are you the eldest?

I am the eldest.

Sisters?

Four sisters.

What did your father do?

He is a cloth merchant.

Your education?

M.A.

From which University?

Sagar University.

In which subject did you do your M.A.?

Philosophy.

When did you have the inner inspiration for spirituality? At what age?

It was always inside me. I cannot remember when I felt it for the first time. It has always been with me.

So until your M.A. you stayed with your family and then you decided to renounce this world?

No, I have not renounced the world. I am not in favor of renouncing anything.

Take Vinoba Bhave, for example. He has renounced the world. He does not have a paisa on him. Take Gandhi-ji. Are they not sannyasins?

I do not believe in renouncing the world. And my vision is life-affirmative, life-positive.

What do you mean by a life-affirmative, life-positive vision?

The religion that has existed until now has been life-negative: renouncing life, condemning life, saying that life is meaningless and that you must search for the goal beyond this life.

Is there a goal beyond life?

No! Life itself is the goal. There is nothing beyond it. So to live life in its totality, in its entirety is – according to me – religiousness. Life itself is divine. And to know the mysteries of life is the way to attaining this.

What attainment? When there is nothing beyond life, then what do you attain?

We attain life in its totality, in its wholeness.

What happens when we die?

Nobody dies.

There is no death?

There is no death! Death is a fiction, a falsity.

But a man dies, or does he not?

Life only changes form.

Do you believe that in life everything reaches its end?

All things are. There is no beginning, and there is no end. Everything is. But life changes form, it appears in new forms. This change itself creates a false notion about death.

Whether this is a fiction or not, we always reach to an end with life. A tree dies after some time. Animals die, birds die, human beings also die. At the level of the body we all die.

A tree dies, but that is not the inner experience of the tree.

But a tree also has life.

There is life in a tree. Everything has life in it. Only others feel it as death. You have always seen others dying, you have never seen yourself dying. No one has seen death happening within himself. It is always the other who dies. Life changes form. Others feel that something has died. Nothing can die. Everything is.

Are you trying to say, in other words, that only the body dies, what is inside does not die?

It changes form.

But the body dies – the human body! Do you accept this?

Only the form changes.

What would you call this? We call it soul.

You could call it the soul.

Once this body dies, is it possible to contact the soul again?

There is no such possibility because, nothing repeats itself. Everything is always new and fresh.

You have said in this pamphlet that there is a need to pour new life into spirituality, religion. What do you mean by "pouring new life"? Is there something wrong with the religion in India?

Everything is wrong.

But in India there are so many religions! If you say religion**, then I have one religion; some other person has another religion...**

It applies to all religions as we understand them.

So everything is wrong?

The concept of religion that has persisted is completely wrong.

In India?

Everywhere.

No, about foreign countries we cannot say anything.

It is not a question of the religion of this country or of foreign countries. The kind of religion that exists up to now in the world... It is not a question of Buddhism, Hinduism, Christianity or Islam – the way religion has existed until today, like an organization, like a church, in a ritualistic manner – that is wrong. According to me, religion is a very personal thing. There can be no organization of religion.

So there can be no organized religion in the world?

Organized religion is not possible. As soon as it becomes organized it becomes wrong. What I mean when I say "wrong" is that it becomes political. So these names – Islam, Hindu, Christianity, Jaina, Buddhist – these names, these organizations, are not religious. These are all political. There cannot be many religions, just as there cannot be many sciences.

Only one?

Only one! Because truth is one and it is universal.

In other words, in every religion truth is one and the same, but the ways to attain to truth are different. According to my understanding religions are ways.

No! Truth cannot be attained in different ways. There is only one way, and that is through meditation – which is to attain to no-mind and awareness.

It is not that religion does not teach meditation. In religion meditation comes, fasting comes, self-denial also comes. Religion and spirituality are one and the same thing. Without suppressing oneself, without purifying one's bad deeds, how is this possible?

You cannot wipe out bad deeds.

But a man commits bad deeds.

A man does commit bad deeds.

And he cannot be blamed for that because God has created him. Has God created us or is there no God?

The creator is not separate from the created.

This I know. If there is no difference between the two, then we are one with the creator, the one who has created us.

No, No. There is no creator.

No one created us?

No one has created us. There is no creator beyond and apart from creation.

I am coming to that point. This is the real thing. I am asking: is there anyone who has created us? Is there a God?

No! No!

There is no God?

No. There is no God as a creator.

No one else can be the creator!

This whole energy of creativity – as I see it the meaning of God is this entire creativity.

I am not talking of creativity; I am talking of the creation.

Neither is there any creation nor is there any creator. There is only creativity, the energy of creativity.

Many, many thanks.

9
A Collective Vision of Religion

My beloved ones,

This country has had a long history of misfortunes. Society's lifestyle, society's consciousness has become so ugly, so distorted and insane that it is difficult to make any sense of it. And it seems our sensitivity has also diminished, so we cannot even see the ugliness. We cannot even feel how distorted life has become. We cannot even see that humanity is losing its humanness more and more every day.

This happens. When you get used to something over a long period of time, the mind loses its capacity to experience it, it loses its sensitivity. And sometimes an even more peculiar thing happens. Not only can we not really see the things we are used to, even if we do get a glimpse of something good, we find it difficult to see it.

Once a fishmonger was passing through a perfume market. He was used to the smell of fish; he had no experience of perfume. As soon as he started smelling the perfume, he covered his nose with a cloth and thought, "This is really troublesome; how did such a terrible smell come to be here?" In that perfume market the most expensive scents were being sold. But as he was walking through the market he started feeling more and more disturbed, and finally he fell down unconscious.

All the shopkeepers came running. They thought that perhaps he was tired and suffering from the heat. They started bringing good perfumes for him to inhale, thinking perhaps he may regain consciousness. Those poor shopkeepers didn't realize that he was suffering from the smell of the perfumes, and that was why he had fallen unconscious. The more perfumes they gave him to smell, the worse his condition became.

At that moment another fisherman passed by. He said, "Please stop! Can't you see this man's bag? Can't you see his basket? He is a fisherman and I know what is happening. Please remove all your perfumes!"

Then he sprinkled some water onto the unconscious man's basket, the basket from which he sold his fishes, and brought the basket close to his nostrils. Soon the man opened his eyes and said, "This is a real perfume! This is the real smell! These crazy people were making me smell all sorts of things."

The sensitivity of a society dies in the same way. This is what has happened in this country. In this country, thousands of years of thinking have completely disconnected human beings from collective consciousness, from social consciousness.

All the teachings in India make people extremely selfish; they do not make them feel part of the collective consciousness. In this world a man earns money for himself, builds a house for himself, searches for his liberation in the other world, searches for his heaven. He doesn't have any connection with anyone else. Even if the teachers in India have made us understand that we should be kind to others, and not cause unhappiness to others, it is not because that is a good thing to do in itself. The reason they give is that if you make others unhappy, you will go to hell, and if you don't make others unhappy, then you will go to heaven. So the basic motive, the fundamental inspiration, is how to get to heaven, how to achieve liberation. Hurting others is not in itself a bad thing, the bad thing is that maybe you won't achieve liberation if you hurt others.

India has talked so much about nonviolence, but it has not developed the basics of love. Obviously there must be a fundamental error in this teaching of nonviolence. The teaching of nonviolence says do not commit violence because then you will lose heaven, by being violent you are committing a sin and this sin leads one to bondage.

The teaching of nonviolence does not include the idea that others might feel hurt or unhappy, or that you should love others so they don't feel unhappy. Concern for the other does not exist in the teaching of nonviolence; it is only about "me, my ego, my selfishness." That is why although India was the first country in the whole world to propound the philosophy of nonviolence, there is no trace of love in this country. This is very surprising. We talk so much about nonviolence, but there is no place on this earth where there are so many people devoid of love. There must be a reason for this.

Our teaching of nonviolence has its basis in self-interest. There is no thought for the other in it. If we knew that even if we hurt others, it wouldn't prevent us from going to heaven, then we would not experience any difficulty in hurting them. And if we discovered that hurting others helps us to get to heaven, then we would really look forward to hurting others.

"My own welfare" is the basis of all our worldly teaching, and also the basis of our religious teachings. And in my vision, a person moves ahead on the path of meditation only when he drops the sense of "I" and accepts the concept of "thou," the concept of "everyone." The way to godliness is to move from "I" to "thou" – to expand our vision of life. We worry so much about having a better life and happiness, whereas in fact it naturally happens that when someone thinks about a better life, happiness, and the welfare of all, his own unhappiness immediately disappears.

One of the bases of sorrow is selfishness. One of the bases of sadness is how much someone is thinking only about himself.

An emperor had fallen ill. No treatment seemed possible, he was on his deathbed. All the doctors had failed to cure him. Then someone said that a sannyasin lived far away, and maybe he would have a solution.

That sannyasin was called. He said, "No, I cannot give you the solution. The cure is very simple, but I am unable to tell you what it is. Please forgive me."

The emperor said, "If the cure is simple, why can't you tell me?"

The sannyasin said, "I cannot tell you, but...it is also simple. But you will not be able to follow it, many problems will arise. But you can be saved, death is not certain."

The emperor caught his feet. He said, "Please tell me the cure."

"No!"

The court, the queens, the entire capital stood there, wringing their hands, saying, "Please don't leave, please tell us the cure."

The sannyasin said, "Since you won't leave me alone, I will tell you. Ten thousand children will have to be beheaded, and the emperor will have to bathe in their blood, only then can he be saved. I am going. I cannot say any more. The emperor can be saved. Collect ten thousand children by the following date. On that day, at this time cut their throats, bathe the emperor in their fresh blood, and he will be saved."

The date he gave was six months away. The emperor said, "No, I do not wish to be saved. Ten thousand children will have to be killed! And an unknown sannyasin – how reliable is he? Whether I am saved or not, those ten thousand children will be killed! And even if I am saved, how long will I live? I will have to die some day. I am already an old man, but ten thousand children! Their lives are yet to be lived, how can I end their lives?"

His family tried to convince him, the courtiers tried to convince him, the intelligentsia of the capital tried to convince him: "Your life is more valuable than the lives of those ten thousand children. As long as you are here, then not just ten thousand, but ten million children are safe in this country. If you are not here, nobody's life will be safe."

He was such a loving king, so intelligent; he was filled with so much mercy, so much compassion that the entire country prayed that he would be saved, regardless of the ten thousand children.

Reluctantly the king had to agree. The children started being collected. The palace started filling up with beautiful small children. The king could not sleep. Day and night he thought about what he was doing. What will happen? Day and night he could see nothing but children. Ten thousand children were coming from many villages. And in every village people started praying for the king to be cured beforehand, so the children could be saved. Some people started cursing the king, wishing for him to die before the given date so that the children would be saved. The whole country was concerned about only one thing, and the king also had the same worry in his heart.

The six months came to an end. The final day came. Ten thousand children were collected. At daybreak, as soon as the sun rose, their throats were to be cut. Outside the palace the children were lined up in a row. Naked swords started flashing in the sunlight. The king came down. He saw the children standing in a row. The time had come, the swords were about to be raised and the children were about to be killed. Immediately the king shouted, "No! No child will be killed! I am prepared to die."

The children were saved. And the king got better. It was amazing how well he became. His illness was finished.

The sannyasin was called and asked how this could happen even though the children had not been killed. He said, "There is only one reason. For six months the king was not able to think about his illness at all. So many children were going to be killed – just that one thought kept coming to him. The attention went away from 'me,' away from the self, away from the 'I.' His thinking had been stuck around 'I.' That was his pain, his suffering. That was the illness."

If someone can't sleep, they can't get better. Doctors say that if they can sleep, then everything will be all right. What is the connection between sleep and healing? There is no connection, except that in sleep you forget you are ill. In sleep there is a discontinuity with the idea that "I am sick." There is no other connection. A person moves out of "I" in his sleep. That is why sleep is essential; otherwise you would go mad. "I," ego, is the center of craziness; it is the secret of madness. If you want to become mad, then "I" and "I" and "I"...

It is essential to move out of "I," otherwise you will go mad. That is why sleep is important. And in a country where people sleep less, then alcohol becomes essential because it allows people to forget themselves. There is no other way.

But alcohol and sleep and unconsciousness are not lasting ways to forget, because you will become conscious again. How long can the effect of alcohol last? Again consciousness will return and again everything will start. Sleep will end and again everything will start.

But there is a spiritual approach called love. Someone in a state of love is always far away from the "I," the ego.

Why am I saying all this?

I am saying it because if a seeker of truth is only a seeker, then he will not be able to get out of the ego, he will never be able to drop the ego, because the center of his meditation will be "I": How can "I" become silent? How can "I" be liberated? How can "I" attain liberation?

People ask me, "How can I become silent?" I tell them the entire world is so restless and disturbed, and in the middle of all of this how can they think about how "I" can become silent? Don't they even feel ashamed to ask this? Imagine, if the whole of Mumbai was sick, if everyone was on their sickbed: what would you call me if I were to ask how I can become healthy? Would you call me a stone or a human being? If everyone is hungry and I ask for food for myself, what would you call me?

Understand that in the middle of such a sick society, such a restless life, if someone starts asking how to be silent, how to attain truth, how to be liberated, know well that they will never achieve it. And even if it were possible for them to achieve it, it would not be the liberation that people like Mahavira, Buddha, Krishna and Christ would accept for themselves. They would never embrace it. If sick, disturbed people can claim this kind of liberation, know it is not the kind of liberation good, healthy people would want."

Someone asked Edmund Burke, "You do not believe in God, you do not pray in the temple, you do not worship, and no one has ever heard you talk about theology, so will you be able to go to heaven?"

Edmund Burke replied, "If good people get a place in heaven, then I will get one, and if bad people get a place in heaven, then I wouldn't want to go there." He explained, "As far as I understand it, wherever at least ten good people gather together, then even if they are in hell, it won't remain hell for very long, it will become heaven. And wherever ten bad people gather, then even if they are in a place called heaven, it will be heaven only on the sign – within ten days it will become hell.

"I am not saying that I want to go to heaven. I would like to go to a place where there are good people, where there are loving people; that place will be heaven."

There is no one who can love in this country. That is why it has become a hell.

I am saying things that will disrupt and change everything that has been going on in the name of spiritual discipline, in the name of moksha, in the name of salvation and religion. The concepts and ideas I am talking about carry the seeds that will be able to bring about a major revolution, which will replace every concept this country has been revolving around up to now. Because what we are seeing today is a result of it revolving around those centers, those axes. This result is not accidental. Everything is interconnected, linked.

India was enslaved for one thousand years, and this was no accident. India does not have a collective consciousness, so what else could it be other than enslaved? That it has now become independent is a miracle, is a wonder! In fact it is puzzling. It can only be because of somebody's compassion, some international circumstances. We do not have the capacity ourselves; we do not have any sense of being a collective whole.

We do not have such a thing as a collective soul. We have "I" and "I," "you" and "you," "they" and "they": I go my way, you go your way, and he goes his way. And we don't even know that our ways are crossing. If I go my way, I am blocking you, if you go your way, you are blocking me.

If all of us here start going out of this door at the same time, if we all want to go out, then that very desire will result in us all blocking each other. But if we go out one by one, if we wait and give way to each other, then we can all get out.

When I am giving way to someone, then I am also creating a way for myself. But when I am just looking out for myself, then I am getting in my own way and also getting in someone else's way.

Life is a collective process. So India needs to create a collective vision of religiousness. Meditation, spiritual endeavor, has to be linked with society. The individual shouldn't be made to stand against the collective consciousness. He should stand in harmony together with the collective consciousness.

Who will do this? How can this happen? How to break these wrong, misguided five-thousand-year-old notions? It is not within my capacity. It is beyond the capacity of any one individual. And it cannot be done in a single day either. But even if ten of the weakest of the weak join together and start working in one direction, then what is a small seed today, can become a huge tree tomorrow.

And we should remember that if seasonal flowers are planted, then although within two months the flowerbed will be full of flowers, after another two months it will be empty – with no flowers, not even any plants. People who want to grow large trees which can provide shade for thousands of people to rest under should drop the idea that: "I will plant so many trees so that within my lifetime thousands of people will be able to take shelter under them." This crazy idea has to go. This is the ego. Nevertheless they should start the work, even if it is just a small beginning.

And remember that even the smallest thing has a value. It has so much value that it is difficult to measure because, in the end, at the ultimate conclusion of life, there is no difference between a small thing and a big thing. Even small things play their part. A tiny incident can be more valuable than we can imagine.

When Napoleon was six months old, a wild cat jumped onto his chest when he was lying in bed. Could you ever imagine that one wild cat can influence the history of the world? Or that something like a cat climbing on the chest of a small child can have some historical value? It has no value. The servant came and shooed the cat away.

But the six-month-old Napoleon was scarred for life with the fear of cats. He was not scared of fighting men with naked swords, he was not scared of lions, but in front of a cat he would tremble in fear of his life.

Napoleon lost a war when his enemy tethered seventy cats in front of his army. As soon as Napoleon saw the cats, he shivered. And he told his comrade, "Today victory seems difficult; as soon as I see cats, I lose control." He was defeated for the first time! Historians say that Wellington defeated Napoleon. Psychologists say that the cats defeated him. And I agree with the psychologists – historians don't know anything.

Can such a small, useless incident – meaningless – have such a huge impact? To talk about what has happened as a result of Napoleon's defeat would take a lot of time. If Napoleon had not been defeated, what would have happened? The world would be entirely different. If Hitler had not been defeated, the world would be different. If Napoleon had not been defeated, the world would be different. And Napoleon would not have been defeated if that cat hadn't climbed onto his chest. A servant sitting outside could easily have shooed the cat away, and the history of the world would have been different. Nobody would ever imagine that one servant shooing away a cat could be so important.

In this great interdependence of life, this inner connectedness of things, this interrelation of all living things, even a small thing has the same value as something big. In this respect there is no difference between the value of the sun or a lamp. Sometimes a lamp can be more valuable than the sun, sometimes the sun can prove to be smaller than the lamp. The arithmetic of life is very strange. A small piece of work can have huge consequences. And if some work goes in the right direction…

We can assure ourselves of only this much: that we are to take the work in the right direction. If a few friends gather courage and work together, then don't be surprised if within ten or fifteen years a revolution in the moral consciousness of this whole country is created. Consciousness is ripe for this – just like a house can be ready to burn, just waiting for a spark to set it alight. Anyone creating a spark will set off the fire. And if this fire starts, then this country can find a fresh, bright new way of life.

I am going from village to village, meeting hundreds of thousands of people. From their eyes, from their very being, from what they say, it seems to me that they are ready – as soon as someone calls, as soon as someone throws a spark, as soon as someone tells them…

Things die of their own accord; sometimes it is simply a matter of giving a push. What is left anyway? Nothing of the old tradition is alive, just corpses remain. If someone gives them a push, they will fall over. Those corpses are in no condition even to say, "No, we are not going to fall," or "Please don't topple us." Those who are propping them up are also hoping that someone will topple them over so they can be freed from the burden of holding them up. But they cannot muster the courage to stop propping up the corpses. They are always waiting for someone else to do it – this person or that person, but someone else. And meanwhile life goes on deteriorating every day.

Think a little in this direction. There are no fixed formulas for how to do this work. There is no sect, no organization, no creed; just some threads, some fundamental points like getting people in this country to think for themselves, rather than believing. And I am not saying they should think in a certain way. Saying *how* they should think is the first step in creating sects – be it Jaina thinking, Hindu thinking or Mohammedan thinking. No, I am saying *think* instead of believing.

The question of a sect does not arise. There is no question of a sect because the question of sect arises only when there is a particular kind of thinking. No, this question is entirely different. It is not a question of belief. Independent thinking has to be promoted. Not blind faith but seeing eyes have to be created. People should not be looking at the past but have an orientation toward the present and the future. The individual should not be centered around his ego, but surrendered to the whole. The meditator has not only to take care of his meditation, but also to look after the consciousness of the whole – because after all, I am not alone, you are not alone, we are all joined in some greater oneness. Your unrest will eventually become my unrest, and my disturbance will eventually become your disturbance.

This whole vision is not a dogma or a creed; it is just an intense force of thinking, a wind blowing through the whole country. Then thoughtful young people will find their way, make their way. We should not tell them where to go. All we can say is: "The way you have been going in the past has not helped you reach anywhere. Stop for one second and see where the journey of the last five thousand years has landed you." If we can do only this much – that people stop and look – then they will be able to see for themselves. The only trouble is that no one is stopping, nor is anyone stopping them. So we need a movement, an upheaval in the country.

Movements happen in the world, revolutions happen, but fundamental, basic movements and revolutions do not happen. If someone rescues a person from one sect, then he tries to get him hooked into another sect. Actually he only rescues him so that he can be caught in another. As I see it, we have to create a human being who is incapable of getting caught up in any sect. This kind of freedom, this kind of liberation has to be created. If we do not create this capacity in people, then irresponsible, chaotic behavior is bound to emerge.

Freedom is a discipline, a development of consciousness. And chaotic, irresponsible behavior is just a frenzied reaction to bondage.

If we don't want to create this kind of behavior, then we need to develop our life energy, our consciousness, in the direction of freedom. If we sit quietly, freedom will not just come by itself. Bondage will go, but it will be replaced by licentiousness and chaos. All the threads of life will disintegrate, and everything will fall apart. Before this happens it is essential to let consciousness grow within.

All I can do is to go from village to village and tell people, "The house is on fire! You need to wake up!" But how far can I shout to inform people? This message needs to be shouted from the rooftop of every house in every village, to the entire country, to the whole world. So for this, it is necessary to invite friends. Whoever finds it appealing, in whichever way they find it appealing… There is no fixed way to do this. Whatever way people like – in whatever direction they see they can do something, can ignite some spark – they should do it.

If they want to work with the Life Awakening Center, then they should work with it, and if they want to work separately, then they should work separately. If they feel that some work can happen with the friends who have already gathered, then they should work with them. If it doesn't feel possible to work with these people, and if ten friends would like to work separately together, then they should work separately.

The question is not with whom and how. The question is the work. It is not a question of a name, or an organization, or an affiliation. People can work in whatever way is best for them. If they feel like giving some momentum to the work with the friends who have gathered under the name of the Life Awakening Center, then they should give it. If tomorrow they feel that this is not possible, then they should remember that only the work is important, only the revolution is important. Neither the Life Awakening Center nor I myself have any value. If it seems that this work can happen with me, then good. But if it feels that I am too dangerous, that I will become an obstruction in the way of the work, then I should be dropped immediately. Only the revolution is valuable: neither individuals, nor a sect, nor an organization is important.

But a revolution must happen in this country. If you feel a thirst for it, if you feel that it should come, then do something. How you do it is up to you, and in whatever way you do it. If the result is that there are changes in the values of the country, if the old fixed views are shaken up, if this country can be liberated from its slave mentality, then that work is good – the revolution has started, the steps of revolution have begun. So think in this direction. Meet together and see what is possible, what can be done.

I am a very impractical man; I don't know anything about how things work, how houses are built, how shops run, how someone earns – what he does. But I know something else: how a person can look up toward the sky, toward the sun, how he can see beauty. But a man who just looks at the sky is not much use because one has to walk on the earth. And I don't know anything much about the material world. You may know about it. If your hands can strengthen my hand, then the same thing that once happened in a certain village will happen again. I will tell you about it and end my talk.

An emperor invited everyone in the country for a feast. The whole country seemed to be going. People were gathering in groups from every village and setting off. The villages were emptying.

A blind man and a lame man were sitting together, very sad. How could they go? The blind man could not see, and the lame man could not walk.

Then an old man said, "You idiots, you should join together. Otherwise you will just sit here, and you will miss the king's invitation to the feast."

They asked, "How can we join together?"

The blind man could not see, but he could walk. The lame man could not walk, but he could see. So they joined together. The lame man sat on the shoulders of the blind man, who started walking. And they both reached and participated in the feast.

But in another place there was a different problem, and no one knows if a solution could have been found. A deaf person and a mute person were sitting together. The deaf person could speak, but could not hear. The mute person had heard about the invitation from the king and that everyone should go, but he could not say to his friend, "We have to go." The deaf person could speak, he could have said, "We have to go to the palace," but he had not heard about the invitation. Both just sat there, pulling each other. The mute person kept pulling the deaf one: "Come on!" The deaf one kept resisting: "Where are you pulling me? Sit down quietly! Where do you want to go?"

Both missed the meal at the palace.

Now, I don't know what will happen with me! Whether we will join together like the blind man and the lame man, or we will be like the deaf and the mute one. One cannot know. Right now it is like the deaf and the mute men's story. Let us see how it goes! If it becomes like the blind man and the lame man, then the journey is possible, this revolution can reach the palace.

I do not want to say more than this. You will have to think about the rest of it – only this much for now. Think, and meet up with the others here. Strengthen the hands of Durlabh-ji bhai. I can see, but I do not have legs. If you want to make any use of my sight, then you will have to offer your legs, your feet. If you do, then the revolution will reach the palace, there is no doubt about it.

I can see the way to the palace but I do not have any legs at all. So you have to think: can your legs be of any use? If it is possible, then I am ready to ride on any legs – there is no question whether the legs are of a weak or a strong person, of a woman or a man, of a poor person or a rich person; no question whether they are of a Hindu or a Mohammedan. They can be the legs of anyone, but they should be legs, and they should be capable of walking. That is enough.

That is all I want to say. There is nothing more to say right now.

10
The Art of Work as Meditation

I would like to say two or three things.

One thing we need to keep in mind and understand is that if some work is big, significant, and someone is interested in doing it, then that person should already have some inner qualities. Only then can he move the work forward; otherwise not. If we were some ordinary organization providing services – or some other kind of social organization – then it would be a different matter. With the kind of message we want to bring to people, our workers should possess some qualities which reflect that work. Only then can the work reach others properly; otherwise it cannot.

For example, when we are running a meditation camp with twenty people working there, those twenty people should have some depth of meditation; their transformation should be obvious from the way they behave. They should stand out; otherwise it will be very difficult to accomplish the work through them. So a special kind of worker should be there. I also have the idea that in the future there should be a separate meditation camp for workers, because they miss out, they cannot get the full benefit of the camp – they are so busy with their work.

If they are just like other people, then although the work may get done through them, we will not get the results we could have expected from that work. So far we haven't looked at this, but something has to be done so that we are able to prepare an entirely different type of worker. And I am ready to do whatever work is needed for this to happen. Some preparation has to be made for the work you are to do, because if a very new idea has to be brought to people, we will also have to prepare a new kind of person. And we cannot expect this from others; much more should be expected from the people who are interested in doing and spreading this work. The way we behave, our demeanor, should be different.

For instance, there is deep respect in my heart for everyone, however unimportant they may be. If a similar respect is not there in the hearts of the people doing this work, it will become a very contradictory affair. The work has to be done of course, but that work in itself is not going to bring much value; it is not going to be in tune with the vision I have. In my heart there is the same respect for the most ordinary of people as there is for a tirthankara or a *bhagwan* – a blessed one. If there is not a similar respect for ordinary people in the hearts of those who are going to take my work forward, then they cannot take my work very far.

What I mean is that one part of the work is mechanical and anyone can do it: a book has to be printed, a book has to be sold – that is the mechanical part of the work. The other part is very alive, very revolutionary. Only if it has reached deep into your own life can it reach others, otherwise it cannot.

So concerning this, whenever there is a meditation camp or a meeting, our worker friends should always have a separate meeting together as well. They will have their own issues, their own problems that they won't get time to talk about. If not today, then maybe tomorrow, we should start having a small meditation camp for the workers: a camp for three or four days with twenty to twenty-five people. There, it will be easier for them to be with me. They won't have such big responsibilities, so they will be able to solve their own issues – because they are dealing with many issues and it is very important that they should be able to talk to me about them. And I cannot do all these different types of work alone. Even if I pull all my energy together, what can I alone do? The fact is that if the work is to be done properly, we will have to create many individuals who will be able to communicate it.

One way they can communicate it is to present it as dead propaganda: somehow or other managing to bring it to people by "beating a drum." There is no point in doing that. When the message travels like that, it dies before it arrives. The other way is for the worker to be so alive that anyone who sees him feels, "If he became interested in this, then I should also be!" But if one of our workers gets upset over small things, gets offended, gets angry, starts fighting about trivial matters, then how can he communicate the things that we want him to? So the right direction…

Today the work is not so huge, but if we have the right group of friends, then if not today, then tomorrow, it can become vast. Even if I put all my energy into it, it cannot bring vast results unless there is a group of friends helping.

Whether there are five hundred people here or five thousand I will put in the same amount of energy. From my side, it will make no difference to the amount of energy I will put in. But for the maximum number of people to take advantage of it, we will have to build a group of friends. And it should be such a group that no matter what type of person comes, anyone can have the opportunity to contribute his work. There is nobody on this earth who cannot contribute something work-wise. Hundreds of people are eager; everywhere people tell me they would like to work. So what can I tell them? What work shall I give them to do?

There should be a group of people who can make use of their offers, who can use their labor. We should be able to make full use of whatever help people are willing to give. But you can only do that when... For example, say a new person comes: he has come because he felt my influence over the last three days, something made an impact on him and so he comes to you. But if you listen to him with indifference or you just say, "Yes, okay, we'll see," then you will lose someone who might have been of tremendous help. When the person comes with enthusiasm, the doors of your heart should be open for him in a loving way. And this is the opportunity: this person could help in your work. But if you are indifferent, and just say, "Yes, okay, we'll see," then that person will leave. It is possible he could have done a tremendous amount of work, we don't know.

Often very small people have done great work. And great people are not born from the sky, everyone is born small. It is the opportunity and the work that makes them great.

So every person – whosoever is eager and in whatever capacity – should be welcomed with great love. We should make use of their contribution even if they are ready just to move a rock from one place to another. And the work is so vast that if we work hard for ten to fifteen years, a climate of revolution can be created throughout this whole country. This country is ready; the mind of this country is ready. If we do not manage this, then it will only be because of our weakness, our misunderstanding and our incompetence.

The youth of today in this country have no direction in their lives, no guidance. They are not going to stop – they will keep going – but without guidance, without any direction. Wherever the country goes, they will go. If we gather a little courage and make an effort, then they can find a way, a direction. And this is not only the situation of the young people here; it is the same with young people all over the world. If our experiment is successful here, then it can also reach many more people out there.

So firstly, your interest has limits. You have come because you are interested in yourself, because you want to become peaceful, silent. But I want to tell you that always to be only interested in yourself is a kind of sickness. It is okay to have a little interest in yourself, but a very self-centered person can never become silent because this is also a cause of his unrest. This "I," "I," "I" – "I should be all right," "I should become this way," "I should become that way" – if someone is thinking about this too much, that in itself will not allow him to be peaceful, silent. If we feel something is the truth, if something feels right to us, then we should come out of our bubble of "I" a little, and make some effort for this truth to reach others as well.

You will be surprised to discover that the day you become interested in others, you will find that the cause of your restlessness, your sickness of "I" has decreased by fifty percent – just because you have become interested in others.

So the person we call religious has one fundamental disease: he is only interested in himself. And in all the communities that have become very "religious" in this way, everyone has become very selfish. Religion is the hand behind this: people forget that someone is standing right next to them. And they don't understand that life is so interconnected that this attitude is as stupid as it is in this anecdote...

Three men were sitting in a boat. One of them started making a hole where he was sitting. The other man shouted, "What are you doing?"

The first man said, "I am making the hole where I am sitting. What does it have to do with you? I am not making a hole where you are."

At this, the other two became silent. What he was saying seemed to be right: he was making a hole where he was sitting, so what concern was it of theirs?

But if someone makes a hole in the boat, then it is not a question of his or your place, because the boat is not separate, it is one boat. The hole is going to drown everybody. If your neighbor is making a hole... We are all sailing together in the same boat. Our life is one collective boat. If anyone is making a hole in it, then you shouldn't think, "*He* is making a hole so what does it have to do with me?" Life is an interrelationship, it is so interconnected that a hole made anywhere is a hole in *your* boat. The opposite is also true, any hole plugged by anyone is a hole plugged in your boat.

So one kind of interest is limited to yourself – you want to be more peaceful – and another interest is more expansive, its concern is for a peaceful environment. That peaceful environment will also be there for you, but your motivation, your thinking is on a wider scale. If you remember this, you will feel a difference.

All the religions born in the East are centered around the individual; none of them are centered around a group. Christianity is the only religion that is group-centered. Looking at the differences that exist between the group-centered thinking of the West and the individual-centered religions of the East, one wonders how they compare. They both have a kind of incompleteness about them. Because Christianity became absolutely group-centered, there is no central role for the individual left in it. And all the religions here have become absolutely centered on the individual so there is no vision of the group left in them.

Because he is interested in his own peace, in his own bliss, the truly religious person becomes interested in everyone else's peace and bliss. He is neither self-centered nor group-centered. He is interested only in peace and bliss. And he understands very well that, on the larger scale, his peace and your peace are not two different things – because on the larger scale the boat is one.

So the meaning of a worker is one who understands that now he is not just one person meditating for himself. Instead, what he has come to realize is that meditation should be spread on a wider scale.

It is necessary to give some thought to how meditation can be spread. Right now the work happens without any thought; the work is being done by friends with no thought behind it. And up to now I have had no role whatsoever in the work that is being done. It has been the friends' work and they have been doing it in the way they have thought best. They have achieved a lot. But now I feel I will have to get involved in the work. Perhaps only then it will have a good sense of order, otherwise not.

So whatever thoughts, ideas and reflections you may have about this, sit together in a separate meeting and discuss them. There are also small, specific issues, and you should discuss those as well. Your own particular issues will surely be of a different kind, so it makes no sense discussing them in the main gathering.

Everyone who is eager to spread this work should start thinking from this perspective: What preparations can he make so that this work spreads far and wide? It is not just a question of spreading the work. It is only through your own growth that the work can reach others. There is no question of creating an organization; there is no question of making a very centralized organization.

There will be a functional center. And it should be seen just as a functional place – because when a center becomes too organized it starts creating many kinds of obstacles. So we should spread the work so much, it should expand so much, that it doesn't even feel that there is a center. The center will be everywhere and nowhere – because if a center is too entrenched and strong, its depth and strength will come at the expense of weakening other branches, other centers.

If the capital, New Delhi, becomes very strong, it will become strong only by weakening the state capitals; otherwise it cannot become that strong. So the stronger it becomes, the weaker the state capitals will become. That has dangers. Finally it becomes centered in the hands of just a few people; in the hands of one individual, or in the hands of two, three, or four people.

So it is not a question of creating this kind of centralization, even though a functional center is necessary. But be fully aware that it is only a functional center. We should be working so hard in all the different centers that they are almost self-dependent and self-sustaining. They should look after themselves, they should think for themselves. We will provide as much support as we can from the center, and take as little help from them as possible. This should be our approach: that we take as little help as possible, and give as much help as possible.

And in different places there will be different circumstances, there will be people who think differently. So, whatever their plan, whatever work they want to do, if we feel that it is not contrary in any way to our vision here at the center, they should be given the opportunity to do it. Whatever work they want to do, they should be allowed to do it. And we should help them as much as possible to work in a way that is entirely free and self-sustaining.

Many people will become interested in the work; different types of people will become interested. If we only want "the right kind of people" to work, we will be mistaken. All kinds of people will come to work. We should just take care that there are no people with attitudes contrary to our work and vision. That is all we need to be alert about. And the doors should be open to whoever comes, so that everyone can come in.

In organized institutions a danger starts creeping in – and we do not want to create an institution that is like the other institutions that prevail around the world. It starts to become dangerous if an institution falls into the hands of one, two, three or four people because then they start living in the constant fear that someone new will come and displace them, remove them. And as this tendency starts creeping into every institution, this mentality closes the doors and the work suffers.

My proposal is that we won't have any positions or special status. We don't want to create anything like that – then there is no need for anyone to worry. Our work is such that if we hold on to the idea of position and status within this group, how will we be able to bring about the revolution we want to? This whole revolution is about destroying these ideas.

So at least *we* should have enough understanding that we are immediately ready to step down and take another job whenever someone comes along who wants to do our job and can do it better. If there is that much welcome in our hearts regarding the work, then it can grow tremendously.

Right now such small things come to my notice. Every day someone comes and tells me this or that. It amazes me. They are such trivial things, and if situations arise among us based upon them, if all sorts of problems arise, if all sorts of worries come in – and it really does amaze me – then it will be very difficult for the work to expand extensively with all these situations. So there is a need to consider all of this very openly as well.

And if some conflict arises between workers, among friends, then gossiping about it among each other should stop. It should be discussed when we all are sitting together. When all thirty of us are sitting together, if anyone... Let us suppose someone has done something wrong, and someone else has something to say about it, then they should say it in front of everyone. You shouldn't gossip about it among yourselves because in this way it spreads like a disease. When we all are sitting together, that is the time to say, "Agarwal-ji, such and such a thing seems to be wrong and we don't like it." Sitting together we can all reflect on it. Maybe Agarwal-ji is right. Then, together we can all decide that what he is saying is right, and that you are worrying unnecessarily. But if he is wrong, then we can tell him that to do this will be damaging, so please drop it.

And we should be ready to do that. What is the big deal in dropping or not dropping such small matters? If we are afraid of dropping such things, then how will other people be able to let go of all the things that I am telling them to leave behind? In their case, I am attacking the very core of their lives; it is almost an attack on their whole lives. They are supposed to be letting go of ideas that are thousands of years old – ideas that they have been hanging on to – and meanwhile, if we keep getting caught up in these small things, then it will become very difficult.

There is only one thing to be remembered in this regard: such things are not to be discussed among you individually. That creates unnecessary bitterness. We should talk about them when we all come together, in an open and straightforward way, and in the context of the work – that such and such a thing could become a hindrance so we want to talk about it.

And really keep in mind that perhaps at this stage you cannot foresee how big the work can become. Perhaps you may be able to guess it in two to five years. No one ever is able to estimate how large some work is going to become. If only people could see that beforehand, then the work would expand very fast, and would expand with fewer hurdles. But we never see it. People rarely have the foresight to see how large some work is going to become in ten years' time.

In 1920 or 1921, Gandhi was staying with Gokhale in Kolkata. Gokhale was worried about accompanying a man dressed like a sadhu onto the stage. He was worried that people would laugh – because until then the Congress Party consisted only of well-dressed, properly dressed, people – barristers, and suchlike. Gandhi was not like the other people in the organization. Should Gokhale go with him or not?

Thinking about it, Gokhale made some excuse that he had a headache and couldn't go. He had no idea that by going on stage dressed like a village farmer, Gandhi – by wearing such clothes, by standing there in the role of a poor man – would cause a revolution in this country. No one ever imagined that. Gokhale certainly didn't envisage it.

Whatever kind of work has happened in this world, there was never any inkling before of just how much it would expand. If it could have been seen beforehand, Gandhi could have been spared an incalculable number of difficulties, and the work that took twenty-five years could have happened in fifteen. But we never foresee this. Only when something has already happened do we see what the possibilities were.

The idea you have become interested in can bring about a very far-reaching revolution. Keep the bigger picture in your mind rather than thinking about yourself. And focus on how to move this huge work forward without any hurdles.

You should also be aware that you have an enormous responsibility. As long as I am saying whatever I am saying to small groups, it will not cause trouble. But the day large numbers of people start coming, then the problems will start coming too. That is for certain! And the more these ideas take hold, the greater the dangers and problems will be. They will grow in the same proportion. You should be prepared for this; when you start talking about change and revolution, you should already be prepared for this in many different ways.

You have an enormous responsibility. Right now, I don't see that you are really ready. The day you are ready, the responsibility will be waiting for you. And as for me, I have to pause at every step, wondering who will take all this responsibility. If it is all to rest on your shoulders, who is going to be able to bear it, to sustain it? The sooner you can be ready, the sooner I can start speaking to the right people. What would have been said in two years' time can be said today. It is a message that needs to be brought to every village, to each and every home.

How to spread the message? What needs to be done? You need to sit down and think about all of these things together because one, two or three people won't be able to manage everything. And the work will expand more as people who have a wider, universal understanding come. The more people with many diverse talents, many different qualities come, the more the work will grow.

So your organization should do its work remembering that it is just a meeting place, nothing more than that. Your work is simply to make it possible for many different people to come: people with different perspectives, different types of people, people from different groups and classes. You have to think about how to use them in the work. That is what you need to pay attention to. And if we can extend an invitation to many people in a very loving and welcoming way, then there is no reason to doubt the success of the work.

The whole vision of what I am talking about today is directed toward religion. If not today, then tomorrow, I will have to speak on other aspects of society as well – financial aspects, political aspects. Society lives as an undivided whole.

If change is to be brought to its whole perspective, then we will have to look at all its different aspects. I am talking about religion because it is one aspect. And statements of the same revolutionary intensity are needed as far as every aspect of life is concerned, so we can present a complete revolutionary plan to the psyche of the country.

If tomorrow I start presenting my vision on politics, on economics, on society, on education, then we will need many different kinds of people in the work, even though we cannot imagine right now how essential those people will be. Today many such people already show their enthusiasm, but we don't have work we can ask them to do.

Many professors all over the country have become interested. If we prepare, then in the near future we can organize a separate meditation camp for them, and in that camp I will talk only about what can be done in the field of education. Young people have become interested: we can organize a separate camp for college students; we can talk to them. Many politicians in this country have become interested: if not today then tomorrow, if we are working on a bigger scale, we can make a separate camp just for them. We can talk straightforwardly to them; we can tell them a few things!

But all this is possible only if we allow every type of person to join in. In the future, there will be different approaches for different types of people. Right now there are so many questions that I don't answer just because the people I need to speak to about that subject are not here. Then what can I say? For example, there is not a single day when someone or other doesn't ask a question about education. But what is the point of talking about education until I am speaking to the educators? So much could be done in this area.

For tomorrow there are one or two questions on politics, but what is the point of responding to them unless I lay out the entire political plan according to my vision? And to whom should I say all of this?

There are many aspects to life and the workings of a country, and a complete revolution can happen only when it embraces all of those aspects. But for that we have to be more prepared. For example, take this meditation camp: four hundred people have come, and there could have been two thousand. We need to give this some attention. And you will be surprised to know that these four hundred people, these same people, would have benefited even more if two thousand people had come, because the greater the number of people, the greater the energy field, the greater the atmosphere that is created.

And because life is always experienced when there is expansion, the more expansive a situation is, the better. If there are ten thousand people meditating near you, with you, it will make a difference to your meditation. If you are meditating alone, it will not be the same. This is because with many people you start feeling some clarity. A certain psychic atmosphere is created: the reflections of so many people, the waves of so many people's minds, the vibrations of so many people's minds create a milieu.

Whichever village Buddha went to, ten thousand bhikkus would go with him. You may ask what point there was in moving around with such a crowd, but because those ten thousand disciples had been prepared in a special way, they would change the whole atmosphere of a village. They had a special type of consciousness, a special kind of eyes, a special kind of feet – the way they walked, the way they stood, the way they talked... Ten thousand silent people: wherever those silent people went, they filled each village with amazement!

Once they were staying near a city – ten thousand people staying outside the city – and the king wanted to meet them. He asked his ministers, "How far away is it?"

They replied, "You can see – just near those trees over there."

The king became suspicious. He took out his sword. "Are you trying to deceive me? You are saying that there are ten thousand people over there, but it doesn't look as if there even one single person. Such silence! Ten thousand people are staying just a stone's throw away, just near those trees, and the night is so silent. I feel suspicious." He took out his sword. Maybe it was a conspiracy…

The ministers laughed and said, "Keep your sword in its sheath, it is not a conspiracy. But please come! These ten thousand people are an entirely different kind of people." The king went and he was amazed to see that ten thousand people were sitting under the trees, absolutely silent. No one was talking.

Now this king is entering a psychic atmosphere where, even if he wants to prattle, he cannot. Ten thousand people are silently present. No one is talking. They all are sitting silently. Among them, he has the chance to pause – and he changes. He has never seen anything like this. He could not even imagine that such an environment is possible.

Many different kinds of work can be done. I have the idea that there could be a "consciousness attack" in the villages. But for this we will need people. My idea is that two thousand people stay in one village for three days. At present we conduct meditation camps. If we have two thousand people ready – who we think have made some progress in meditation, who have become peaceful, who have understood the vision – then we can all go to a village, a village of say ten thousand homes, and those two thousand people can become guests in the homes of the villagers, explaining with folded hands that they are making a "consciousness attack" throughout the village. Entering a village of ten thousand homes, these two thousand people will become guests, one for every five homes.

Those two thousand people will stay for three days, each talking to the people in those five homes in his area, and in the evening we will have a meeting to which our two thousand people will bring all the children and housewives of the entire village. The close association with those two thousand people – the way they act, the way they talk, their thinking – will create an atmosphere in the village.

Why should we have meditation camps in the forest? The only reason we have meditation camps in the forest is that we don't have people who can go to the cities and create the right atmosphere there. When we have two thousand people we can "strike" a village. In a year we can go to twelve villages. And in those twelve villages we will be able to create such a total magic for three days that the whole village will be awestruck, and a palpable difference will take place in its life.

So the work can take many forms, many dimensions. But it can take shape only as your collective strength grows, as more of you gather and think of new ways.

Today's gathering has been called because I have been thinking that from next time, the camps should be for four days instead of three. The first day should be for all the friends. One day should be spent with them, and the camp will start the next day. Then I can do something for them, and they can think and reflect in this direction. And in whichever village we are meeting, we are gathering together, there should be a one-hour sitting for the friends of that village who have become actively interested in doing the work. There should be a get-together for them in which we can think together about how we can expand the work there. Whoever has any proposals should bring them and explain to the others how the work can move forward according to their ideas.

Think it over, contemplate it. If you want to ask anything more about this, please ask.

Just recently those boys in Jabalpur did some good work. They worked well. If young people become interested… And you have to make them interested. Just recently fifteen or twenty boys created a group in Jabalpur to take our literature from door to door. They got a very good response. Wherever they went, they received a very good response; they had a very good response.

A friend has a plan for a weekly bulletin, so those boys are starting it from January. They are getting ready to publish it in Jabalpur. It is a small newsletter of six pages, and all the information can be there.

Osho,
The work is very big.

The work can become very big. And the more ready you are, the greater the direction I can give to it. It is all in my sights; nothing is impossible. So much can happen; so much can happen that within fifteen or twenty years we can create an entirely different atmosphere in this country.

Osho,
Is that why you have said that we workers should do the meditation experiments deeply?

We need to prepare a very particular group of people.
[At another meeting]

Osho,
Many people feel that you say something, and then after a while you say something different. Then they are unable to understand whether the first thing is true or the second. It seems doing your meditations brings transformation over a long period of time, but

so much time is wasted in discussions. Now one example is that people have started wondering whether to keep your photograph or not. You may be thinking about this in a different way, so the programs turn into discussions from the very start.

During the program meetings, anything can be asked – whatever it is about.

Osho,
So if the talk is about something a long way in the future, then maybe it will never be understood, but if some idea is to be carried out, then at this time it should be given all our energy. Later on if it doesn't seem to yield results, it can be given back to the person and they can be told it didn't work. But if it is to be done, then at this moment it should be done with full intensity.

Yes, with total intensity. Because whatever has to be done, the understanding… For example about my photograph: I am getting hundreds of letters every month asking for my photograph. From where can I send the photograph? If I don't send it, people write again saying, "Can't you even send us one picture?" So the only way is to make the photographs available, so whoever wants one can have it. How can I send the pictures? People even come to my house asking for my photograph. Where am I to get the photographs from? How am I to keep them, and send them? And how many should I keep?

The best thing is to keep photographs on the stall, and whoever wants one can have one. And if someone doesn't want one, there is no problem.

Whatever the matter may be, it should be given some thought.

How can I say no to anybody? Someone has come saying he wants a picture of me. So what should he be told? And someone else sends a letter asking for a picture. Now some things have to be done to get that picture: money has to be spent, then the letter has to be posted – and that costs more money. What does all this mean? If the photograph is not sent, then the person becomes unhappy because a picture has not been sent.

Osho,
Okay, so all of this should be taken care of by some kind of a club?

Yes, I said that; make a club, have three or four friends in it, and then the matter will be taken care of.

Whatever people wish for and whatever we can arrange, we should.

Osho,
Sometimes the workers get caught up in the idea of whether arrangements should be made for what people want or not.

Yes, this should be thought about.

Osho,
About the pictures: maybe people will misuse them. What if people start worshipping them?

What happens is that our minds never quite catch the right point; it always swings to one side or the other. Either we worship the pictures or we become afraid of the pictures – afraid that something may go wrong if we give someone a picture.

This mind of ours! It either wants to create statues or destroy them, but it never just accepts them naturally. A statue is a statue, it doesn't need to be worshipped and it doesn't need to be destroyed. A picture is a picture, there is no need to worship it and there is no need to avoid it. Mohammedans have avoided this so much that if you create a picture of Mohammed, immediately there will be fighting and riots. If you simply hang a picture of Mohammed in your house they will set your house on fire. Now isn't this just creating the other side of the stupidity? And it was started for this reason: it was started to prevent idol worship, to prevent someone worshipping a picture of Mohammed.

Swami Satyabhakta built a temple in Wardha. He put statues from all the religions in the temple, including one of Mohammed. Immediately there was a riot, and finally the statue had to be removed. No one can create a picture of Mohammed. Creating a statue is simply out of the question. So there is no authentic picture of Mohammed anywhere. Now, isn't this another kind of foolishness?

What I am saying is why don't you look at things in a simple way? A picture is a picture. What is the big deal about it? There is no need to worship it and there is no need to be afraid of it.

Osho,
In fact, there is a fixed idea in the minds of the workers of how you should be.

Yes, that too is very difficult, that too is very difficult. We will have to demolish that too. We will have to destroy that idea.

Osho,
Even after listening to you so much, we are still wondering why you are allowing your photographs to be taken for people. Why do you need photographs? Why are you fond of photographs?

Yes, we should understand all of these things clearly. We need to understand all these things clearly. People certainly have an idea about how I should be.

Osho,
Our concept is of how a sadhu, a religious man, should be.

Yes. And whatever concepts you have, have been created over thousands of years. I am not that kind of a man at all! I will break your concepts over and over again. It has to be made very clear to you that I am not that kind of man at all. I don't belong to any of these categories. So I am not afraid if someone keeps my photograph. What is there to be afraid of?

Osho,
What if someone tears it up?

That's fine; there is nothing to fear about that. Even if someone spits on it or stamps on it, what does it matter?

Osho,
What if someone worships it?

If someone wants to worship it, what can we do? In fact, I am fighting against the mind that wants to worship. But if someone worships it, what can we do? What does it matter? It is okay, it is their wish.

Our fight is against the mind that wants to worship. The worshipping attitude is stupid. Even so, if someone is mad, he is mad; if he worships, he worships. It doesn't matter! And if he doesn't worship my photo, he will worship someone else's photo. What difference does it make? If a certain mind has a worshipping mentality, it will worship. And the mind which opposes it, which feels afraid of worship, is the same mind that wants to worship. It is not a different mind; it is the same mind as the one that wants to worship.

Now in so many places people come and tell me that there are fears that a sect will grow up around my teachings. To this I say that it is the minds of those already in sects which are talking in terms of fear. The most interesting thing is that the person who tells me this, is himself part of some sect – and yet he is afraid that a sect may arise. If this man were to worry about this after he had become free from his own sect, then that would be understandable. Then, yes, that man would be talking some sense. But he is firmly rooted in a sect. And his fear is never about creating a situation where a sect arises; his fear is always that it will be in competition with his sect. So the basis of his fear is that another sect is coming: "There is already so much competition for my sect and here comes one more." This is the fear. He is not afraid of sects, he is already rooted in a sect – and that is the fear. That is the fear.

So we should discuss all these matters, and understand them clearly.

Osho,
So should the workers have a small meditation camp?

Yes, we will have a meditation camp. There should certainly be a meditation camp. That will be beneficial. Just for some twenty-five to thirty friends. All these things have to be made clear. Everything should be made clear about me, also.

Osho,
Yes. In this way, your message, your ideas, will move forward in the right way. Only if we absorb your ideas, can we bring it to others.

That is certainly right.

Osho,
What happens is that you say something and we take something else to people. This way we ourselves help create wrong ideas about you.

Yes, it happens, it happens.

11
Making Meditation Centers

Osho,
Our idea is to make a meditation hall and a guest house. I would like to ask you about the funds that we are thinking of collecting, the one and a half million rupees which is our estimate. What is the real point behind all of this? And while working on this project, what about the Life Awakening Center? What is the advantage of having all these places? Please explain this to us.

You have asked a very difficult question.

Osho,
You have given answers to every difficult question!

There are many factors. Firstly, society will probably never again be in the same situation that it is in now. Over hundreds of thousands of years, only once in a while does a society reach such a state of transition, when everything is changing, where the new replaces the old. These moments can be a blessing or a curse. It is not that the new is always right in every situation. The old is wrong in every sense, but the new may not always be right. And when the old crumbles away, a thousand alternatives come along. If a wrong alternative is chosen, it can become a great misfortune.

So this has to be properly understood: whatever the circumstances, I am against the old, but I am not always in favor of everything that is new. The old should go. It should not wait for even a single moment. In fact what we call "old" is something that has overstayed its time, something that should never have remained in place for so long. But when the time comes for the old to fall away, societies like ours, which have never said good-bye to the past, face a difficult situation. We don't know how to dismantle the old in a healthy way, with a healthy mind. This means that whenever we have to demolish the old, we can only do it in a feverish state, in a frenetic way.

But remember: the old can be demolished in a frenetic way, but the new cannot be created like that. To create the new, a very peaceful and healthy mind is needed.

So in this moment, the most essential thing is not what we should or should not do. Before taking any decisions, the most important thing is that the country needs a peaceful and healthy state of mind. Then, the next step is to ask: "What shall we do and what is the best way to set about it?" The question is not that our car is standing at the crossroads of life and we are wondering which way to turn. The question is whether the driver is conscious or not. This is more important – because if the driver is unconscious, any road will lead to danger, and how can he choose the right way?

Everywhere, in every aspect of life – be it in politics or policy, literature or art – the old way is on the verge of extinction, is breaking down. Without our doing anything it is breaking down. The new will have to be chosen. It is not as if we have a choice right now about whether to choose something new or not. A situation of sheer helplessness has been created in which people have to choose something new. The old has lost all reason for existing. It has lost its very base.

There are two types of people in this country: those who want to hang on to the old out of insecurity – at least it is known, it is familiar – and those who are eager to discard the old at any cost for any new thing that comes along, those for whom anything new is bound to be okay.

I am neither of these types. And that is why my problems are many. I feel that the new has to be chosen, needs to be chosen – every day it needs to be chosen – but who will choose? In this country, for thousands of years, we have been making mistakes as far as this is concerned.

For example, for fifty years before 1947 the whole country lived in the hope that when it became free, everything would be all right. Even the people we call highly intelligent explained to everyone that the British were the cause of all the country's troubles, and when they went the troubles would also go.

This was absolutely false. But maybe when they said it they did not understand it was false, maybe their intelligence could not see it. We hung all our hopes on 1947: "When we get freedom we will get everything. As soon as the British go, all the troubles will also go. Slavery is the cause of all our problems: once that goes, everything will be okay." That is why, when we woke up on the morning of 15th August, we were eager to see if everything was okay now or not. But nothing was okay.

Now twenty years have passed. Now we know that the British were not the reason for all our problems. Maybe they were one of the reasons, and that reason was still there because all our other problems were sustaining it. And all those problems are still present today. There has been no change in the mindset of the country.

This country is now saying that if socialism comes, everything will be all right. Again we are talking the same insanities. Even when socialism comes we will still find ourselves unable to believe that nothing has changed. It will be the same as it was before, when we thought that slavery under the British was the cause of all the tension and chaos – even though that was absolutely untrue. In fact, we can't even say that if the British hadn't been here, we would be in as good a shape as they left us in. When the British took hold of this country's reins the situation was so bad that it is difficult to imagine it now. When they left us, they left us in much better shape.

Now we have the idea that capitalism must somehow be done away with, that this is the root cause of all our problems. But if we destroy capitalism, we will once again be in a mess. And once again we will have the experience that even though capitalism has gone, our dreams have not come true.

Our dreams cannot come true. They do not come true like that. This country does not have a mind which can think, which can see to the very depth of things, which can investigate and understand them. There are very different realities, and we are not aware of this.

For example, there is a big house and around it are some very small huts. Anyone standing at the crossroads could say that the big house is only so big because the other houses have been reduced to hutments. Everyone could agree with that. But this is absolutely untrue, and the reality is just the opposite. The ten small huts only exist because the big house is there, otherwise they would not exist at all. Because when a big house is being built, a wealthy person is making it, an engineer is working on it, a laborer is carrying sand for it, someone else is digging holes, someone else is cutting wood... When a big house is being built fifty small houses are erected nearby because of it.

But the politician standing at the crossroads will say that these houses have remained small because that one big house has been built: "If this big house had not been built, then you too would have had big houses." But you should remember that the logic of life is quite the opposite. In the first place, if the big house did not exist, then the possibility of those small huts existing would not be there.

In Buddha's day the population of the country was only twenty million – and if the country had followed the ideas of people like Gandhi, then still today the population of the country would only be twenty million, not more. But today India and Pakistan together have seven hundred million people. How are these seven hundred million surviving? Capitalism has created wealth. But you cannot see this with a frenetic mind; to see this, a very sane and peaceful mind is needed. And only when we have achieved this sane and peaceful mind do I believe we will be able to use capitalism to bring about socialism. Right now we are ready to fight capitalism in order to bring in socialism; we are ready to destroy capitalism to bring in socialism. My understanding is that when capitalism is a complete success, then it will inevitably transform into socialism. Socialism is the next step after capitalism. But to see this, immense understanding and a silent mind are needed.

I have given you this as an example. But in the same way everything in this country is entangled, confused – be it politics, religion, ethics – whatever it is. I do not insist that people should follow what we feel is right. It is more important that the right thing is understood, that a heart which is capable of understanding is created. And only when the heart understands that by doing things in a certain way they will be put right, should things be done in that way. But a silent heart that is capable of making decisions between the right way and the wrong way does not exist right now in this country.

It is not necessarily true that something can only happen when the whole country has a peaceful mind and heart. It takes only a few people to make life move forward, a very few people. If the names and contribution of just two hundred people were taken away, mankind would still be stuck in the same place as it was some two hundred thousand years ago. We would not have even learned to come down from the trees. The genius of around two hundred people has given an impetus to the entire world.

So this has been my constant feeling, that there should be meditation centers in all the major cities in this country – places where we are not concerned with what is right, but where we are helping people achieve clarity, where their minds can become silent so that they can start seeing how things really are. Neither their prejudices nor their previous biases or karmas will be in the way. They will have a clear vision and the ability to use it.

If we can create even a small group of people in every major city who can see things clearly, it will be a precious asset in this period of transition. And I believe that this may prove to be the most valuable thing of all.

For this, to create a silent mind, a silent being, we have to create, to provide the right ambience, the right atmosphere, and the right place. And for that to happen, many things need to be looked at. We have spoken about meditation halls, we have spoken about meditation centers. It is essential that all the major cities have such a place, which is neither Hindu, nor Muslim, nor Christian… The place should be for everyone. It should exist for anyone who wants to become silent.

In these places, silence can be supported in all kinds of ways. Different things can be arranged for small children; literature can be produced which will help them to go into meditation. A thousand ways can be found…

The thing about devices is that… For example, if someone today looks at a painting from the West, he will see it has been created by an unhealthy mind.

Recently when I was a guest in someone's house in Pune, they had bought two expensive paintings. They asked me, "What do you think?"

I said "I will not say anything. Sit and look at this painting for half an hour and then let me know how you feel."

Half an hour was a long time. After looking at that painting for even five minutes your head would have started spinning and you would feel as if you were in a madhouse. A painting like that doesn't have a soothing effect.

If someone looks at a Picasso painting and starts meditating on it, they can become mad, not silent. But if you meditate on Buddha's statue for five minutes, even if you are mad you will begin to feel a change. You will become peaceful. We can create climates of silence with statues and paintings. And then there are the dances of the Dervish mystics. I would like to have places all over the country where everyone can dance. We are already dancing, the whole world is dancing. The world cannot be prevented from dancing, and any community which prevents dancing will suffer great harm. While dancing, the dancer can become silent or he can become restless. It is a question of the movements and the rhythm. Dance can provoke sexuality in you and it can also take you away from sexuality. Even people watching a dance can become sexual.

Just now a girl returning from England told me that she had gone to see a musical about hippies. The cast was dancing and during the dance they threw off their clothes and were naked. At least twenty percent of the boys and girls present were so mesmerized by this that they also threw off their clothes and became naked – inside the theater, from among the audience. She said she was very surprised by what had happened, because it is okay if someone dancing in the play becomes naked, but what was happening to the audience in the hall?

Dance will do something to you inside. Whatever you are looking at will affect you within. If someone is watching the dances of the Sufi Dervishes for half an hour, they will find that all their mental worries have disappeared. The movement, the speed, has been created in such a scientific way that it soothes your mind and makes it silent.

So to me, a meditation hall has a very different meaning. We can make sure we have pictures in the hall which silence the mind, which purify the mind when you look at them. We can have dances which quieten the mind and make you sane and healthy when you watch them. We can arrange for a certain kind of songs, a certain kind of music – a veena playing. A certain type of teacher should be born there, a certain type of child should arise – and the same goes for old people, husbands, and wives. We should start touching all aspects of life there.

There were many meditation halls in the past, but they had an aura of discipline, they were escapist. If someone went to the temple, he would be escaping from life. I would like temples which will take a person deeper into life, not encourage him to escape from it.

So the main thing is to set up such centers where all aspects of life can be touched upon, where work in all directions can happen, and where we make it possible for people to dive into silence from every direction. Such a set-up is possible. It will not very difficult. The strategy that has made people restless is also a set-up, but a set-up that has created this madness.

So a meditation center is needed. I don't know about money matters, Ishwar bhai and all of you will understand that. I won't get involved there. I just know that if you are able to create such a set-up, then you will be able to do something for all the future generations of this country as well as something for yourselves; something valuable, which will have a lasting effect on the consciousness of the country.

Some literature will also be needed. Whatever literature there is right now in the name of religion is absolute rubbish. Because of this literature, anyone with any intelligence will not be able to become religious. What we call "religious literature" is repulsive to anyone intelligent. You have to be retarded to read such literature! So we need literature which touches the intelligentsia of the country – something which can enhance the country's brilliance, make it juicier. These centers can also become a base for publishing and circulating such literature.

Now we have ways and means which we never had before, which were never there before. We have them now, but we are still unable to use them for the benefit of mankind. Buddha had no alternative but to walk – and walk for forty years. But even though he went around for forty years, he still couldn't get further than Bihar, and he only went to Varanasi once. The world is so big and Buddha had no other answer.

If someone like me has to wander around like Buddha, then two and a half thousand years will have been wasted. In such a situation I will not be able to do more than Buddha managed. But technology has developed in these two and a half thousand years. This means that now a film can be made so that my message also reaches villages which I have been unable to visit. In the villages where we cannot arrange to show the dances we are doing in Mumbai, they can see them on film. It may not be possible to take paintings to all the villages, but the whole country can see a film of the paintings that we have in the Mumbai meditation room. There is no reason why not just the whole country, but the whole world cannot be connected. Radio is a medium, television is a medium. Now media are available that the old world could not use because they did not have them.

But instead we are using them, not for our benefit but rather as a curse. So there is a great conflict. People who meet me these days say, "The cinemas should be closed!" It is not a question of closing them. This medium exists, it cannot be stopped. The question is not about banning them; the question is about their right use: how to use them rightly. At present such a powerful medium like the cinema is being used in a wrong way.

I have heard a saying, a French saying: "Whenever something new is invented the devil is the first to take it over." Good people remain idle bystanders, just shouting that something is wrong. Who is stopping them from stepping in? But no, they go on having meetings with the so-called saints, they go on deciding that such bad posters should not be allowed – but who is stopping them from putting up good posters? And why can't they put up a nice poster to replace the bad poster and force it to disappear because nobody wants to look at it? No, their only concern is that there should be no bad posters. They will complain that bad films should not be shown, but who is stopping them from making good films?

But we can't even imagine such a thing. We can't imagine what would happen if someone like Buddha were to appear in a film! First we would say that a buddha would not appear in a film. Why not? After all a buddha can talk, a buddha can walk, so, why can't the whole country watch him talking and walking on film? The whole country could watch it.

But the bad person is the first one to take possession of a new invention, and the good person just keeps on complaining. The good person has always been impotent, absolutely impotent. He doesn't do anything; he just keeps shouting that this terrible thing is happening, that this bad thing is happening. He never does anything. If a bad person starts a fire, a good person doesn't even bring a bucket of water. He just keeps on saying that a terrible thing is happening, that this should not have happened.

In my understanding, good people have to be empowered. The fight against evil cannot be resolved through talking. All the media that are being used by bad people should also be used by good people.

I am amazed! I can go to every village, and walk around... If I go to a village and even if ten thousand people come to hear me, it is like adding a drop of color to the ocean. It will never change the color of the ocean, the ocean is so big. Even if I work hard, in my whole life I will not be able to meet all of the five hundred million people in this country face-to-face. But now there is no reason why this cannot happen. What was impossible in the past is now possible. It can become possible now.

How can religion make use of the latest technology and science? Not only do we need to think about this, but we also need to do something to make it happen. Those one and half million rupees are a very small amount; you should regard it as a beginning and keep moving on. If this can be done, a great revolution can happen.

Children are watching films, and you are telling them not to watch them. I don't see any reason to say no to them. They should actually be made to watch films. Children can watch films, but there is no reason why they shouldn't watch films which can enlighten their lives. Why shouldn't they sing film songs? They want songs. Now children are doing the twist or some other dances, there is pop music – all this is going on. I believe children should dance, because a child who cannot dance is already old. He should dance. But again and again we shout, "No! This dance is not good!"

But where are the right kinds of dances? Either there is no dancing or there is the wrong kind of dance. I tell you that between these two alternatives, the wrong kind of dance will always be chosen. There is no other solution. Where is the right kind of dance? Bring it, and the wrong dance will automatically start disappearing. It needs to be undermined.

My understanding is that up to now, the good has not been attractive so the bad still is. It is surprising that the bad is so attractive and the good is not. When death approaches, a person starts going to the temple, otherwise he doesn't go. Yes, a film theater may have the name "Maratha Temple" but that is another matter! If someone goes there that is a different matter. Otherwise he only goes to the temple when he is old and approaching death. It was not attractive before, it did not provoke anything in his being. When he starts becoming tired and defeated, when all the other attractions start to disappear, maybe then he will find religion attractive.

This means that all the religions up to now have been attracting dead people, not living people. But the power is in the hands of the living.

I would like each of these centers to be a nucleus, a center from where we can touch all aspects, all the dimensions of life so in ten to fifteen years we can lay a foundation for the birth of an absolutely new society.

And regarding the work: I have been moving around talking continuously for ten years, and I have been observing all types of people and what type of person can do a particular type of work.

Recently I was staying in a jungle, and there was a sculptor who had once been very famous, but who had become fed up with the world so he had started living there. He is one of the top five or ten sculptors in the world. He doesn't have money to make statues, but whenever someone gives him some, he makes one. He has a wonderful talent, but he has no cement or concrete to make a statue. He told me he would like to make statues all around the lake near where I was staying. He showed me all his plans, his models. They were amazing! But he doesn't have any money.

I told him "If I make a center, I will invite you to come and make statues all around it."

He said "I would spend my entire life there, because I don't have any other work. Once I get my bread, I don't need to do any other work; I can make statues my whole life."

There are sculptors, musicians... But only inferior music sells, because the customers are worthless people. Slowly musicians start selling music that is more and more inferior, because that is what sells in the marketplace; that is what fetches a good price. We should organize things so that we can provide the opportunity for excellence to flower in all the major cities. Then we can give birth to the best, even if it is only on a small scale.

Meditation is the collective result of many things. Meditation is not something that you do only once in a while, and then go back to acting in any old way for the rest of the day. Meditation is not like that.

My understanding is that if you want to enter into meditation, you should change the color of the walls in your house because certain colors may not allow you to meditate. If you have painted the walls red, yellow and black, and then you sit there with closed eyes, within five minutes you will start feeling restless. The clothes you wear are also meaningful. We are living at a very physical level. We talk about the soul and other things, but actually we live at the level of the body, which is physical.

The centers which will be created should investigate all aspects of life, they should research everything: what clothes should be like, what the color of the walls in the house should be, how the houses should be, what kind of trees should be near the house... We need to look into everything. And when everything is taken care of, meditation becomes such an easy thing – nothing else is so easy. Then it may not even be necessary to do it as a separate practice. How the food is, the clothes are, how the houses are, how the gardens are, how the person stands, sits down, and how he talks... If you just remember what it is that brings you to peace and serenity in all these areas, then it is not necessary to go separately into meditation. All these things will become a thread for the meditation inside you.

So meditation has an entirely different meaning for me. And right now the people I am talking to about meditation are the wrong type of people, because the world they live in and the way in which they are living have nothing to do with meditation. It is a question of their having some correct guidance, but if they don't even have that, what can they do?

I have a complete vision in my mind. If the people who agree with it put in a little energy, then it can be fulfilled. Otherwise there is no problem. I will keep on doing whatever I can do. It makes no difference.

Now I have some people to whom I can allocate some work, who can be of immense help, because I cannot remain in one place. If I settle in one particular place, it will be costly. I will keep on moving, but some people can stay put, and this can be very useful for the work. But to keep them in one place, plans and arrangements need to be made.

So think about it. It could start in Mumbai; the model could be created in Mumbai. Then it could be started in other cities in the country. Everything that is significant takes time; its influence is very slow. If we sow seeds of seasonal flowers, they will start flowering after a month, but after two months, they will be finished. So this is not an easy process where things can happen immediately, today. I feel that this is often why work doesn't happen – because our aspirations seem to be very seasonal. We want things to happen immediately. If they can't happen now, then we give up, thinking, "If it cannot happen now..."

This is a long journey, and it is a journey which doesn't have an end. We give it a push and then we are gone. Then someone else gives it a push and they are gone – and the journey continues. The journey is infinite. If the only thing a person leaves behind him at the end of his life is that he managed to push mankind a little toward bliss, toward benediction, I believe that person will experience great peace because of his efforts.

If we don't manage to do this, remember, it is not possible to remain neutral: you will still be pushing. But you will be pushing toward chaos, toward something harmful. You are alive, so your pushing is going to affect life. The question is, in which direction will your pushing take life? Will it take life toward the beneficial, toward the good, toward bliss? There can be nothing more gratifying than the fact that someone is able to do something for the good of all in their lifetime, for the well-being of everyone.

Buddha used to say to his disciples: "When you meditate, don't think that the peace you get from meditating should only be for you, otherwise you will never be peaceful – because the feeling of 'I,' of 'me' is restless." Buddha said: "When you find peace in meditation, then pray that it comes to everyone. Don't think that just 'I' should get it because the idea of 'getting it for me' is the basis of unpeacefulness, of restlessness. Wish that it may be shared, that everyone may get it." He said: "While meditating, ask that whatever peace descends should be shared with everyone, spread to everyone, spread far and wide. Don't keep your ego in there. And when you get up from meditation and experience silence, peace, pray that it should be for the well-being of everyone, that it should spread to everyone."

The interesting thing is that the person who wants to limit this peace to himself not only cannot spread it to others, he cannot even allow it to reach himself. And the person who wants to spread it to everyone manages to spread it to everyone, and then finds that by sharing it, it has also come back to him. There is no question about it, it has already reached him.

Osho,
Good and bad, life and death – what is all this? Why is it there? For what? What is the solution? How can this be renounced? How can this be understood? How can this be attained?

The questions we have are not real questions. In our questions are things we take for granted. One is that we believe everything must have a purpose. We take it for granted that everything must have a meaning. A flower has blossomed and we ask, "Why have you blossomed?" The sun is radiating light and we ask why. But neither the sun nor the flower will answer. The flower will go on blooming and the sun will go on radiating – and we will go on destroying ourselves asking such questions.

The questions people raise are so childish; they are based on a fundamental misunderstanding. We assume that everything must have a meaning. But doesn't it occur to you that if everything had a meaning, life would be so rotten that you cannot even imagine it. In life, whatever is beautiful is without a reason. Whatever is beautiful is purposeless.

If I love someone and I start asking the meaning of love, then that love has disappeared. When we are asking questions we want to understand everything with logic. If we understand things in the language of reason, then life will become very sad and useless. All the happiness of life exists only in those things which are purposeless. A person is dancing. What is the purpose? He says dancing itself is the purpose. Someone is singing a song. What is the purpose? He says singing itself is the purpose. The birds are singing in the morning and flying high in the sky. What is the purpose of this? Flying itself is blissful; there is no other meaning.

Why should there be a purpose in the first place? What is the need for everything to have a meaning? My understanding is the opposite. My understanding is that as our awareness deepens, even things we thought had a purpose start becoming purposeless. And in the end the whole world becomes just a play, a *leela*. Purpose doesn't exist, only the play is left. But our minds don't accept play, they accept work. There is a difference between work and play. Work has a purpose; play doesn't have a purpose.

The strange thing is that we get bothered by work, and yet we only accept the concept of work, of purpose. Even when we are playing, we want to turn it into work. If a few children are playing, the grown-ups want to ask them, "What are you doing this for?" – because when adults are playing, they play with some money at stake. Then it has some purpose: "We have won fifty or we have lost fifty." Otherwise why bother? There is nothing to be gained.

Children are playing and they don't understand why you are asking them what it is for. Playing is enough in itself, it is sufficient. Beyond that there is no question! You ask the question because you have forgotten how to play. You don't know about play. For you, only work is left. If the shop is there, there is a purpose; if the temple is there it is for a purpose.

People ask me, "Why should we go to the temple? What will we get from going there?" In fact they will only go to the temple if it proves to be like a shop. If they can get something there, then they will go. Now if a person goes on questioning like this, what will the end result be? In the end he will ask, "What is the meaning of my being here?" Then, except for suicide, there will be no other solution. So for this question of yours, the final answer is suicide!

12
Facing the Ego

If a few people can give me some idea of what points they want to discuss, then I can say a few things.

Osho,
One of our ideas is that with all the economic problems we are facing here, we could request friends from all the places around the country where you have been speaking to donate whatever small amount they can manage to help the Mumbai center.
I would like to suggest that all our friends and well-wishers pay an annual membership fee, a fixed amount. This will help a lot toward improving our economic situation. We can even keep the fees at eleven rupees annually, which is not a big amount in my view. All of our members, our well-wishers, who feel that we are working toward some good, can pay a fixed amount which is collected annually, so that the organization can keep going.
The way our organization has been working up to now is that there is a trust with trustees, and those trustees nominate a managing committee which runs everything. But until now there is no constitution as such. This means that it has not yet been decided

which committee members do which work, and how the work is to be distributed among them.

I think that another committee should be created and that all the finances of the managing committee should be handed over to it. Then the life members and other supporters should make a constitution together and the work will be able to proceed accordingly. There should be some kind of elections. The committee should not function simply by nomination. The life members should elect the committee and whoever wants to work should come forward.

Also, if there could be some arrangement where we could get time to meet you once a week, it would be very good.

There are three or four things.

Firstly, it is fine to make some arrangements for those who want to come and see me. It can be done in two ways. The easiest way is for you to decide on a day of the week. I will come and sit outside for two hours on that day, and anybody who wants to come and meet me or sit with me, can. That will mean there is no need to make an appointment. Just decide on a day. On that day anyone who wants to come and meet me, can, and anyone who wants to just sit with me can do so. There will be no need to get anyone's permission.

Secondly, make a list of people who do some work, or contribute in any way. You can give a copy of this list to Laxmi, marking the names of the people who should be able to see me under any circumstances. You can categorize them one, two, and three, so it is easier for her. Otherwise there will be a problem. If twenty appointments have already been made for a certain day, and then one of these people of yours calls, naturally there will be no slot free for him to meet me. He is bound to be hurt. He will not be concerned with those other twenty people, he will not be concerned with our time, he will not be concerned if I am sick, he will not be concerned with anything – and his situation is also understandable. In six months, he is asking to see me only once and he cannot!

So keep a list here. The reason people get upset is that even if they are doing a small job, in their minds they expect some reward for it. If they are running meditations in their houses, they want compensation even for that. Those meditations are not happening there out of their joy.

You have only been facing one difficulty so far in finding workers, and in a way it will always be there. I tell you constantly to drop your egos. But egos are not dropped. And listening to me, you feel that you don't need to take anyone's ego into account. But you will have to take notice of people's egos if you don't want to have the problems that you are facing now.

Hearing me, it appeals to you not to take any notice of the ego. But if someone has given you one thousand rupees, you will have to fulfill his ego to the same extent. If you don't, he will create trouble! It is not so much a question of meeting or seeing me; he will express it in some other way. He will ask for a seat at the front, or to go in first when he comes to see me, or to be able to see me whenever he wants.

If you run things only paying attention to what I say, these troubles will go on multiplying for you. Arrange things bearing the people in mind, not just paying attention to what I am saying. Be aware that if you have received something from somebody, or you have asked someone for help in any way – if you are using people in any way – you will have to make arrangements to fulfill their egos.

I cannot help you directly to fulfill anyone's ego, because it is not possible for me to support the disease I am putting my whole energy into fighting against. So it is your thing. You will have to take care of that. Arrange to take care of the people who are getting offended. Arrange to take care of those who are helping you. Prepare a priority list. Take care of all of this – it is your area. Don't involve me in any of it, not even by mistake.

This is what people desire, what they are interested in. Wherever something happens around your so-called saints and monks, everything is taken care of for such people, and then they are satisfied. If there are twenty of you sitting here, and one of you has given some help, then I am expected to say, "Desai-ji, come here and sit in the front!" That I will never do. And you mustn't do it either – it creates trouble! I will never say that. On the contrary, if Desai-ji tries to come to the front, I will stop him and tell him to stay at the back: "You have come late, so sit in the back!"

But you should take a little care, otherwise you will have problems all the time, because when you ask someone to do something for you, don't think he is giving you money or helping you in some way because he loves your work. And it is not that he *doesn't* love your work – but that is always secondary. First, is his ego. If you place his ego second, you will create trouble. Then he will look for many ways to create trouble.

So at the root is only this: if you have to go on receiving help from people, you should pay attention to taking care of all their needs. I don't say that you *should* go on asking for help. I also don't say that it is essential for *you* to manage this work – I don't say that either. But if you want to run it, then you will have to take care that people's egos get some satisfaction. If you are having a meeting, send them special passes. If you are having a get-together, send them a special invitation. When you publish a new book, send them a special copy. When they come here to see me, give them special priority. Whatever else is happening, make it special for them. Then all these kinds of problems will disappear.

And there are not so many people who complain like this. But if four people start complaining, soon it begins to feel as if it is coming from forty people, because they tell it to one person, then to another, and then to another... they just go on spreading it.

Here, whenever someone wants to see me, an appointment is given after checking with me first. But if you always have to ask me, you will get into trouble, because I know that even though this person has given ten thousand rupees to you, he is useless – that he just will waste half an hour of my time. So I will certainly refuse to see him! No, just don't ask me! Take care of all of this yourselves. Whosoever you want me to meet, just allow them to do so. Whosoever you don't want me to meet, don't allow them. Don't ask for my advice about it – because right now you are checking with me first, and you are getting into difficulties.

It is not Laxmi's fault or anybody else's. Laxmi comes and informs me, "This man is asking for this much time to meet you. Shall we give it to him or not?" I tell her not to give that much time; five minutes will be enough. But he is not satisfied with five minutes, even though there is nothing about him that is worth even those five minutes. He has nothing to ask and he isn't interested in doing anything about himself.

The problems are arising because right now you are asking me. Stop asking me! Take that responsibility for yourselves. If Laxmi asks you instead of me, then you will have no trouble. Then you will be able to arrange everything: who should see me, who should not see me.

And things *are* like this. Someone who hasn't done something to help you is not the one who will go around complaining. If someone like that couldn't meet me, you wouldn't be bothered, even if it might have been really necessary for that person to see me. But if an unnecessary person who has done something for you cannot meet me, you will be disturbed.

If you run these things by asking me, the trouble will continue. You should manage this whole business by yourselves. Then there will be no trouble at all, because the people who could have harassed you will be getting the chance to meet me, and those poor fellows who can't do anything for you won't even come back to complain. They don't have enough status to complain – and anyway you would not value their complaints.

You don't value complaints; you value the person behind the complaint: "Who is the person? He has done such and such a favor; how can I go back to him again? He has given ten thousand rupees, now how can I go back to him again?" Or you worry that when you do go back again to ask, he will put a whole list of complaints in front of you. But someone who has not given a rupee – who doesn't have a rupee to give – is not going to complain, nor will you value his complaints. He won't come to you and you won't go to him.

So this is the whole cause behind all these troubles. Arrange all this on your own; don't leave it up to me. If you leave it up to me, there will be problems, because I will see that this person has already met me ten times. I am asking him to meditate, but he is not willing. He is again calling to say that he wants to meet me, for the eleventh time. I am going to refuse. I cannot take into account what he has or hasn't done for you.

So this is not a complex matter at all, but if you keep me involved in any way, you will have trouble. And it is just three or four people who keep this whole thing going round and around. If you want to leave it up to me, then you should have the courage to tell them that the appointment is being checked with me. And then if anybody is responsible for the "no," it is me. You should tell them, "What you are doing for us is not a reason for meeting Osho. Whether you meet him or not depends on him."

If I feel it is necessary to see that person, I will see him immediately. If I feel it is unnecessary, just a formality... And for most of the people coming to see me it *is* just a formality, not necessary at all, but just something they "ought to" do. If you give them complete freedom and don't stop them, there will be no complaints, but then they will be wasting my time. And that is more harmful to you.

It was like that in Jabalpur. There was no hindrance whatsoever, so I would be seeing people from morning till night. If someone came and sat with me for three hours, I was tied up for all that time. Then it became a habit for people. They wanted to come every day, regularly. So their times became fixed: "At five o'clock so-and-so is coming…" and without fail they would come and sit with me every day at that time. And even those who came every day felt hurt if you stopped them.

Don't leave it up to me at all. Create your own system and make a list of all your acquaintances. Allow those you want to meet me, to meet me, and don't allow those you don't want to meet me, to meet me. Or if you want all of them to meet me, let them all meet me. Don't worry about it. It is not such a big problem. But you should not have to face difficulties and inconvenience.

Osho,
What about setting aside one and a half hours each day to see all of these people?

No, you don't understand what I am saying, you do not understand at all. You have no idea. You will find the same people sitting here every day during that one-and-a-half-hour session. They will certainly waste my time – and it will be the same people every day.

Osho,
Yes, that's right. It happens that way; I have seen it happening.

It will be the same people sitting every day for one and a half hours. I have no problem with that, I can put aside those one and a half hours, but it will serve no purpose. And if you think that the people coming will be those who complain, you are mistaken. Those who complain will want special appointments – personal and in private. I warn you that this one-and-a-half-hour session will be attended by those poor souls who have never complained to you.

I am saying this from my experience. The people who come in these one and a half hours will be those who never complain, who are happy just listening to me in the discourse meetings. And the demands of those who have been complaining for a special, private time will continue, because the reason for their complaints has nothing to do with meeting me. They already listen to me in the discourse meetings and in the meditation camps. No, it is because they want a separate individual meeting, and that won't be the case during that one-and-a-half-hour session.

It already happens. In the meditation camps we keep a time at noon for people to meet me, but instead, I end up meeting people all day, because those special people, as you call them, say, "That one and a half hours is for everyone. Keep at least ten minutes separate for us." They don't want to be with all those other people.

But it is very interesting: Who are "all those other people"? That one and a half hours of my time is gone anyway, and those who wanted separate time, those complainers, want time in the morning.

Every day during the meditation camps I am talking up to eleven o'clock at night. You have no idea: I get back to the place where I am staying by half past ten, and they are already there, waiting for me! I arrive back from the morning discourse and they are already there. What begins at eight o'clock in the morning goes on until eleven in the night, without a pause. There are the three discourse and meditation meetings, the noon time for meeting me personally and then those who want a special time are also there...

So the difficulty is that the people you want to set this time aside for are not going to come. And you will take up that much of my time without solving anything. I have already tried it and seen that it doesn't solve anything. You don't understand the real issue. It is not about meeting me or seeing me. The real issue is that their egos need some satisfaction. So do something about that; nothing is going to be solved by letting them meet me in an open session.

Yes, if you can make a personal appointment for them to meet me, they will be satisfied. And don't worry that it is inconvenient for me. My time will be taken up in the same way as it is now. So you needn't worry that it will be inconvenient for me if you decide to do this. I won't be inconvenienced. The only difference will be that right now only those who need time get it, and in future those who don't need time will also get it. It makes no other difference. The time I spend will be the same. So there is nothing to be sad about; the time I spend is going to be the same.

It is impossible to imagine how difficult it is. I sit down to have my meal, and if you don't stop them, then ten to twenty people will come and I can't even eat. And if you prevent them, they will be hurt.

The doctor has said that nobody is allowed to sit here when I am eating. Himmat bhai had come and was sitting with me – and he always comes when I am having my meal because then he can talk about everything conveniently. These people, Jhaber and others, were bringing my meal in and saw Himmat bhai sitting there. So they took the meal back thinking to bring it after he had left. Now Himmat bhai goes around saying that I gestured not to bring the meal because he was there. And he keeps phoning everyone saying that he won't go to Woodlands again because he has been turned away. Nothing at all has been said to him. But these people certainly took the meal away, and this became very hurtful for him. Now what are we to do about all this? The problems are strange – even eating becomes difficult! When twenty people are sitting here, they are bound to start a conversation. If you come in and I don't say, "Welcome!" then it hurts. But even if I don't do more than saying "Welcome!" to twenty people while I am eating, it becomes difficult to eat.

So the hurts are not so much about seeing me and meeting me – because after all that is what I am doing, meeting people the whole day, with the demand increasing all the time. What I see is that if you let someone see me today, he says he wants an appointment once a week. If you let him see me once a week, he says he wants time every three days. And he is not at fault. He feels good, he finds it blissful. So how to take care of all this?

It was because of this that we devised a system in this country called darshan, where there is nothing to be said, you can only see the master. But be aware that you cannot get any help from a master by merely being in a public darshan; you can only *have* darshan. If I am to help you, I will have to give you time. And if I have to give you time, then we will have to make a choice about how to use it; people will have to be chosen and also the time will have to be divided. All that will have to be done. Otherwise we will just have a darshan: come, see, and leave!

That is what was happening with Ramana Maharshi. He was available for people all day long, there was no difficulty. But what help can he give? He is sitting, lying down on his wooden bed, and people are coming and having darshan from morning till evening. Even if he is sleeping, the darshan is still going on.

But my outlook is scientific and I think time must be made for those who need help, those for whom I have to work. But that time should not become a habit, something that you need every day. When you need it, then of course yes – then there is no question. I am also clear about who needs it. That is why I even send messages to call such and such a person to come and see me, because I am aware who is in need and what they need.

So, there are two things. If you leave it up to me, this trouble will continue to some extent. And the strictness you see in Laxmi is not her strictness. That is from me. Anybody who has to say no to you is bound to start looking like a bad person, and it is not so. We feel that such a person should speak lovingly, but even if the person speaks lovingly, the love won't be seen when they say no.

And the person who has to do that all day long also has a limit to their love. You don't feel that way because you are alone when seeing that person, but the person has the same work all day long – morning till evening – meeting this person, meeting that person. Somebody asks for an hour of time, somebody else asks for an hour and a half, somebody says he only wants half an hour. Now if that person has to say no… And somebody has come from Chennai, somebody else says, "I have come all the way from Kolkata and I want an hour's meeting." That person has to refuse from morning till evening. And the person who refuses is bound to look bad to the one who gets the no – no matter how sweetly it is given. And in any case that person's sweetness will disappear soon, because it is routine work.

I have tried giving this work to many different people. Raman bhai was doing it and people started feeling that he was harsh, that some soft, loving person was needed. So I gave the work to the person who used to complain, Anup. And then he became a harsh person to others. Now Anup complains about Laxmi. What to do? The work is like that!

It is not so much a question of the person; there are some kinds of work which mold the nature of a person. Work also has its nature. Now, someone who has the job of refusing and preventing people all day long *will* start looking harsh – and will become harsh. The whole structure of that work is such that it will do this to him. Yet still I am saying that whoever is doing this work has to be careful to do it with as much love as possible. But I know that it makes no difference to the complaints; the complaining will continue anyway.

So you should start telling everyone that it is not Laxmi's fault, it is nobody's fault – my decisions are being followed. For those whom I feel it is necessary, I immediately give time; for those whom I don't feel it is necessary, I don't give time. If I don't give time, you should understand that you don't need time and that anyway you are not following my suggestions.

So either gather that much courage, or else don't leave this up to me – just make your own arrangements. If someone can manage better than Laxmi, if someone feels they can manage more sweetly, let them do it – there is no problem. Keep one person just for this; their whole work will be giving or not giving appointments to people. And then you will have some idea: within two months you will see that complaints have started coming about that person.

The difficulty has to do with economics. What I mean by economics is that the time is limited and the people are many, hence the problem. The whole difficulty is economics. How many people can you manage to fit in to meet me in a day? As you go on increasing the publicity, the number of people eager to meet me will go on increasing – and I will remain one. The available time will be the same and the work will go on expanding, so the difficulty is bound to grow. If there were some fee, the problem would not get bigger. The more people that came, the more you would increase the fee, and then there would never be a problem for you. Understand this; otherwise you are not getting the point about the difficulties.

Two hundred people used to listen to me. Now twenty thousand people listen to me, but the time I have available is the same. So what do you want? Now these twenty thousand people want to meet me. My time has not grown a hundred times; it remains the same as it was before. So how will you make all this clear to these people?

There are only two ways. You can make the decision that our workers and the people who support us financially or some other way are the only people to meet me, and not others. Then that category will be satisfied. That is one way. The other way is to leave it up to me; I will meet with those I want to and I will not meet the ones I don't want to. This too will be a category. But I think my category will be meaningful. Your category cannot be meaningful.

Start putting it out in this way: that it is not a question that I will simply meet someone just because they want it.

Osho,
But people think if they do your work they should be able to meet you.

Our workers and friends still don't understand this. Whenever someone complains in the future... Publish this in our three or four papers, and inform all the friends that I will not necessarily meet someone just because they want to meet me.

Osho,
It depends on the wish of the master.

It depends on my wish. When I feel that an appointment is necessary for you – that it will not do for you to go without meeting me – that you need some kind of help – *then* I will meet you. So leave it up to me. Just give some intimation by telephone and leave it to me. The difficulty comes when people feel they want to meet me and somebody stops them. That is the problem. I receive letters where people say they want to meet me, and someone in the middle is preventing it. No one in the middle will be preventing it. Make this clear to them. This will reduce the problem.

The second thing you should remember is that when you approach friends for help, you should make it clear to them from the beginning that the help is unconditional. Remind them again after receiving the help from them that there are no conditions attached to it, that there are no obligations on your part: they are giving this out of their love. If the person says that he is not giving out of love, note it down. Tell the person that you want to keep a note of who is giving out of love, unconditionally, and who is giving with conditions – expecting that those conditions will be met afterward – so that you can fulfill them satisfactorily. So note down that you have taken ten thousand rupees from this person on the condition that whenever he wants to meet me, you will have to arrange it. And then fulfill that condition. If the help is unconditional, then note down that it is unconditional. Then the person won't be able to complain later on.

So make some arrangements like this, because it will go on growing. You have no idea how the number of people will keep increasing. The work will reach outside of India, people will come from far away. The work will reach in every nook and corner of India, people will come from here; so you will certainly have to make choices. Whether you choose to make them according to money, according to meditation or according to intelligence, you will need some criteria to decide which category of people should be allowed to meet me. Otherwise it will become impossible.

And I think there are only two ways to manage this. One is that you leave it to me and don't blame someone else in the middle. That person in the middle is only representing me; he is only passing my message on to you, he has no other role than that. Where is the trouble in that? The trouble arises when a complaint comes and you start wanting to take it onto your own shoulders and not let it fall on me. This is when the trouble starts. So let that blame fall on me; that will create less trouble for you in the long run. In a year or two it will become clear to people that this is how this man is: if he wants to meet you, he meets you, if he doesn't want to meet you, he doesn't meet you. The decision to meet me doesn't come from you, it comes from me.

With Gurdjieff, what to say of months? He would not meet people for years. It wasn't just that he would not meet them, he would give you a time, invite you to meet him, and then not show up. You may have traveled a thousand miles to see him because he had fixed the appointment, he had told you to see him at five o'clock on such and such a date and in such and such a place. You would be sitting there waiting at five o'clock and he would send a message that he couldn't come.

After a few years people understood that if you went to see him, you traveled all those miles at your own risk – it was not certain that he would meet you. And it was not just with individuals; he would arrange a public meeting, go to the meeting at the right time and announce that he would not speak that day. Soon the complaints stopped, people understood that if you wanted to listen to this man, you had to go with the understanding that he may or may not turn up; he may or may not speak.

So the trouble at the moment is that in order to protect me, you take the blame onto yourselves. You might say, "Taru may have made a mistake; Desai-ji may have made a mistake. Osho is very loving; someone in the middle must have been the problem." Never say that. Say that Osho is such a man – wrong or right however it may be. He meets whomsoever he wants to; he doesn't meet those he doesn't want to. And whoever you take help from, make the issue of conditions clear. Ask them to tell you if they have any conditions so that you can remember them and avoid any complaints. If their help is unconditional, tell them you will remember that they won't be complaining. That is the first thing.

The second thing is regarding management. Two or three points about this should be understood.

Firstly I am not so much in favor of elections or of too much of a constitution. I don't believe that any work can be done through elections. Yes, elections can happen and they might appear to be important work, because elections are no small thing. But the work will suffer. Yes, it will be fun, and it will generate interest among the workers. The possibility to get ahead or behind, up or down will be created, but that will not get the work done. I don't believe that it will get the work done. In this world, if you want to get the least possible work done, then have a system based on elections, because an election itself is such a big job that nothing else gets done.

So I don't believe in elections. If the work is going to be done, I believe in direct nomination from the top. Yes, if you want to satisfy people, if you want to satisfy everyone, then elections are the way. But this work is an altogether different matter. If you are trying to satisfy everyone, then it's okay. You have a thousand members, you go for elections, everybody will feel juiced up, and everyone will come to the meetings because there will be opportunities for defeating others, for winning, for forming parties and groups. But it won't get any work done! As far as doing the work is concerned, then this won't help and it will just brings politics into your inner world. So I am not at all in favor of elections. I would not like to put you into that situation. I am in favor of direct nomination. I would not like to put you into that complex situation called an election.

Neither do I see any sense in constitutions or such things. These things are good where there is no work to be done. If you do not want to do any work, but to appear to be working, then there are the Lions' Clubs, the Rotary Clubs. No work is needed to be done there, but there are chairmen, and deputy chairmen, and presidents, and vice-presidents – and it just goes on and on... Everyone is engaged in "great work" but no work is being done. What has work got to do with it? So I have no interest at all in that kind of thing.

This much I know: make a constitution, make a system and take care that the work can happen in an orderly way, but don't even think of having elections. Forget about it! Don't even accidentally consider it.

Secondly: certainly do something about distributing the work. We all say there should be a system of distribution, but distributing to whom? Whosoever is interested in doing some work should come forward and offer. Rather than elections, people should come forward and offer themselves. If Anand bhai feels he can do this work better than Ishwar bhai, then he should offer himself to the committee. Then I think that work should be passed on to him; the committee should give it to him for six months: "Okay, for six months show that you can do it better. If you can do it better, we will happily let you keep the work, because after all, Ishwar babu is also only doing it so that it can be done as well as possible."

I believe that making an offer is much more worthy and intelligent than an election. An election is a very paradoxical thing. You make efforts to get elected and yet at the same time you try to show that you have no interest whatsoever in position and all that; that it is all just for the sake of the work! An offer is just the opposite. You are not canvassing anybody; you are simply offering to do this work better than such and such a person. You are offering the fact that you have more capacity for that work, more knowledge about it, more time for it, so the committee should give it to you for six months on a trial basis. The committee should appoint you for six months as an experiment, and if you do the work better, then they should let you keep it. If you don't, then you should give the work back.

So try to extend offers. This, I feel, is a more worthy and religious way, and more humble, although it looks the opposite. It looks the opposite if someone stands up and says he can do this work better than Lehroo, but for me it is actually being more humble if a person is so straightforward and authentic.

What is happening at the moment is just the opposite. You don't say you can do it better, you say that Babu bhai is not doing it right. What you really want to say is that you are more intelligent, more worthy; that you can do it better than he can. But instead you say, "Babu bhai is not doing it properly." This solves nothing. Nothing! It is more honest to say you can do the work better, so it should be given to you to try. That way you don't have to slander others. And also, you will have to think twice about whether you really can do it better. Just to say someone is not doing it right doesn't require any thinking. What is the problem in saying that so-and-so is not doing it right? But before saying you can do it better you will have to think a thousand times and take a very considered step.

So if you are to bring an end to this daily worrying about each other in this committee, the only way is for you to make an offer, and to prove yourself by doing the work out of your own joy. You will make a commitment for six months, and you will show what you can do by doing it. There is no problem: let the work be divided; let the work be distributed to those who offer.

And remember one more thing: whenever someone does any work, there are two aspects to it. One is the difficulties inherent in the work – and these never occur to us. The other is the mistakes in the work – and these we *do* take note of! We also don't take note of the results. So whenever you are thinking about asking to take on someone else's work, you will realize that it is better to think about all the aspects of the job first. It is better to think about all of the difficulties: how you are going to organize it, what the results are at present, how much the person who is currently responsible for it is actually doing... Then, only after understanding the whole thing will you be able to make an offer, otherwise not.

So, simply let go of all these things within you. Always come with the offer of wanting to do some work. Then you should get that work. And I am ready for things to be that way; there is no need for elections. When a person is saying that he can do some work, what more evidence do you need that he will do it right? Can the votes of twenty-five people prove that you are capable? Do you need to explain to twenty-five people that you are a worthy person? Why? Just stand up and say, "These are my qualifications and I want to do this job." Then you should be given a part of the job, or any other job, on a trial basis.

So certainly there should be division of work – but among whom? Start offering yourself for it. It will be a new experiment – and it will be very valuable. And I believe that elections are not good between friends. Elections create enmity, they destroy friendship. To offer yourself is good; you are being direct, and also courageous. And it brings the responsibility back to you, because afterward the committee can ask you how many of the problems that you used to complain about have been eliminated in the past six months, and what you have managed to do. So certainly divide the work in this way.

But I also think that if one person is doing some work, as far as possible don't divide it. There is plenty of new work that can be started, there is no shortage of work. For instance, at the moment Ishwar babu is looking after all of the publications. Lashkari-ji has said that he has experience in publishing, and he has his own press, so he has offered to look after it. But I think we should start a separate publishing division with Lashkari-ji called Neo-Sannyas International Publications, and we should entrust him with that. There are so many books waiting to be published that even if you start ten separate divisions, you would not manage it all. Let Ishwar babu look after what he is already looking after, and we will give Lashkari-ji another job: to start Neo-Sannyas International Publications.

So these are two things to be aware of; otherwise someone makes an offer, the previous person is taken off the job and if the new person is unable to manage it, soon everything will be in a mess. And who knows whether the person you took off the job for six months wants to take it back? That will depend on his thinking. We have so many new jobs. The necessity to divide a job should arise only if we don't have enough new jobs. But the jobs are many, so start a new publication.

Recently some people have been thinking of starting a new English magazine, *Sannyas*. Create a new committee for it; why go on putting everything on Ishwar babu's shoulders? The funny thing is that we talk about dividing the work, and at the same time we go on putting everything onto him. We go on piling everything onto the same three or four poor people who do all the work. If you want to start *Sannyas* magazine, create a new committee for it!

We have to build a permanent campus at Saputara, so create a new committee for that. Let the new committee take complete care of it. It should have nothing to do with the old committee. Four different people can do it, and it can be left with them.

I would like us to build a small campus of our own in Mumbai very soon. It should be outside the city, so that at least on the weekends you can be with me for two days. Form a separate committee to organize this. It has nothing to do with anything else, so nominate separate trustees for it from among yourselves. Find the secretaries and everything else, but appoint them – there is no question of having elections for this either. Create a committee for a permanent campus in Mumbai and hand that work over to it.

People say that there is no proper accounting system. If they can show examples of proper accounting in their committee, we can ask Ishwar babu to leave the accounting to those people, because then they will be able to manage it very well.

New dimensions of the work are to be found – and there is plenty of work to be done, there is no shortage of work. Gradually you can separate the publication work into different languages. For example, publishing in Marathi is stuck. Make a separate committee for it. Let them raise their own funds and be responsible for it. Ishwar babu will not be involved with this committee; it will raise and manage its own funds. After all, in the end all the funds are doing the same work. So it is okay to do things separately. Separate the Marathi publishing, then gradually separate the Gujarati, the Hindi, and the English publishing. Gradually divide them.

So this is the whole difficulty so far, that no one comes forward to take on some work. And I believe it is you yourselves who are spreading the complaints about the accounting and other things, because who else would say that your accounts are not correct? And it is incredible to think that someone says this to you, and you just listen quietly and agree that the accounts are not right. If the accounts are not correct, then Ishwar babu alone is not responsible; you are also responsible. If you had replied convincingly that the accounts were perfectly fine, then the other person would have been silenced. But you say, "Yes. This is correct; the accounts are not right."

And what is not correct in the accounts? And why don't you do something to systematize them? What is the big deal? There is no big deal. The person who tells you that the accounts are no good just says so because he doesn't want to give you what you are asking for. And you agree with him because then you don't have to admit back here that you have been unable to bring any money: "What to do? The accounts were not right." And so the matter is over. He gets his solution, he has been spared from having to give you money, and you have been spared the responsibility of having to bring some money in.

I have been hearing that the accounts are not right for the last two to three years – and not just two or three years, it has been the same talk for ten years. So there seems no reason why the problem can't be solved. There is nothing to prevent this happening. The only hindrance is that you have a shortage of funds.

If you keep the accounts perfectly, you will get no work done at all. The work is such that if you hand over the accounts to a totally organized, systematic person – Vasan-ji bhai is very systematic with accounts – if you hand them over to him, it will become difficult for you to work, because in the work there will always be some disorder, and if Vasan-ji bhai has to maintain order, then the work will stop. If you do not have a rupee in the bank, and Ishwar babu is sending books worth forty thousand rupees for printing, Vasan-ji bhai will have to stop it because there is no money. Where will these forty thousand rupees come from? Ishwar babu is buying paper from someone promising payment in a month, and then he goes on tossing it around for three months. He is getting things printed and tossing the payments around for four months. He takes from this man and gives to that man; takes from that man and gives to this man – so the accounting cannot be perfect.

If you want correct accounts, you will have to raise more funds. Otherwise you will never be able to balance them. You should have enough funds to do everything properly, so that if you have to pay ten thousand rupees to someone, you are able to pay it on time. Right now you don't have that ten thousand. So there are two possibilities: either the work continues regardless of the accounts, or you have to stop the work and keep the accounts correctly. If you have no money in the bank, the orderly person will ask, "Why are you writing that check?"

Ishwar babu keeps writing checks and they keep bouncing. The checks should not be written because there is no money in the bank. But he says that it will be fifteen days before the check is returned, and by that time we will have managed something. This is wrong – even I know this is wrong – and the person who returns it will also be puzzled, "What is the matter? He says that the payment will be made on time, but the money just doesn't come." If you want to pay this man on time and don't have the money, then you won't be able to do any work if you function systematically.

If you say that the work will be done only when the money is there, then it will never be done. Now what Ishwar babu has done is a total hodgepodge, but it is because there is no other way for him to manage. So we all criticize him, saying that these accounts need to be regularized, but he also doesn't say with total courage and conviction that this is not possible. He also agrees that it needs to be done, because our common belief system places a high value on the accounts being correct. Everyone thinks that accounts should always be correct; it is absolutely the right thing. No one ever says that it is not necessarily the right thing in every situation.

To have correct accounting is actually a big luxury. If you have more money than you need, then the accounts can be correct. If your need is more than the money you have, then your accounts can never be right – there will always be small mistakes.

Right now you have no money whatsoever, and the work is extensive. Ishwar babu has no money at all, but he says we sold literature worth two hundred thousand rupees this year. So how is that literature produced if there is no money whatsoever? He prints one book, sells it, and using that money starts printing another. Sometimes he puts money earned from the meetings into the books, sometimes money from the camps. You say everything should be systematic – money from the books should go to books, money from the camps should go to the camps, and money from the meetings into the meetings. That can be done, but then neither the meetings nor the camps will happen, nor will the books get printed!

So the whole problem is that you have limited funds. And the work is growing by the day. At present there are about one hundred books, and this is nothing. Right now there are five thousand hours of recordings with Lehroo – perhaps they will never get published because I will go on speaking every day, and while you are busy publishing those talks you will not be able to publish those fifty thousand pages from before.

If you want to regularize the accounts, raise funds! But to avoid raising funds, you gossip that the accounts are not correct. They will never be. I warn you that in this work your funds will never be more than you need. It will never happen that your funds will be more than your work. Never be under that illusion. No matter how much money you collect, it will never be enough.

So understanding this situation, you should always defend the person who is doing the work. But instead of defending him you spread the idea that yes, the accounts are not so correct. I simply cannot accept this, because how can anybody know that the accounts are not correct? It is not that he never presents the accounts – they are presented at the end of every year. Everything gets audited; otherwise your trust cannot function. Put the audit report in the hands of everyone who says the accounts are not right. And if you really want to keep the accounts accurate to the last paisa, then raise enough funds so that this can be done. The day you raise the funds to a sufficient level, I will relieve Ishwar babu of the job completely and hand over the whole work to you. But if I hand it over to you now, all the work will stop – this I know. But of course, your accounts will be very correct!

So, for me the work is more important than the accounts. And to you, it seems the accounts are more important. What is so important about accounts and things like that? Whether they are right or not – what really great thing is going to come out of all this? In the end, accounts in themselves have no value. The real question is the work: how can the work grow?

What surprises me about all this talk I am hearing from you is that it is all negative, not positive. Don't worry too much about what mistakes are being made. The greater the work is, the greater the mistakes.

The most maligned person in America isn't a thief or a hooligan, it is the president. Nixon will receive more insults than a murderer. If anyone is going to be the most disgraced, it will be the president, not a hooligan. Who bothers about a hooligan, who bothers to disgrace him? The reason is that whoever does the job gets all the problems. The problems are already there; they don't belong to him, they are all around. It is not Nixon who created the Vietnam problem. The Vietnam problem was already there, and now Nixon is caught in it. No matter what he does, he is trapped, because the world is divided. If he does one thing, some people will be against him; if he does the other then the others will be against him.

No one should ever be under the illusion that he will be spared criticism. If you work, there will be criticism. The only way to avoid criticism is never to do anything. Then no one can criticize you. So, never live in the hope that no one will criticize you. It simply means you are a useless person, that's all. In other words, no one is able to find anything in you worth criticizing; there is nothing to latch onto. You are not doing anything so no mistake can happen, nothing can go wrong.

Put more awareness into the positive; and look for new dimensions in the work.

There is one more basic psychological reason behind criticism. When one or two people do the work, the others feel frustrated – they have no work. There is a natural desire to work; it is natural, and it is good. Now it's okay if Ishwar babu is doing all the work, but then what is Anand bhai supposed to do; what is Babu bhai supposed to do? Then they are left only with criticism – which is also a kind of work! What else do they have to do? So there should be work for them too. If they are to be spared from criticizing, spared of meaningless work, then there has to be some meaningful work for them. Everybody has creative energy, and if it is not used it will be wasted. So expand the work into new areas.

Make a committee, a separate committee in Mumbai, which will not be the responsibility of this working group. Make it from among yourselves, or bring in new friends from outside, but make a committee that works to create a permanent campus outside Mumbai so that one to two hundred people can come and be with me for two days regularly at weekends. Then this desire of yours to meet with me will subside, this problem will be solved, and you will be able to move more into meditation.

Create a committee, and whoever wants to can offer to join it. And that committee should take all the responsibility;

this present committee will have nothing to do with it, and that committee will have nothing to do with this fund – it will have to raise new funds, it will have to make a new trust, it will have to take care of the new issues, and it will have to take care of all its own arrangements. Whatever shortcomings may have been noticed about this committee, they have to show that they won't happen there.

Saputara campus is being created. Recently they talked of it costing one hundred thousand rupees, and a promise has also been received for one hundred thousand rupees, so I have asked Jayanti bhai to look after it. Let Jayanti bhai be on the committee, let Lashkari-ji be there. Mridula Abhyankar has also offered, so those three can be on it. They can include three to four other people whom they would like to work with, or people who offer can join them.

Let them create a campus – a campus outside Mumbai that can be used at weekends. Many friends from all around have started coming, so you will need at least some kind of a guesthouse – maybe where people pay – but at least make arrangements for those coming from outside. Ten to twenty people will be able to stay there, maybe permanently, but later on they will be very useful to you. So one guesthouse will have to be built for about ten to fifteen or sixteen people to stay in. Everyone should be able to stay there, and they can have their meals somewhere else. They can pay for their stay. Create a separate committee to arrange all of this.

With the publishing, separate the publications of Neo-Sannyas International. Start a new Neo-Sannyas International publishing team, and a separate committee to take care of its funding and management. The Life Awakening Center will sell its publications, and it will get commission for doing so. And if Neo-Sannyas International sells something for the center, it will get commission from the center. If you like, the center can take on the whole of the Neo-Sannyas International Publications sales, but make your own arrangements for publishing and management and funds. Make proper accounts for all of it – show how it can work.

Create a separate committee to take care of all the expenditures here at Woodlands. Why go on putting all of this onto one person? Make a separate committee for this and let those people take care of it. And in two, four and six months all the committees can meet and discuss everything together to see who is doing what, and whether you can give any support to each other.

Divide the existing work later on. Right now, start with the new work. For example, delegate responsibility for what is published in Marathi; create a separate committee for it. Publishing in English is still new. Separate it; there is no problem in doing that. Slowly separate all the languages.

There are so many jobs. For example, I think you should start selling audiotapes. But leave that to Ishwar babu, and what will the result be? There is so much work put onto one man's shoulders that I sometimes wonder how he manages everything! Yes, there is a little problem: he notes things down somewhere in his diary and it is all a hodgepodge, and he goes on doing everything. There are dozens of other matters in his diary. He takes care of the correspondence too; he is attending to correspondence until late – one o'clock in the night – until Guna really tells him off! So there are bound to be problems, and it is a shame, because there is so much loaded onto one head, and nothing but criticism comes his way.

Make separate arrangements for audiotapes, make a separate committee for it, because gradually audiotapes are going to start selling as much as your books. There should be a separate department that produces only tapes – that makes them professionally and sells them. They should be produced in advance. If a blank cassette is available for fifty rupees in the market, then sell it for sixty rupees – ten rupees will pay for the cost of recording and all other management expenses. But the tapes should be prepared in advance, and sold in the same shop as our books are being sold. Make full sets of all the discourse series, because if I travel around less – and I am going to go out less – then your tape sales will increase rapidly.

In so many places people are listening to me on tape machines. It is amazing. Recently I heard that in Amritsar every Sunday three to three hundred and fifty people regularly gather and listen to my tapes. Didn't five hundred or six hundred people come every day recently to listen to the series of talks on Mahavir Vani in a packed hall? So everyone will start listening to them.

Have a separate department which will be solely responsible for the tapes. They should make recordings. Now there are long-playing records, which can take around forty minutes of a talk. Those who cannot purchase tapes can buy a gramophone for one hundred and fifty rupees in any village. Long-playing records should be produced; there should be separate arrangements for that. All this work should be divided up.

Now that there are sannyasins, they should be allotted certain work that they are the best people to do. If we distribute all this work, it will reach hundreds of thousands of people. And in this way, we have also used the capacity of the people who want to work. We can think about this later in more detail.

Now, here, we have a gathering of friends: how can the work they do in their own professions benefit our work? Think about it, because my understanding is that if the work is to be big, to expand, it should have some permanent resources. Any work that depends on day-to-day requests does not last for long. Now all these people are so intelligent, are good at thinking rationally, have businesses, professions, their own industries, so think about the work from that angle. If you want, you can take a loan from the government and start a small-scale industry. There are sannyasins who will be able to take care of the whole work in return for food and clothing. This can become a permanent source of income for you of from ten to twenty-five thousand rupees a month. If there is some work related to exporting, think of that. If it is not possible from Mumbai, get that work done in some rural place outside and send twenty sannyasins there.

You should acquire some permanent resources.

The financial potential of the books is so great that if you can make full use of it you will not need to ask for anything from anybody. You will never need to ask for anything from anybody. It will not be difficult to keep a register of five thousand customers in India, and as soon as a new book is published a copy can be immediately sent to them from the press, cash on delivery. It is not difficult to have five thousand such people. It really is no problem; it's only a question of choosing five thousand such customers from all over the country whose names can be registered with us. As soon as the book is published it can go to them, straight from the press, cash on delivery. And they will be very happy, because people keep writing that they cannot get the books easily. They ask for them, but it all takes months. They will be very happy to get new books directly from the press as soon as they are published.

Don't print less than ten thousand copies of any book. Five thousand copies should go directly from the press to your listed customers. Then all your expenses will be covered, and you can sell the remaining five thousand copies easily, without a problem.

You are pricing your books at four times the production costs. If you spend five thousand rupees on printing, then even after giving forty percent commission and deducting all the expenses, you should still make five thousand rupees. If you print twenty books a year, you will easily make one hundred thousand rupees. There is no question about it. And those twenty books are to be gradually printed in all the languages.

And Babu bhai: treat the publishing very professionally. Spend money on advertising them properly – in the same way as you do for any of your private products.

You don't realize that in India, even if you print three thousand copies of a book, you cannot sell all of them even in five years – even the largest publishers can't manage that. And you are selling three thousand copies in two months – and everything is disorganized! I have talked to the largest publishers and they say it is very difficult – it is an achievement – to sell even three thousand copies of an edition in five years. Who reads in India? But you are able to sell out in two months. A book comes from the press, and within a month you have to start telling people that it has sold out. Five to seven of your books are always out of print and customers are writing to you every day wanting them.

You should make everything professional, as any publisher does. It should be organized completely professionally. If you organize the publishing professionally, you can earn half a million rupees annually from the books.

Then advertise them properly, spend money on advertising them, because the whole system today… You should think about the books in exactly the same way as you think and act in your own business. If you spend five thousand rupees printing a book, you should spend a thousand rupees advertising it. And the advertisements should be all over the country. There is no reason why you shouldn't sell one million rupees-worth of books every year very easily. There is simply no reason.

Soon the books will be published in foreign languages – and you don't realize that books published in India can bring in the most money from sales in the West. In the West it is very difficult to find a book costing less than forty or fifty rupees: if it has two to two hundred and fifty pages, the price will be equivalent to forty or fifty rupees. You can print it much more cheaply here because the labor charges are negligible. And once you have found a market for the books in the West, you won't need to bother about what people say to you here. You won't need to go around asking them for anything, and even if they want to give you something, you can decide whether you want to take it or not.

There will be no difficulty at all in finding a market for the books in the West, because the books there are all rotten and worthless. Books that are being published under the name *religion* over there have no value, no meaning.

So organize the work and distribute it to different committees. For instance, this involves foreign countries, so make a committee to arrange and look after all the publishing for outside India. Why impose all of this on Ishwar babu? That committee will make the contacts, write to the publishers – and now we have our sannyasins out there, they will be helpful to you. Print the books here and sell them in the West. A book produced here for five rupees sells for fifty rupees in the West. And I think also, that once you are well organized, we can even print and sell some books that are not mine but which I think will be useful to seekers in the West. That also will be quite useful for you. Tapes can also sell very easily in the West. There is simply no difficulty with this.

So create a new committee for this. Create a new committee for the work outside India that will only take care of that work, and which will take care of all the reading, writing, and correspondence – everything connected with that. Offer yourselves for this work; call a meeting of all the friends and invite offers. See who wants to take on what work. Then they can take it and look after it.

If someone shows how good they are in some new work, then I can ask Ishwar babu to hand over some of the old work to such and such a person. In this way there will be no problem for anyone about handing over work in the future. But right now there is a problem: whom to hand it over to? Will the person we hand it over to be able to handle it or not? As far as I can see, someone who really wants to do something gets involved very quickly. So choose something to do and get involved with it.

Then there are the meditation camps. Keep a separate committee for them. Then there will be no need for you to discuss the camps; the committee will look after them – where a camp will happen and everything else along those lines. And because I will be staying here longer now, more and more camps should be organized near Mumbai. My idea is that in the future we should have three or four camps with both the dates and the places permanently fixed every year. Then people will know that on those days the camp is happening. And even if people arrive without advance information, there will be no problem. Create a separate committee to organize this.

As of now, you have to organize four to six different series of my talks. Make a separate committee for this, and then don't interfere with it anymore.

And every committee has to take care of its own funds. The problems start when you want to take on a project, and you want the funds to be given to you as well. Then you make problems for others and for yourselves also – and that is why that work is not being given out to others. The difficulty, as I see it, is that you all ask Ishwar babu to share the work, and his problem is not that there is any difficulty in dividing up the work, but that right after asking for some work you immediately ask for the funds to pay for it. And the funds are not there. You can't divide the funds, so the work also doesn't get divided, and then the work gets stuck.

For example, you are asked to take over the Marathi publications, so you ask for some funds to do the work. But he doesn't have any funds; from where can he give them to you? So that project gets stuck and stops there.

Take the work, but don't talk about funds. Start arranging your own funds. And when you go to people, tell them that now you are taking care of this part of the work, and if they can help with the funding you will give them complete accounts: "I am taking money from you with the guarantee that you will have complete accounts with no errors." And I also believe you will be able to say it quite confidently when the work is in *your* hands. When the work is not in your hands – when the accounts are kept by one person, the work is done by another, and you are the one who goes to collect that money – then how are you supposed to reply? You will have no idea about anything.

So do things in this way. I don't see any big difficulties there. And problems are quite natural in work that is growing. This work will grow to be so vast that in two years' time it will be beyond your imagination. So don't get bogged down in small, trivial matters, get busy with helping the work to expand. I do not see that there is any real difficulty, that there is some complexity anywhere, or some problem.

So think along these lines a little.

Enough!

13
Beyond Office Politics

We must remember that when we create an organization, the organization itself should be unique and revolutionary – because the organization is being created with the sole purpose of spreading the vision, and one of the essential aspects of spreading it will be that our organization is in harmony with that vision. If this organization becomes just like any other organization, any other institution – if the same kind of politics, the same kind of disagreements, the same kind of envies and jealousies also run through it; if the same sicknesses, the same influences are here too – then the radical revolution we wish to bring about will falter at its very first step.

So first we have to develop the feeling that this is a circle of friends. And if we can establish that first, then whoever joins in later will become a part of that way of doing things. The system we have had so far has been faulty; hence the wish to remove it. If we can manage to create it properly, then the vision, the work, will remain alive. Individuals will come and go – one person will leave, another will join us – but when a new person joins ten workers who have already been here for some time, he will become a part of what already exists, and the vision will continue.

So it has to be created after some good preparatory thinking. And the constitution has to be written in such a way that it is not very complex, so that no one creates problems because of those complexities and as a result has everyone hustling and bustling around him. The reason being that then it will be difficult to take his job away from him, and it will also be difficult for him get along with others. So all this has to be kept in mind.

Secondly, the system has to be such that not much importance is attached to someone's position. The positions are functional – there is no great honor in having a position, nor any value. We have to establish this as a clear convention: that there is no value in a position. Otherwise if someone becomes a secretary, who knows what he may think he has become! The system has to be such that to hold such a post is not something special. It is just that many friends are doing the work, and for convenience's sake we give one of them that title. Our attitude, our behavior, our system has to be such that "position" does not gain any sort of status. This has to be kept in mind.

We have to lay the foundation so that all office holders, all the friends, everyone doing the work, are able to work as one team, in one harmony. A thorough foundation has to be put in place. There should be no question of leadership. No one should have the idea that he has some personal responsibility, that he has to personally achieve some target by himself. He is doing it for everyone. Even if he is a representative somewhere, he is a representative on behalf of everyone. And we don't have to give anyone personal glory for something they have done. Whatever has been done, has been done by the center. We have to break the habit of someone feeling that *they* have accomplished something and talking about receiving special status because of it.

So once we have created a system, whoever joins us will know that no work here receives personal recognition. We don't even have to thank someone for having done some work. The center has done the work, not you; we simply have to forget personal names as far as this is concerned. A meeting took place and this much work has been done – that's all. Some work has been done by Premchand bhai, some has been done by Ishwar babu – but mentioning their names has to be dropped, because that is the beginning of politics.

That kind of politics comes in from the beginning. Its journey begins from this place: who did this and who didn't, whose name got a mention and whose name didn't. We have to remember that whenever a mention needs to be made, say that the center did it, the friends of the center did it. Even when a book is published names should be abolished. The publisher should be "The Life Awakening Center" or "The Secretary of the Life Awakening Center." The secretary's name should not be given. Whosoever is the secretary at that time will be the publisher. Then no one will ever feel that his name was once there, but now it has been removed. When a name is changed – today it is this person's, tomorrow it will be that person's – a chain of misery and pain begins.

One thing we have to remember is to get rid of the idea of "the person" completely – because at least our own institution should be a proof of the revolutionary vision that we are sharing with society. There simply is no "person" in it – there is no Bisan-ji bhai, there is no Ishwar bhai, there is no Jayanti bhai. There are only friends here, and they have no identity of their own. They are not to be thanked, nor are their names to be mentioned. Whatever credit there is belongs to all; whatever fault there is, belongs to all.

Keep this in mind: when we give credit to individuals, then faults also have to be assigned to individuals. That becomes a cause of fighting. Today we say Harshad is doing very good work, and Harshad is pleased. And tomorrow when the work goes wrong, we will say Harshad is doing a bad job. Then that will be a cause of suffering. Don't accuse individual people. When we praise an individual, we haven't been asked *not* to praise him. And when we give someone credit, naturally the blame will also go to that same person. Then it becomes a cause of misery and fighting. What happens then?

We give credit very easily. But when it is time to blame, we have to do it in a cunning way; we have to talk in a roundabout way. You want to blame someone, but you don't use his name. Then you talk, going around it and the other person also answers in a roundabout way. And everyone understands what is going on, but at the same time we don't let anyone understand. This doesn't help anything. But it all begins with praise; it doesn't begin with blame. It starts when we begin honoring someone personally.

The idea of the person has to be erased completely. There is no place for it. The credit belongs to the center not to a person. If Kanti bhai is here today and gone tomorrow, nobody will even notice. And there is nothing to gossip about because even when he *is* there, nobody will notice. Even when a person is here he goes unnoticed, and then when he is not here, that certainly goes unnoticed. When a person is very obviously here, then a problem arises when he leaves. His leaving means that things get a little shaky. It becomes a subject of discussion: who was here and who wasn't here, why he left, and why he shouldn't have, and so on. So from the very beginning there should be no question that somebody *is*!

We should proceed with a clear understanding that whoever is joining the center is coming after leaving himself behind –

that is how he joins, starts participating. And the day he wants to elevate his ego he is no longer a member. If we are clearly able to create such an environment, then we will be able to say, "Premchand bhai, your ego is coming in, so you are no longer going to be a member." We will be able to sit down and say this very lovingly; otherwise it will lead to other, very different things, which are not a part of our work.

So get rid of the idea of "the person" otherwise we will never be able to avoid politics. It will keep coming up – every year or two. Whenever new people join, it will come up. And new people will be coming, they will come every day. Whenever they join, this idea of personality will arise, because if position and status are involved, new people will try to be in the forefront. The new person wants to overpower, and the old one, who has a position, will try to hinder him. Between this hindering and the attempt to overpower, a conflict will be created. And in this conflict the institute will suffer, the work will suffer.

We should set things up in such a way that whenever someone leaves, it is not noticed, and whenever someone joins, it is not noticed either. And only when we have created this will the attachment to position, the clinging, end – because from the very outset "position" will mean nothing. There is no reason for you to cling to a position because you never received any honor for it. No one will even know that this Kanti bhai is the president, that he is the head, and that this person does this... No one will know about these things. It is simply not something to be known. All our official positions will be just between us, internal. There will be nothing to talk about outside. They are to be internal and functional: someone has been assigned a job to be done.

So all these insights should be included in whatever constitution you make. This understanding should be our basic ground.

To do the work that is waiting for us, we have to take care of all these matters. I feel that the work can grow so extensively that it can become a movement. So many thousands of people are eager, and eager with a love that is rarely seen for anything today. If we fail to make use of this, it will be because of our lack of intelligence.

Recently, people in Indore said it was more than thirty years since they had seen so many people – well-educated, intelligent – gathering together in one place. All of them had an eagerness to understand, a thirst that has not been seen for such a long time: three thousand people in the hall, some eight thousand standing outside – even standing in the mud – all listening for an hour in pin-drop silence! There were no arrangements to keep any kind of order, no volunteers, but everyone was standing quietly by himself so that nothing would get in the way of his listening. When people are taking such an interest, then if we don't build on that interest and eagerness, the mistake will be all ours. And to go on discussing these trivial matters – which don't have any value or meaning – makes no sense.

So one more thing to remember: don't start playing trivial games. No trivial matters are to be raised – because whatever we bring up gains strength. We should be raising the most important matters and giving them energy.

I often feel that whenever there is nothing significant happening, we automatically get occupied with trivia because we need to be occupied. These problems which arise are nothing special; but then we start getting preoccupied with trivia.

So there should be important, significant work clearly in view, which we need to develop. The work can grow so vast that if we make a little effort for ten years, an atmosphere can spread throughout the whole country. And this atmosphere can influence, can impact, every aspect of life – religion, politics, society, the establishment, young people, adults, married life, the family – everything. What I am saying can be applied in every dimension, and results will start coming from wherever we apply it.

The next thing to be looked at is that at present, my energy is not being spread efficiently. In some villages five hundred people are listening to me where five thousand could have listened. And the only barrier is that they didn't get to hear about it. That is the only obstacle. It is a very small obstacle that can easily be overcome. In Mumbai we should take special care of this, because the results of whatever we do in Mumbai are seen throughout the country. I come across people everywhere who say they heard me for the first time in Mumbai, and when they returned home they started creating an energy field there.

Recently I went to Varanasi. I was there for the first time, but the meeting was so big. People said there were never so many people in Krishnamurti's meetings. It is fifty years since the Theosophical Society's hall was built there. One of their trustees said, "In fifty years – and I have heard people from Annie Besant onward – this is the first time that the hall has been full. It has never been full before. I always used to wonder why we had built such a large hall. I could never have imagined that people would even be standing outside the hall. This is the first time we have had to provide seating outside. For the first time in fifty years I felt that this hall is small."

Now, this was my first visit there, but someone there had heard me in Mumbai, someone somewhere else... Even if someone had not heard me themselves, they had been told about me by someone who had heard me.

So one thing: we should make sure that what we do here becomes a model, because the news travels from here and it can give people a lead, a suggestion. It will become a model for others as to what is to be done, how a meeting should be organized, what kind of arrangements should be made, how many people should be involved, what should be there, what shouldn't be there and so on.

And secondly, we should organize our publicity in a scientific way.

What is happening now? I spoke in Varanasi. A group of a thousand to two thousand people there heard me, but since then there have been no reverberations in the rest of the country. What I said, how many people heard me, what effects it had – there has been no report of it anywhere. It was a local affair, and it stayed that way. It should have created reverberations around the whole country, because it is this same echo resounding again and again...

Tomorrow I will go to Satara. If the news about Varanasi had reached there, then a group of people in that village would already be waiting to hear me – eager to know what happened, and what didn't happen there. So we should use the radio, the newspapers, as much as we can. Otherwise, for my part I am making an effort – and I will continue to do so – but a thousand times more could have been possible.

In other words, my undertaking is happening in almost exactly the same way as Mahavira's or Buddha's did two thousand five hundred years ago. Nothing has changed since then. Mahavira went to a village, he spoke and the matter was over – because there was no way at the time to create reverberations. Twenty-five centuries have passed since Mahavira spoke and now his echo is still not worldwide. And what he said, and its echo too, is becoming fainter with each passing day.

But now, with just a little organization, an immediate effect can be created. Today all the means are available, today there is no shortage of ways as there once was. And because of the lack of means in the past, they had to use ways which have caused tremendous harm.

What really happened? What means did Mahavira and Buddha have at their disposal except to go around and speak? So they had to prepare people who could take their message to the masses. And those people spoiled everything. They had to prepare ten thousand sannyasins to carry the message. They were ten thousand different types of people, so they took ten thousand different messages – and the message became meaningless. The society that resulted was developed by those ten thousand people. It was not developed by Mahavira or Buddha. What could one man do?

Today we have the possibility of sending the original message directly. No medium is needed in between. So instead of Jayanti bhai taking my message, the radio can do so more efficiently and more accurately – and it brings it exactly, verbatim. Mahavira and Buddha had to use the old way; they had to send messengers. People still don't understand what the function of their messengers was. Their only function was to be postmen; message carriers. What could Mahavira have done alone? One man running around, traveling on foot for thirty or forty years – what more could he have done? All he could have done was just to keep running! Somehow these messengers managed to carry at least something of him, and in that way they passed something on.

But what these people passed on turned out to be just confusion. It was bound to be confused – and it was. For example, yesterday I spoke on trust. If ten of you pass on what I said then to others, great confusion will result – because in the first place, you yourselves don't fully understand what I am saying; your inner ambivalence about it is still there. And then, with that unresolved ambivalence, you will try explaining it to others – and they have their own inner ambivalence. So everything will become topsy-turvy. Who knows what final form it will take?

So that is not needed at all today. Everywhere people are suggesting to me that I should prepare some people "to take my message." That is a completely wrong idea. I am not going to prepare anyone. In the first place, no one will be ready to take my message. If someone is ready to assimilate what I am saying for themselves that is another matter. No, I have to deliver my message myself. So what has to be taken care of is that nobody comes in between, and my message reaches people. It is when people come in between, that trouble is created.

I don't want to have anyone coming in between. And now that the message can reach people directly, there is no need of a messenger.

We have to put our total possible energy into this, as much as we can, even though the results may not be as visible today as they will be five years from now.

Osho,
What about the article the editor of Nav Bharat Times ***has written?***

Don't worry about it. And don't worry about the controversy that will arise either. It should happen, it is good that it happens. We want controversy, because that also creates reverberations. Don't worry what Karanjia says or writes, don't worry at all, because anything written by people...

Just recently I received a letter from Ujjain about that little booklet someone published about me. The letter said, "The person who wrote this book has done us a great favor, because after reading it we *had* to read your books. And we found what we had been searching for our whole lives. So whoever that gentleman is, we want to thank him."

So that's how controversies are! The person who stirs up a controversy is connected to an entirely different group that I would never have been able to reach directly. For example, if

Karanjia creates a controversy about me... Do you think I would have ever been able to make a direct contact with Karanjia's group except through Karanjia? If a religious monk starts talking against me, there is no way I would have been able to establish any relationship with his group except through him. The group learns about me only through hearing the monk speak against me.

It has to happen through one way or the other, because there is no way I can have any direct contact with them myself.

However much energy we put into other ways of working, we should put much more into journalists, the radio and other media so that our point of view becomes known in the country, and people become aware that such a thing exists. What people think about it is none of our concern – "it is right" or "it is wrong." If they think it is wrong, there is no harm in it, because even if they think it is wrong, if not today, then tomorrow, they will have to come to me. And by discussing it they will be able to conclude what was wrong and what was right.

Osho,
Our idea about trustees, etcetera, was that every year...

If, for instance, there are twelve trustees, then a third of them, that is four people, should be renewed every two years – because we need both continuity and stability.

Osho,
That post of secretary, what shall we call it? Secretary? Convener? Can we call it whatever else we want?

There is no harm in doing that. For example, there are eight people. Assign a department to each one of them. Then they can make their own subcommittee of three people. Those three will not be members of the Working Committee.

Jayanti bhai is on the Action Committee. Jayanti bhai, Harshad and Ishwar babu can form a committee of their own. For example, Jayanti bhai looks after the publicity. It is up to him; he is responsible for it. He can take on whomsoever he thinks appropriate and start his work. And Jayanti bhai will be the representative on the Working Committee; contact with the Working Committee will be through him.

So carry out your work as you feel best. You will have a separate subcommittee of your own, of which you will be the convener, and you will also continue to be a member of the Working Committee – because there should be a Working Committee which can coordinate everything overall, which can take decisions about what work has to be done and then distribute it.

If you take someone on, it should be a unanimous decision. And take on one person at a time; the unit has always to be kept as a unit. For example, if you want to take on Harshad, do so only when all eight members of the Action Committee are unanimous. Take people in only when there is total unanimity. There is to be no question of voting – that one is in favor and seven are not. Only take someone in when the team decides unanimously, otherwise not. And keep quiet about any decisions so no harm is done. In the meanwhile, you can make better use of that person by taking him into different subcommittees.

Osho,
What about the situation with the other group? Did we make a mistake in the way we dealt with them?

There was no mistake at all. You couldn't have done anything else under the circumstances; nothing else. You didn't make any mistake, the situation turned out well and there was no particular trouble. So the right thing happened; there is nothing to think about. There is no issue except that whenever a group creates some organization and another group comes forward to replace it, this kind of difficulty starts.

And the second thing is that those who started that organization were not connected to me. They couldn't have been. I was a stranger, and they were all strangers. I had no prior contact with them. They created their group and made all the arrangements, but they had no understanding of my way of thinking or of me personally. They had nothing to do with me. It was just that my ideas appealed to them, and so they began their work. Naturally, it couldn't have been in accordance with me. And that was nobody's mistake. They did their best, but it couldn't have been in accordance with me. Just as many other groups have done things, they also did something.

But the group that is coming together now is of an altogether different nature. So the set-up that has to be created now is completely different.

Until yesterday it was all just a natural flow, growing by itself. But it was bound to fall away from me, they were bound to fall away. That is what happens. I was someone who appealed to them, so they formed their organization and started their work. But they didn't ask me anything about the constitution, they didn't ask me about anything they were doing. They had no inner connection with me in the work. I was aware that they were doing something for me, but I had no other information at all – I couldn't have had. And also I was not interested, and I knew that my taking an interest in that group wouldn't be good either. When another group comes along with different feelings – having understood me – then my connection with it will be different.

So that was a very different situation, and it is inevitable when anything new is born. It cannot be avoided. It was absolutely inevitable. But they created a ground, a base, and that allowed you to come to me. Their work was to create the ground, nothing more. Once that was done, they were going to become a hindrance.

Anybody else could have been in their place. It is not a question of individuals at all. In my view, things have less to do with people, they always have more to do with the circumstances. Whether it is A, B or C makes no difference. Anyone else from Mumbai could have been in the place of those three, and if any other group had been in your place, still the same thing would have happened. In this whole story of life, things are not the way we think they are. For example, we think *we* are doing something, but it is not so.

It is all an inevitable part of life, and if we understand this, then we no longer put blame or praise on people – those very feelings disappear. In fact it is not a question of blaming or praising people. Things just happen in a certain way. It is natural. And if instead of me there had been someone else, then these three people would have worked for him instead. In the beginning they will be patronizing. It is natural, because they are launching that person, they are doing his work, *they* are spreading the news of him! Without them that person cannot be launched. So they feel, "*We* are launching him."

So it was bound to happen, it could not have been different. And it is all unconscious. The mechanics of the human mind are such that any three people – any Tom, Dick and Harry – will feel the same. Then when they have launched the person and spread his work, they will feel a kind of ownership over him. And then when another group comes... And it will come, because through their work of spreading the word another group will inevitably arise, and the original group will have never thought about that. It is an inevitable outcome of their own work that another group will come – that is the reason they were doing the work.

So soon after, as the new group arrives, the original group will start becoming cautious about promoting the work further.

They will begin to be afraid: "Here comes a new group! It speaks differently, it talks about things differently." So then they won't want to spread the work further; a kind of exclusiveness will be created: "Not too many people should be allowed in; so-and-so shouldn't be allowed in." Soon they will notice that a new arrival is talking in a way that doesn't fit in with them, which can become a cause for trouble, so they will begin to create obstacles.

But the day the original group starts creating obstacles, from that very day its death has set in. Now it has become afraid of promoting the work it has been promoting because the people who will come as a result of any further promotion will replace them. Scores of problems will arise, so the original group will resist. It will not give work to the new group, it will not respect the new group, it will create hurdles, and it will create all kinds of trouble. And it is not aware of any of this.

No individual is responsible for all this; that is why I am calling it a kind of mechanism. It is in-built. And when hurdles are created for the new group, it will fight back; it will start noticing lots of mistakes, even mistakes that are not there. And the mistakes that *are* there will be seen as much greater than they really are. But the new group will have no idea what it is doing either. Only when it is running something will it come to understand; and that too only when an even newer group arrives, not before. And by that time it will have forgotten the mistakes it had pointed out to the previous group.

Mistakes are there because they are part of the work; they are not there because they are part of the people. The people are irrelevant; those mistakes are part of the work.

For example, Sohan came to see me. She had wanted to meet me alone but Raman bhai had no interest in arranging it. She asked me, "Why can't I see you alone?"

I told her, "Don't think about it now. When I come to stay at your home, then you will understand."

Recently she was here and she started saying, "It looks very strange that some woman comes to my house and wants to see you alone."

So I said, "You know all this. Raman bhai was the one who found it strange before. Now *you* are worried why a certain woman wants to see me alone: why can't she see me with you? So it is not a question of you, it is not a question of anyone. This is how the human mind works."

This is the working of the human mind. Now she is not aware of this. She is not aware because, for herself, she is so sure that there is no harm in her meeting me alone, but about others!... Do you see how things happen? First Raman bhai appeared to be the cause – because Sohan felt there was no harm in her meeting me alone, so: "Why does Raman bhai get in the way? This man is not good!" Now *this* is a different story. She is clear that she was not doing anything wrong before, but: "It doesn't look good to people that some woman comes and sees you alone." And that woman is also clear that she is not doing anything wrong. "Why can't I meet him alone? Why I am being hindered?" This is what I call the mechanism of the human mind.

So there should be no trace of blame or praise. The understanding has to arise that "things happen as they happen." In me there remains no trace whatsoever of who did what. I see that anyone would have done the same, so the matter is finished. It is not a question of "this poor man." No, it had to happen; hence, there is nothing to be concerned about, nothing to think about. The matter is over. You have to move on from things. Don't think about what happened, what didn't happen. What was to happen, happened; what was not meant to happen did not happen.

What we have to think about, now that the experience is over, is how to use it, what understanding we can get from it so it doesn't happen again – because it *will* happen again. So if you pass through an experience, benefit from it. If you don't benefit from it, the experience is wasted, because now you have taken the other position and you are not making use of the first experience. You have adopted the same position that the others did before.

In five years' time, or maybe even two, a new group of people will come. And every new group will start seeing mistakes, because it is not aware of the whole scope of the work. It doesn't know what work a certain person is doing. No one notices; the work happens very silently.

So mistakes are seen – "This mistake, and that mistake have happened about such and such" – because the person is interested in finding mistakes, he is not interested in the work itself. Someone did not receive his book, something did not happen for such and such a reason – he sees all of that. Tomorrow when he is on the other side of things, he will notice that fifty thousand rupees are due to be paid. Then, whether a book has arrived or not becomes a secondary issue. Paying the fifty thousand rupees is the real issue.

That is what Raman bhai was doing – and you will have to experience these things for yourselves. The real problem was paying the money, and it became such a big problem that whether someone got their books or not was pushed to one side. "Let us first take care of this money!" became Raman bhai's main focus. The mistakes happening around delivery were not important in comparison, and they were bound to arise because something more important was being dealt with. Should the attention go to that, or to more minor issues?

So if we can learn from this experience, it is of great significance, and it will become an example that is helpful for the people coming in the future. Then we will be able to act with more understanding. That is exactly what we are *not* doing right now. Only this much awareness has to be gained from the experience. Don't worry about whether what happened was right or wrong; just become aware of what happened and if we can avoid repeating it. More than that is not necessary.

14
Liquid Organization

Osho,
Now is the time to put things into concrete terms and act. In that respect we wanted to know what sort of a constitution we should have. There is no doubt that it should be flexible. Should the registration be now or after some time? Should it be done in India or at the headquarters in New York? What should be the preamble of our constitution? What are the basic functions of each of the international presidents, the continental president and secretary, and the national one? How should the two be interconnected so that that work can be more perfect?
Then, what practical action do we need to take regarding the meditations, and the healing? Please tell us a little about how these things are to be organized, in regard to Neo-Sannyas International. What is the distinction between the activities of N.S.I. and the Life Awakening Center to be? How are they to be organized so that there is no overlapping between them, and the people who specialize in a particular branch can devote themselves to it? How do we choose those people and give them specialized work?
And in all this respect, we want there to be some sort of a camp for all the sannyasins we have, so that we can give them this message,

a practical share of exactly all that we want to, and some training during the period of the camp.

Anything more, Madhusudan?

Osho,
No, we only want to be enlightened on these points.

So, first make a body for framing a constitution. The constitution must be as liquid as possible – not only flexible, but liquid. It must be absolutely nonpolitical. There should be no inner politics. Normally any constitution will create inner politics. It is to be absolutely nonpolitical. There is bound to be an organization, but it should be as unorganized as possible, with no elections.

So, more or less, don't think in terms of solidity and practicality – because the more solid you make it, the less liquid it will be. And the more practical it is, the more you will have to organize it. Let this be a new type of brotherhood. There has never been a world organization of sannyasins. There have been sectarian organizations, and sectarian organizations can be more solid, because they have a framework. This is going to be just like a brotherhood: so many religions, so many philosophies, so many types of people will be there. If you make it too solid, then it will not be so open to all. So let your solidity be only formal – for example a mala and the robe: that is all. The innermost being must be completely free.

So frame a constitution, and never shape it according to any other constitution. Remember, don't make it a constitution just like so many other constitutions. Neither make it an eclectic one: something from here and something from there. Create a fresh conception. And when you are creating that fresh conception of a world brotherhood, always remember the word *brotherhood*.

All the posts are just appointments from me and they are functional. There is no hierarchy. By holding a post, a sannyasin is not higher than others. All the posts are functional. That is, I have given some work, some particular work to be done; so he is more responsible but not higher. Make it clear in the constitution that our posts are only functional, and all the posts will be appointed by me, so there will be no elections and there will be no hierarchy. Even the international president is not higher than any sannyasin in the brotherhood. He is just more responsible. He will not have any rights but only duties. So no rights should be written, because there are not going to be any rights at all. He will have only duties. He will be responsible, he can be asked things, and he will have to answer.

Let this be really clear: that there are no rights. With any post there are no rights at all. You will have only duties.

When you think about what will be the president's position, make mention of the duties: that these will be his duties and he should be responsible toward the whole brotherhood. Then anyone can ask, "Have you done this?" but he will not have any rights. He cannot say, "I have this right because I am so-and-so."

Make it clear. Then it will be a brotherhood and not an organization. Then the posts will be functional – and when posts are functional, without any rights, then I can change anybody, anytime. With rights, one becomes addicted to the post. When there are only responsibilities and duties, whenever one is freed from his post he feels more freedom. It is not a loss at all.

And this will be the rule: the one who fulfills his duty better will be freed sooner.

So this is a golden rule?

A golden rule!

One who cannot fulfill his duties in a better way will have to carry the burden; he will stay on the post longer.

So this constitution must be a new one, with no rights, and with new conceptions involved. Whenever someone is freed from his post, he must rejoice. We must create this feeling; otherwise appointments will be difficult.

So there is an intrinsic relationship: when there are rights, elections are suitable; when there are no rights, then there is no need for elections. When there are rights then appointments, new appointments, will be difficult. When there are no rights there is no question. One is just freed.

No one can resign from his post...

That is number two!

...because no one can resign from his duties. Resignation is only relevant when there are rights. So no one can resign.

Think according to, along, these lines and make an absolutely new framework. Don't think of registration first. Let there be the framework. If it can be registered, that's all right. If it cannot be registered, then let it be unregistered, because with registration there are laws. Every constitution cannot be registered – and this is going to be something completely new. So don't think of registration at all. Frame the constitution. If it can be registered, wherever it can be registered – in India or in America or in Switzerland, wherever laws permit its registration – we will register it there. And if no laws permit it anywhere, then it will remain unregistered.

And this will be a good thing: first frame the constitution, then we will look where it can be registered. If it can be registered nowhere, then we can appeal to some governments: "This is a new constitution and a new type of brotherhood, so create laws for it." But we are not going to change according to the laws. We will rather remain unregistered.

So make a body and think about it. And always remember that something new must evolve. Something completely new...

There have been organizations which only frustrated humanity. There have been anti-organizational thinkers who have not done anything. So something completely unorganized *and* with an organization is needed – because both have failed. Too much organization fails; too much of an anti-organizational attitude also fails. The one cannot work because of the organization; the other cannot work because there is no organization. That's why I use the term *liquid*, flowing. When there is a need you are organized; when there is no need you are not. With need, there is fluctuation.

So the president is not always a president, only when he is functioning. In a particular situation he needs to be the president; otherwise it makes no sense to call him a president. Our posts are functional. When there is a meeting, you are a president; when there is no meeting, you are no one. You must not always carry the presidential post: it is not a twenty-four-hour function. So whenever there is a need, you function as an organization; when there is no need, you function just like a brotherhood. When you are meeting just informally, no one is a president and no one is a secretary, and no one...

This must be added: "All these posts are functional. When we need to, we function like that." The organization can work in an organized way when there is the need, and is just unorganized when there is no need. If the need is more, the organization will be more organized; if it is less, then the organization will be less organized. So it will be always fluctuating. Nothing is fixed.

Really, in life nothing is fixed. We fix things because we cannot function without fixing. But that fixing goes against life and always creates an anti-life attitude. Love is a liquidity; marriage becomes fixed. You cannot function with love; you can function with marriage, but then marriage becomes dead.

Love has been tried. It becomes anarchic and society cannot exist along with it. But if society cannot exist, then love, in its turn, will also not exist. It will not be possible. Love needs a society, but society cannot exist with love and love cannot exist without society. These are human dilemmas. Society creates marriage. With marriage, love cannot exist – only society can exist – but without love it carries no meaning.

It is the same everywhere: you cannot do without organization, and with organization you will not be able to do it! That's why I emphasize liquidity – and because there are not going to be any elections I will force you to be liquid. If there are elections, then liquidity will be impossible. Me alone, I will just be reshuffling, so soon you will not be fixed with someone as president, with someone as secretary. Things will be changing. Within one or two years, you will be well acquainted with this liquid atmosphere.

And something about what you are going to do... Make some wings. For healing, make one committee. This committee will be an international body. Make separate committees so they can form their own liquid working constitutions. You need not bother about them: just make a mention in your constitution that there will be a body for healing and there will be a body for meditation and there will be a body for education, etcetera. And make separate committees so that they make their own constitutions. They make their...

...constitution within the constitution?

...exactly. Then it is more liquid. If you fix it in the main constitution, then they are not at freedom. Let them be free.

And everywhere all the posts are appointed by me, even in those committees – the chairman – everywhere.

This movement is going to be exclusively spiritual. Each individual member is free to participate in any politics, in any economic program, can hold any views – because we have no views. As Neo-Sannyas International we have no views. We are not anti-political. We are just exclusively spiritual.

So no one is barred. Anyone can express his views. Those views can even be contrary to those of any other member, because we are not concerned. Politics, economics...other than spirituality we are not concerned.

Only as far as spirituality is concerned can anyone hold any views, but they should never assert them as being contradictory to other views held in the brotherhood. Anyone can hold any views as far as spirituality is concerned, but he should remember that all the "contrary views" are not contrary but complementary. This is going to be our standpoint; otherwise you cannot make a brotherhood.

A Mohammedan will be there, a Christian will be there, a Hindu will be there, a Jaina will be there. They can have their views, but with this condition: that their views are not inimical to anyone, they are only different. There is every possibility of other paths toward the divine. This possibility must be always remembered – always – otherwise there can be no brotherhood. Even a quite opposite view – which appears quite opposite – can lead to the divine. You travel your path, let others travel their own.

This organization will not convert anybody. There is going to be no conversion – no conversion! If someone changes his mind, that's his affair. We are not concerned. If some Mohammedan becomes a Buddhist, let him be. We are not concerned.

So this non-converting attitude must be clear.

And Jeevan Jagruti Kendra, the Life Awakening Center, and Neo-Sannyas International... The Life Awakening Center is an institution of all those friends who are not sannyasins. Neo-Sannyas International is only for sannyasins. So the Life Awakening Center is a feeding institution for you, because through it people will come and become sannyasins. It is a feeding institution; you are a specialized wing. So The Life Awakening Center will continue.

Sannyasins can be in the Life Awakening Center but non-sannyasins cannot be in N.S.I. Someone can hold a post in Neo-Sannyas International and also a post in the Life Awakening Center – sannyasins can be in both. But non-sannyasins cannot enter N.S.I.

There is bound to be some overlapping. But one thing should be clear, that the Life Awakening Center will work in a generalized way. Your work will be specialized. This specialization will concern the transformation of individuals into sannyas. The publication of literature – especially for meditation, for sannyas, for occult training, for yoga – is your specialization.

So if I express economic views, you are not to publish them, you are not to be concerned with them. If I express some political views, you will not be concerned with them. The Life Awakening Center will do that. Your work will specialize in every direction that is sannyas-oriented, everything concerned with sannyas. That will be good, and it will be easy for you to work, because soon you will have some specialized literature.

A Gandhian, who may not be convinced with my anti-Gandhian attitude, can be a sannyasin and can be a member of Neo-Sannyas International, because Neo-Sannyas International is not concerned with my political views. Whenever someone asks about my political views, just say that you are not concerned with them at all.

So create your own specialized literature soon. Have your own magazine, first an international magazine in English, then in national languages, and then in regional languages. In this way,

N.S.I. sannyasins can work more easily, because all that creates unnecessary discussions will not be in their way at all. They can just drop it: "That's not N.S.I.'s concern." Your concern with me is only in one particular way: as far as spirituality is concerned. So meditation, healing, occult training, yoga, parapsychology… You must have a wing for parapsychology and parapsychic investigations. There is much; you can work in many dimensions.

Ashrams are to be created all over the world, and these ashrams must also have a completely new shape, a new form. Just as our constitution is going to be new, our ashrams should also be new. They must have something original about them. For example, they are not going to be just retirement places. In a way, they will be factories and labs, research centers for occult, yoga, parapsychology. We will create a laboratory in every ashram, a research lab, with all the scientific implements, instruments – because N.S.I. will try to make religion as appealing as possible to the scientific mind. Of course religion cannot be totally scientific, but the beginning, the jumping board, can be made scientific and then one can go beyond.

So this will be one thing: to make religion as scientific as possible. And another will be to make science as religious as possible.

We can create a world university for all this work to be done, and national colleges and regional schools: one university, then national colleges and regional schools. And only then the word *university* becomes meaningful. These universities are not universities, "one that belongs to the universe." These are all colleges.

One university, many national colleges – one national college for each nation – and many schools, regional schools. Schools will be affiliated with the colleges, and the colleges will be affiliated with the university. So make provision for it; we will create another wing for this.

Any work which is done by Neo-Sannyas International will be done by sannyasins. No one can join its work otherwise. N.S.I must have some bearing on current problems too – in a religious way – because current problems are political, economic. So when I say, "Neo-Sannyas International will not have anything to do with politics," I don't mean that it will not have any bearing on current problems. But the way, the method, will be religious. It will not be political. For example, the wars going on in Bengal and in Vietnam…

So there are two attitudes: either religious people should become political, or they should not be concerned at all. Both of these attitudes are dangerous. The moment religious people become political they are no longer religious, because the very working of politics is irreligious. You cannot remain religious in day-to-day politics. Then you are only deceiving, you are only pretending to be religious. Because of this, the contrary view became prevalent: the anti-political attitude that one should just be closed. And when one is closed to day-to-day problems, to existential problems, one becomes dead and the movement can never come alive. Then you cannot make it a great movement in which the whole world is involved. Then it becomes a secluded movement for some people, for only few.

So Neo-Sannyas International is not interested in politics, but it is interested in man, and man is political, he has political problems. How to help man with his political problems in a religious way? We will invent methods and techniques to help with political problems, economic problems, religiously.

The first thing is that we will never be partisan. For example, this Bengal massacre: we can create a worldwide prayer movement for it. In a way, politicians are totally impotent. People are dying, but politicians are completely impotent, they cannot do anything. And because we don't know any other dimension of doing, the whole world becomes just paralyzed, and anything that we do is just a tantrum, childish.

So this will be one of the basic understandings: "Man alone is not enough," and "Man cannot solve his problems alone" – because man *is* the problem. We must seek the help of the divine, of the cosmic force – and through meditation, through *kirtan*, through prayer. And as it helps in healing, it can help with any problem. But you will have to experiment with it.

It can help in any problem. It helps in two ways. The moment you realize that man alone is not enough, you have shattered the ego which creates the problem. The moment you recognize that surrender is needed, you have become a passage, a vehicle, for the cosmic healing force in any problem; not only with illnesses, but with any problem, because any problem is also a disease. It may afflict everyone, but it makes no difference: it is a disease. So we will take any problem as a disease, as an illness. Political or economic, everything is a disease. Mind is defective somewhere, is not able to cope with the problem. Rather it creates more complexities.

We will just create a movement all over the world to help the human mind through divine, cosmic forces. Our technique is going to be altogether different. It is not a protest – because we are not protesting against man. It is not a protest because all the protests are against man, and they create more conflicts and nothing else. They create problems within problems. Against whom you are protesting? The ill mind of man. We are not protesting. So this is not going to be a protest, this is going to be prayer.

Prayer is an opening toward the divine. Protest is against the same human mind which is creating the problems. So for example this Bengal problem: we are not going to protest against Yahya Khan or anybody. This will not be a protest. Every problem is double-sided – it is never one-sided – and every protest is one-sided. It is not that only Yahya Khan is responsible, Mujib is just as responsible. It is not only that Pakistan is responsible, Bengal is just as responsible. Protest cannot cover both sides, but prayer can.

So we are not praying against someone and for someone. We are praying for the diseased, ill mind of man. It may be any problem: our prayer is going to be the same. Just like it may be any disease, but our healing is going to be the same. We are not going to analyze and diagnose the disease. We are not interested in the disease at all. We are interested in the ascendance of divine health. Our concern is with health, not with disease. So we will not make any statements, for or against. We will just pray. And our sannyasins will become a vehicle; they will dance in the *kirtan* and will become a vehicle, a door, an opening for the divine to come to human health. So wherever there is any problem, we will tackle it in a religious way, we will face it in a religious way. We are not going to just escape.

We will have to evolve completely new techniques. This is not even nonviolent protest, this is not a protest at all – because to me there can be no nonviolent protest. Protest is violent. The protesting mind is violent. So you may take nonviolence as a trick, but the protesting mind is violent.

Prayer is going to be the technique. The attitude of Neo-Sannyas International is life-affirmative. We will make each and every effort to make life more beautiful, more loving. We are not against this earth. We are for the transformation of this earth.

We will develop many things. Our centers, our ashrams will be helpful in many ways toward making life more beautiful. As Veet Sandeh has suggested, we can have new types of marriages in our ashram. We can help a new type of marriage to evolve: a spiritual wedding, with the divine force as a presence. We can have marriage counseling departments in our ashrams: how to make life lovelier through meditation – because psychoanalysis has failed, and now no one knows what to do. Everything is a mess.

So we are going to help in every way. For example we can have maternity homes. With the help of meditation, with the help of spiritual healing, there can be absolutely painless birth – absolutely painless.

These are just examples. We will explore every nook and corner of life. "How can we help spiritually?" And we will be there to help.

Our ashrams will be productive. We would not like our sannyasins to depend on this ill society; because the moment you depend on it you can never change it. Productivity is not a value in itself, but the moment you depend on the same society that you are thinking to transform, you are thinking the impossible. The whole movement of sannyasins became just a failure because they were depending on that same society. The moment you depend economically you can have no voice.

So our ashrams must be productive and independent – absolutely. We must be so independent that there is no outer pressure on us; only then you can be a help, otherwise you cannot help – and the society will begin to dominate you.

Productivity in itself is not really a value, but being unproductive will become a "dis-value." So when I say "Be productive," I do not mean the same thing as Gandhi or Vinobha meant. But without productivity you will be dependent, and a dependent sannyasin cannot be a *swami*, cannot be a master. He may deceive himself that he is a master, but he is just a servant of the servants, and those who touch his feet are the real masters. They manipulate him and they will go on manipulating him.

One more point. We will have to create an atmosphere of total positivity in our sannyasins. The negative mind must not be appreciated – never – because wherever there is a negative mind, politics will follow. So no one should say anything against anybody, and if someone has to say something against anybody, let him tell this to that person. Never allow anybody else.

For example, someone comes and talks against Madusudhan to me. I should stop him that very moment and tell him, "Go to Madhusudhan. I will take you to Madhusudhan. Tell this thing to him." Then it becomes positive, it is not negative. Then it helps in many ways. Otherwise a very negative atmosphere will go on running around you. And surrounded by negativity, you will never be able to do anything, you will be just fighting among yourselves – thinking against this and thinking against that.

So make it a point, and tell every sannyasin, "Whenever something negative is going around, stop the very first moment and tell the person to talk to the person concerned. Be courageous to talk to the person, don't go around and around. Otherwise there is fatal harm."

It can always be pointed out that those who are doing something are doing it defectively. Those who are not doing anything can never have the finger pointed at them, so non-doing becomes valued, and the person who is doing something becomes unnecessarily tense and burdened. He is doing, and at the same time feeling hurt every time. So if you are to do something great, never be negative; otherwise the non-doer will be appreciated and the doers will be condemned. Then you create a suicidal movement. Then whole thing commits suicide.

Never be negative. Think along these lines; make some points that every sannyasin should know.

Osho,
What about camps for the sannyasins?

Yes, soon we will have a camp and soon there will be separate camps for sannyasins. The moment there are one thousand sannyasins, then we will have separate camps. Sannyasins can participate in ordinary camps but no non-sannyasins can participate. So those camps will be organized by Neo-Sannyas International, not by the Life Awakening Movement. They will be organized by N.S.I.

Special camps for training the sannyasins?

Yes. We will have another training camp soon.

The question was about training.

Training, yes. That training will be more helpful if we don't have a camp, but have training classes – because in a camp there will be five thousand people, it will be difficult. It will be better to have training schools or training seminars, for a limited group, for thirty – a twenty-one-day period for thirty people – so we can pay them individual attention.

So in the ashrams we can have training seminars for three weeks or for four weeks, for thirty people. Then I will make a training schedule. We will have to train people otherwise it will be difficult. We will have to train them.

At this time we are having that difficulty. Is that how it works?

That is bound to be – yes.

So why not start with training now...

Yes, we will train, we will train.

...so that the pace of work can be...

Yes, we will train, we should have courses. For example, the healers must have a different course. So we will have a general course for every sannyasin to attend. Then we will have special courses: a different course for healers, a different course for teachers, for those who will go and teach meditation. These will be special courses.

So we will also have special courses. One: a three week general training, then, a three week special course. Only then it will be... For six months at least there will be trouble, because we cannot have them now. Let there be at least one thousand sannyasins, then we will begin. Then we will begin.

Sannyas...

I am thinking about it. But I think, let it be in one or two years. It can be helpful and can be harmful also. It can be helpful because we will have to create one step for those who cannot dare to jump into sannyas suddenly, abruptly, directly. For those who are not so courageous, we will have a step in between. That will help. But not now. Now it will be harmful – because all those who can dare, will also not dare. They will not dare. If there had been an in-between step for Madhusudhan, he would be standing on that step! So for one year at least, no step.

So let there be one thousand, two thousand sannyasins, then there will be an atmosphere of easiness, then people will know that there is nothing to be afraid of. First this atmosphere of "there is nothing to be afraid of" must come. Then we will create that step. We can call it *sadhu* or *bhikshu* or... I am thinking to call it sadhu. They will be in a white robe with a *mala*. The robe will be white with a *mala* – sadhu and *sadhvi*.

And that too will be allowed only for a particular period, for example, for one year. Then he will have to decide either to go back, or to go on. It cannot be prolonged forever – because this is only a step, so we cannot allow anyone to stay on that step continuously. He must go on up or back down. So this will be for a period: for six months or for one year. In that one year a person will gather enough courage to jump. No one will go back.

In one year we will think about it. You can make provision for it in the constitution, but we will allow it after one year.

About Osho

Osho's unique contribution to the understanding of who we are defies categorization. Mystic and scientist, a rebellious spirit whose sole interest is to alert humanity to the urgent need to discover a new way of living. To continue as before is to invite threats to our very survival on this unique and beautiful planet.

His essential point is that only by changing ourselves, one individual at a time, can the outcome of all our "selves" – our societies, our cultures, our beliefs, our world – also change. The doorway to that change is meditation.

Osho the scientist has experimented and scrutinized all the approaches of the past and examined their effects on the modern human being and responded to their shortcomings by creating a new starting point for the hyperactive twenty-first century mind: OSHO Active Meditations.

Once the agitation of a modern lifetime has started to settle, "activity" can melt into "passivity," a key starting point of real meditation. To support this next step, Osho has transformed the ancient "art of listening" into a subtle contemporary methodology: the OSHO Talks. Here words become music, the listener discovers who is listening, and the awareness moves from what is being heard to the individual doing the listening. Magically, as silence arises, what needs to be heard is understood directly, free from the distraction of a mind that can only interrupt and interfere with this delicate process.

These thousands of talks cover everything from the individual quest for meaning to the most urgent social and political issues facing society today. Osho's books are not written but are transcribed from audio and video recordings of these extemporaneous talks to international audiences. As he puts it, "So remember: whatever I am saying is not just for you... I am talking also for the future generations."

Osho has been described by *The Sunday Times* in London as one of the "1000 Makers of the 20th Century" and by American author Tom Robbins as "the most dangerous man since Jesus Christ." *Sunday Mid-Day* (India) has selected Osho as one of ten people – along with Gandhi, Nehru and Buddha – who have changed the destiny of India.

About his own work Osho has said that he is helping to create the conditions for the birth of a new kind of human being. He often characterizes this new human being as "Zorba the Buddha" – capable both of enjoying the earthy pleasures of a Zorba the Greek and the silent serenity of a Gautama the Buddha.

Running like a thread through all aspects of Osho's talks and meditations is a vision that encompasses both the timeless wisdom of all ages past and the highest potential of today's (and tomorrow's) science and technology.

Osho is known for his revolutionary contribution to the science of inner transformation, with an approach to meditation that acknowledges the accelerated pace of contemporary life. His unique OSHO Active Meditations™ are designed to first release the accumulated stresses of body and mind, so that it is then easier to take an experience of stillness and thought-free relaxation into daily life.

Two autobiographical works by the author are available:

Autobiography of a Spiritually Incorrect Mystic, St Martins Press, New York (book and eBook)

Glimpses of a Golden Childhood, OSHO Media International, Pune, India (book and eBook)

Osho International Meditation Resort

Each year the Meditation Resort welcomes thousands of people from more than 100 countries. The unique campus provides an opportunity for a direct personal experience of a new way of living – with more awareness, relaxation, celebration and creativity. A great variety of around-the-clock and around-the-year program options are available. Doing nothing and just relaxing is one of them!

All of the programs are based on Osho's vision of "Zorba the Buddha" – a qualitatively new kind of human being who is able *both* to participate creatively in everyday life *and* to relax into silence and meditation.

Location

Located 100 miles southeast of Mumbai in the thriving modern city of Pune, India, the OSHO International Meditation Resort is a holiday destination with a difference. The Meditation Resort is spread over 28 acres of spectacular gardens in a beautiful tree-lined residential area.

OSHO Meditations

A full daily schedule of meditations for every type of person includes both traditional and revolutionary methods, and particularly the OSHO Active Meditations™. The daily meditation program takes place in what must be the world's largest meditation hall, the OSHO Auditorium.

OSHO Multiversity

Individual sessions, courses and workshops cover everything from creative arts to holistic health, personal transformation, relationship and life transition, transforming meditation into a lifestyle for life and work, esoteric sciences, and the "Zen" approach to sports and recreation. The secret of the OSHO Multiversity's success lies in the fact that all its programs are combined with meditation, supporting the understanding that as human beings we are far more than the sum of our parts.

OSHO Basho Spa

The luxurious Basho Spa provides for leisurely open-air swimming surrounded by trees and tropical green. The uniquely styled, spacious Jacuzzi, the saunas, gym, tennis courts… all these are enhanced by their stunningly beautiful setting.

Cuisine

A variety of different eating areas serve delicious Western, Asian and Indian vegetarian food – most of it organically grown especially for the Meditation Resort. Breads and cakes are baked in the resort's own bakery.

Night life

There are many evening events to choose from – dancing being at the top of the list! Other activities include full-moon meditations beneath the stars, variety shows, music performances and meditations for daily life.

Facilities

You can buy all of your basic necessities and toiletries in the Galleria. The Multimedia Gallery sells a large range of OSHO media products. There is also a bank, a travel agency and a Cyber Café on-campus. For those who enjoy shopping, Pune provides all the options, ranging from traditional and ethnic Indian products to all of the global brand-name stores.

Accommodation

You can choose to stay in the elegant rooms of the OSHO Guesthouse, or for longer stays on campus you can select one of the OSHO Living-In programs. Additionally, there is a plentiful variety of nearby hotels and serviced apartments.

www.osho.com/meditationresort
www.osho.com/guesthouse
www.osho.com/livingin

Books by Osho in English

Early Discourses and Writings
The Art of Living
Astrology
Breaking All Boundaries
Compassion and Revolution
A Cup of Tea
Dimensions beyond the Known
Earthen Lamps
The Eternal Quest
Flowers of Love
From Sex to Superconsciousness
The Great Challenge
Hidden Mysteries
I Am the Gate
The Independent Mind
Into the Void
Keys to a New Life
Life Is a Soap Bubble
Love Letters to Life
New Dimensions of Yoga
The Path of Meditation
The Psychology of the Esoteric
Religion's Expiration Date
The Search for Peace
Seeds of Wisdom
Silence: The Message of Your Being
Work Is Love Made Visible
Three Steps to Awakening
Into the Void

Meditation
And Now and Here
In Search of the Miraculous
Meditation: The Art of Ecstasy
Meditation: The First and Last Freedom
The Inner Journey
The Perfect Way

Buddha and Buddhist Masters
The Book of Wisdom
The Dhammapada: The Way of the Buddha(Vols 1-12)
The Diamond Sutra
The Discipline of Transcendence (Vols 1-4)
The Heart Sutra

Indian Mystics
Bliss:Living beyond Happiness and Misery (Shiv Sutras)
Die O Yogi Die (Gorakh)
Enlightenment: The Only Revolution (Ashtavakra)
Krishna: The Man and His Philosophy
Showering without Clouds (Sahajo)
The True Name (Vols 1&2) (Nanak)
The Last Morning Star (Daya)
The Song of Ecstasy (Adi Shankara)

Baul Mystics
The Beloved (Vols 1 & 2)

Kabir
The Divine Melody
Ecstasy: The Forgotten Language
The Fabric of Life
The Fish in the Sea Is Not Thirsty
The Great Secret
The Guest
The Path of Love
The Revolution

Jesus and Christian Mystics
Come Follow to You (Vols 1-4)
I Say Unto You (Vols 1 & 2)
The Mustard Seed
Theologia Mystica

Jewish Mystics
The Art of Dying
The True Sage

Western Mystics
Guida Spirituale (*Desiderata*)
The Great Challenge (Treatise of St. Dionysius)
The Hidden Harmony (Heraclitus)
The New Alchemy: To Turn You On (Mabel Collins' *Light on the Path*)
Philosophia Perennis (Vols 1 & 2) (*The Golden Verses of Pythagoras*)
Reflections on Kahlil Gibran's *The Prophet*
Theologica Mystica
Zarathustra: A God That Can Dance (Nietzsche's *Thus Spake Zarathustra*)
Zarathustra: The Laughing Prophet (Nietzsche's *Thus Spake Zarathustra*)
The Voice of Silence (Mabel Collins' *Light on the Path*)

Sufism
Just Like That
The Perfect Master (Vols 1 & 2)
The Secret
Sufis: The People of the Path (Vols 1 & 2)
Unio Mystica (Vols 1 & 2)
Until You Die
The Wisdom of the Sands (Vols 1 & 2)

Tantra
Tantra: The Supreme Understanding
The Tantra Experience: The Royal Song of Saraha (same as Tantra Vision, Vol. 1)
Tantric Transformation: The Royal Song of Saraha (same as Tantra Vision, Vol. 2)
The Book of Secrets: Vigyan Bhairav Tantra

The Upanishads
Behind a Thousand Names (Nirvana Upanishad)
Finger Pointing to the Moon (Adhyatma Upanishad)
Flight of the Alone to the Alone (Kaivalya Upanishad)
The Heartbeat of the Absolute (Ishavasya Upanishad)
I Am That (Isa Upanishad)
The Message beyond Words (Kathopanishad)
Philosophia Ultima (Mandukya Upanishad)
The Supreme Doctrine (Kenopanishad)
That Art Thou (Sarvasar Upanishad, Kaivalya Upanishad, Adhyatma Upanishad)
The Ultimate Alchemy (Vols 1 & 2) (Atma Pooja Upanishad)
Vedanta: Seven Steps to Samadhi (Akshaya Upanishad)
The Way beyond Any Way (Sarvasar Upanishad)

Tao
The Empty Boat

The Secret of Secrets
Tao: The Golden Gate (Vols 1 & 2)
Tao: The Pathless Path (Vols 1 & 2)
Tao: The Three Treasures (Vols 1-4)
When the Shoe Fits

Yoga
Yoga: The Science of the Soul (Vols 1-10)
The Path of Yoga (Vol.1)
The Heart of Yoga (Vol.2)
Yoga: The Mystery beyond Mind (Vol.3)
The Alchemy of Yoga (Vol.4)
Yoga: A New Direction (Vol.5)
Essence of Yoga (Vol.6)
Yoga: The Science of Living (Vol.7)
Secrets of Yoga (Vol.8)
Yoga: The Path to Liberation (Vol.9)
Yoga: The Supreme Science (Vol.10)

Zen and Zen Masters
Ah, This!
Ancient Music in the Pines
And the Flowers Showered...
And the Grass Grows By Itself...
A Bird on the Wing
Bodhidharma: The Greatest Zen Master
The Buddha: The Emptiness of the Heart
Christianity, the Deadliest Poison and Zen, the Antidote to All Poisons
Communism and Zen Fire, Zen Wind
Dang Dang Doko Dang
The First Principle
God Is Dead: Now Zen Is the Only Living Truth
The Great Zen Master Ta Hui
Hsin Hsin Ming: The Book of Nothing
I Celebrate Myself: God Is No Where, Life Is Now Here
Kyozan: A True Man of Zen
The Language of Existence
Live Zen
The Miracle
Nirvana: The Last Nightmare
No Mind: The Flowers of Eternity
No Water, No Moon
One Seed Makes the Whole Earth Green
The Original Man
Returning to the Source
The Search: Talks on the 10 Bulls of Zen
A Sudden Clash of Thunder
The Sun Rises in the Evening
Take it Easy
This. This. A Thousand Times This
This Very Body the Buddha
Turning In
Walking in Zen, Sitting in Zen
The White Lotus
Yakusan: Straight to the Point of Enlightenment
The Zen Manifesto: Freedom from Oneself
Zen: The Diamond Thunderbolt
Zen: The Mystery and the Poetry of the Beyond
Zen: The Path of Paradox (Vols 1-3)
Zen: The Quantum Leap from Mind to No-Mind
Zen: The Solitary Bird, Cuckoo of the Forest
Zen: The Special Transmission

Osho: On the Ancient Masters of Zen
Dogen: The Zen Master
Hyakujo: The Everest of Zen – With Basho's haikus
Isan: No Footprints in the Blue Sky
Joshu: The Lion's Roar

Ma Tzu: The Empty Mirror
Nansen: The Point of Departure
Rinzai: Master of the Irrational

Responses to Questions
Be Still and Know
Beyond Enlightenment (Talks in Bombay)
Beyond Psychology (Talks in Uruguay)
Come, Come, Yet Again Come
From Bondage to Freedom
From Darkness to Light
From Death to Deathlessness
From Ignorance to Innocence
From Misery to Enlightenment
From Personality to Individuality
From the False to the Truth
From Unconsciousness to Consciousness
The Goose Is Out
The Great Pilgrimage: From Here to Here
The Invitation
Light on the Path (Talks in the Himalayas)
My Way: The Way of the White Clouds
Nowhere to Go but In
The Osho Upanishad (Talks in Bombay)
The Path of the Mystic (Talks in Uruguay)
The Razor's Edge
Sermons in Stones (Talks in Bombay)
Socrates Poisoned Again After 25 Centuries (Talks in Greece)
The Sword and the Lotus (Talks in the Himalayas)
Transmission of the Lamp (Talks in Uruguay)
Walk without Feet, Fly without Wings and Think without Mind
The Wild Geese and the Water
Yaa-Hoo! The Mystic Rose
Zen: Zest, Zip, Zap and Zing

Osho's Vision for the World
The Golden Future
The Hidden Splendor
The New Dawn
The Rebel
The Rebellious Spirit

The Mantra Series
Hari Om Tat Sat
Om Mani Padme Hum
Om Shantih Shantih Shantih
Sat Chit Anand
Satyam Shivam Sundaram

Personal Glimpses
Books I Have Loved
Glimpses of a Golden Childhood
Notes of a Madman

Interviews with the World Press
The Man of Truth: A Majority of One

For any information about OSHO Books, please contact:

OSHO Media International
17 Koregaon Park, Pune – 411001, MS, India
Phone: +91-20-66019999 Fax: +91-20-66019990
E-mail: distribution@osho.net
Website: http://www.osho.com

For More Information

For a full selection of OSHO multilingual online destinations, see osho.com/allaboutosho

The official and comprehensive website of OSHO International is osho.com

For more OSHO unique content and formats see:

- OSHO Active Meditations: osho.com/meditate
- iOsho, a bouquet of digital OSHO experiences featuring OSHO Zen Tarot, TV, Library, Horoscope, eGreetings and Radio. Please take a moment to do a one time registration which will allow you a universal login. Registration is free and open to anyone with a valid email address: osho.com/iosho
- The OSHO online shop: osho.com/shop
- Visit the OSHO International Meditation Resort: osho.com/visit
- Contribute in the OSHO Translation Project:oshotalks.com
- Read the OSHO Newsletters: osho.com/NewsLetters
- Watch OSHO on YouTube: youtube.com/user/OSHOInternational
- Follow OSHO on Facebook: facebook.com/osho.international.meditation.resort
- and Twitter: twitter.com/OSHO

Thank you for buying this OSHO book.